SEARCHING FOR DEXYS MIDNIGHT RUNNERS

NIGE TASSELL

NINE
EIGHT
BOOKS

NINE
EIGHT
BOOKS

NEB 026

First published in the UK in 2024 by Nine Eight Books
An imprint of Black & White Publishing Group
A Bonnier Books UK company
4th Floor, Victoria House, Bloomsbury Square, London, WC1B 4DA
Owned by Bonnier Books, Sveavägen 56, Stockholm, Sweden

X @nineeightbooks

@nineeightbooks

Hardback ISBN: 978-1-7851-2059-6
eBook ISBN: 978-1-7851-2060-2

A CIP catalogue record for this book Prelimis available from the British Library.

Publishing director: Pete Selby
Editor: James Lilford

Cover design by Alex Kirby
Typeset by IDSUK (Data Connection) Ltd
Printed and bound in Great Britain by Clays Ltd, Elcograf S.p.A

1 3 5 7 9 10 8 6 4 2

Nine Eight Books is an imprint of Bonnier Books UK
www.bonnierbooks.co.uk

For the Wilder bunch

'What did he do? He was there. That's what he did.'

Giovanni Cappa, *Mean Streets*

Contents

Introduction

I've been searching everywhere . . .

Bus stop. Early morning. Winter.

In the dark, he leans against the wall, puffing out his cheeks, his work shift over. The collar of his donkey jacket is turned up to banish the pre-dawn cold, his woolly hat pulled down a little further. A sports holdall sits at his feet. A deep, tired sigh sends a flume of breathy air out and upward.

Were this 1979 or 1980 – and were this a suburb of Birmingham, or a Black Country town – you might mistake this young man for a member of Dexys Midnight Runners.

But it's not. It's the opening month of 1983. Dexys Midnight Runners shed this particular look three years back and are currently in the dying throes of their dungarees-and-plimsolls phase. But fashions are slow to change down here in deepest, darkest rural Sussex.

And look at the face under that hat. Its owner is fourteen years old, if he's a day. The work shift he's just finished is his paper round. And the holdall at his feet contains not a classic Stax album or two, but all that's needed today: textbooks, pencil case, packed lunch, PE kit . . . The donkey jacket is buttoned up right to the neck, deliberately obscuring the school shirt and tie beneath.

When the donkey jacket and woolly hat were part of their standard-issue uniform, the eight members of Dexys Midnight Runners were inseparable. Joined at the hip. Hunting in a pack. A handful of years on, this youngest of supposed soul rebels stands alone, without the gang he so keenly craves. Other tribes of schoolkids have formed at the bus stop. Three mods to his left, all in identical fishtail parkas. A pair of goths to his right, sharing the pre-school hairspray. Even the musically unaffiliated have formed allegiances and alliances, trading lines from last night's episode of *The Young Ones* or cadging cigarettes off one another.

Our lad is in a fantasy world of his own, a Midnight Runner in his dreams, imagining himself in the band, quite possibly on second trombone. There's a cacophony of horn riffs in his ears this morning, *every* morning, delivered there at full volume by the Walkman he got for Christmas last month.

In his head, the boy's waiting for his light to turn green. Before that, though, he's waiting for the school bus to come round the corner.

*

Unlike the boy at the bus stop – waiting, waiting, waiting – Dexys Midnight Runners never stood still.

This impatience, this restlessness, came from Kevin Rowland. He wouldn't allow the grass to grow under the band's feet, nor the view to become too familiar, nor anyone to second-guess their – by which we, of course, actually mean *his* – next move.

If it meant starting over, setting off from scratch again, so be it.

Accordingly, Dexys took on a succession of new identities, locked into a near-constant state of flux. New sound, new style, new songs. They frequently changed their clothes, both figuratively and literally.

They – and, again, we pretty much mean *he* – changed personnel frequently too. Sometimes these changes were forced upon Kevin Rowland by mass exoduses, but he never fought against them.

There are very few instances of him attempting to persuade, let alone beg, a want-away band member to stay in the ranks.

Between 1978 and 1985, during the band's imperial phase, dozens of people ran with the gang, Dexys disciples of varying degrees of allegiance and commitment. They were actually a series of gangs, with fluctuating membership and fluctuating fortunes.

As the personnel changed, so too did the nature of the band, the shape of its structure, the tenor of its internal politics. Initially – at least when looking in from the outside – they appeared a cohesive unit, a watertight firm, energised by an all-for-one mentality, albeit with Kevin as their captain and spokesman. This mutated over time. After a mutiny cast the original line-up into history, the reins were tightened. Captain became boss. By the time of the band's second album, 1982's *Too-Rye-Ay*, they were already billed as 'Kevin Rowland and Dexys Midnight Runners'.

That fourteen-year-old schoolkid who was searching for his own little clique back in the early '80s is forty years older now. This time, I'm ready to seek out the actual gang – or gangs – I so admired back then. Whatever became of them? Whatever became of the gang members? Does their tenure in the ranks of Dexys represent the best days of their lives or was it an episode they keenly escaped from? Where are these young soul rebels now that they're in late middle age? And what have they been doing since?

The original eight-piece was chiselled down to a three-strong nucleus by the time of album number three, *Don't Stand Me Down*, when their line-up was plumped by a seemingly endless stream of session musicians heading through the studio door in both directions. Few of them were offered even partial permanent membership. Since then, many more session musicians have come and gone. The Dexys Midnight Runners name has been reduced too; the 21st-century version trades simply as Dexys.

My quest will accordingly concentrate its efforts on that imperial phase, the time of the full, three-word nomenclature, the seven years covering those three untouchable albums – *Searching for the Young Soul Rebels*, *Too-Rye-Ay* and *Don't Stand Me Down* – and the accompanying clutch of hit singles. I'll largely focus on hunting down those who made the most significant contributions to the band's evolution during that period – those who played on that trio of LPs or who formed part of the touring band for a notable length of service. There's more than enough of those for the Dexys detective to go after.

Come with me, why don't you? The passenger seat is free. And that light has now turned green.

Reminisce #1

Railway Approach, Harrow

Close your eyes and imagine. That's the ghosthunter's way.

Imagine it's 1968. Imagine it's just getting dark. Imagine that the two blocks of flats in front of you, here on the approach to Harrow and Wealdstone station, are in fact a single building, a white three-storey pub. Its sign reveals it's called the Railway Hotel.

Imagine the queue outside waiting to get in. In particular, imagine a fifteen-year-old youth, a little bum-fluff on his top lip and owner of an accent that the rest of the queueing punters don't speak with. Tonight, there's a certain soul band playing. If the kid doesn't get in, a particular chapter of British pop music may not get written, a certain band may never form, and certain era-defining songs may not get composed.

But despite being the smallest in the queue, which will end up impeding his view – the lowest head in the club that night, as he'll later sing, keeping an eye out for trouble – he's through the door. A quasi-religious conversion will fall upon him in the next couple of hours. Never mind the sweat pouring down the walls. Never mind the sweat pouring down everyone's faces. Get lost in the groove. Get lost in yourself.

Now open your eyes. The pub has been gone twenty years or so, its derelict shell finally falling victim to the arsonist's match. The two blocks of flats that inadequately replaced it are called Moon House and Daltrey House. They take their name from members of a different band, one that played its first gig on this spot sixty years ago.

That fifteen-year-old boy is now seventy summers young.

And that sweaty night in '68 lives on in song, as the 19:07 from London Euston to Liverpool Lime Street confirms. It roars through the station below, offering a two-note salute. 'Der-dah,' it calls.

'Der-dah.' The opening notes of the main riff of a song called 'Geno'.

Dexys Midnight Runners, March 1980. (l–r) Geoff Blythe, Kevin 'Al' Archer, Andrew 'Stoker' Growcott, Pete Williams, Kevin Rowland, Jimmy Paterson and Steve Spooner. *David Corio/Redferns/Getty Images*

1

Kevin 'Al' Archer

Guitar, 1978–1981

*'We weren't just a bunch of thugs.
We had intelligence.'*

May 1 1980. BBC Television Centre, Shepherds Bush, London W12 8QT.

If you want an example of how Dexys Midnight Runners were in the game but ignoring the rules, just watch their appearance on *Top of the Pops* from the first day of May in the first year of a new decade. 'Geno' has reached number one, a song that glares down at everything else in the charts, rendering all of it insignificant. As presenter Tommy Vance introduces them ('What's number one? I'll tell you. This is – and it deserves to be!'), the band aren't waiting patiently, standing by their microphones, instruments in hand. The camera pans across towards them as they storm on stage. Surely no other band in the history of the show has taken to one of its stages while carrying sports holdalls. And, *most definitely*, no other band has then tossed said luggage all over the shop.

None of the band are as brutal as guitarist Kevin 'Al' Archer who, prior to strapping his guitar over his shoulder, blindly hurls his holdall towards the audience, not even glancing at the group of teenage girls upon whom the bag is about to land. But these boys, this gang, are number one and they don't give a shit. They stand

1

apart, at quite some distance, from the other guests on the show that week, who include New Musik, Hot Chocolate and the Nolans.

Although the shortest in stature of the eight on stage, Kevin Archer radiates more attitude than the rest. While Kevin Rowland is undeniably the chief architect of the band's intentions, of their sound, their look and their worldview, Kevin Archer is the clear number two, the right-hand man, the deputy – or, as the producer of 'Geno', Pete Wingfield, would describe him, 'the great lieutenant'.

Right from the start, nearly two years before 'Geno' hauled itself up the charts, the pair were the twin engines of the band. Their dream – of fusing a punky sneer with a deep appreciation for the sound and spirit of classic soul music – was the spark they hoped would ignite.

The pair came as a partnership. They'd been playing together in the Killjoys, a Birmingham punk outfit whose promising rosebuds – a decent-selling single, a Peel session – never came close to full bloom. When the band imploded, Kevin R revealed his new – and, at the time, decidedly unfashionable – musical vision to Kevin A, wanting his old bandmate to be the first on board, the earliest recruit to the crew. Archer was initially reticent but succumbed to persuasion. Together, the duo spent the next few months scouring Birmingham and the Black Country for musicians who fitted the demanding brief, musicians who would give up everything – jobs, relationships – to become round-the-clock members of Dexys.

As such a fundamentally crucial figure in the band's evolution, Kevin Archer is the obvious candidate to first pursue in my quest. To begin at the beginning. From the start, from the source.

Kevin still lives in Cradley Heath, a Black Country town found halfway between Dudley and Halesowen. One of his bandmates from his post-Dexys band, the Blue Ox Babes, has kindly passed his email address on to me. An exhaustive – possibly exhausting – message goes off from me to him, outlining the nature of my mission and reassuring him about both my credentials and good intentions.

Later that evening, a short message comes back from Kevin, friendly, but politely declining my proposal. And, unlike his change of heart when approached to join the nascent Dexys, he can't be coaxed into reversing his decision. I clearly don't possess the powers of persuasion that the younger Kevin Rowland had at his disposal.

The great Dexys search, this worldwide manhunt to track down the disappeared, has got off to a faltering start. This is undoubtedly a blow. Doubts about the entire endeavour now begin to percolate. Will the rest of the disappeared choose to remain so?

After all, the Dexys story is a tale that was constantly shaded by friction and fights, by mistrust and manoeuvring. Why should I presume that each and every past member would gaily float into my orbit, happy to recount what were, for at least several of them, pained and painful times? Why would they want to prise open the door on the past, to scratch at healed-over scars? Why would they choose to break decades-long silence for me? Will what went on within Dexys remain within Dexys?

Does this grand quest just exist in my head? Will the whole notion just fizzle out, my fireworks pissed on? Questions. Doubts. More questions.

Kettle on. A deep breath. Time to realign my perspective.

Of all those ex-members on my wanted list, Kevin Archer was always going to be the most likely to decline an invitation to sit down and rake over old coals. His particular coals have never completely cooled, containing as they do an unfair share of hurt, disappointment and despondency, the themes of a highly creative musical life derailed by the decisions of others.

Those themes weren't always there. Playing the part of that great lieutenant – and now restyled as Al Archer to avoid any confusion with his namesake – Kevin helped build Dexys from the ground up, recruiting wisely, fine-tuning that holdall-flinging attitude, and writing some stone-cold killer tunes, as credited on the likes of 'Geno' and 'There, There My Dear', the songs that defined the band's first coming.

They were on an irresistible upward trajectory – young men in demand, young men serving a common purpose. 'It was a gang thing,' Kevin would later tell the music journalist Everett True. 'We weren't just a bunch of thugs. We had intelligence. We weren't just yobs or whatever. People saw us as a real group. A lot of people said that to me, which I think is quite a compliment. At the time, groups were manufactured.'

After their first independently released single 'Dance Stance' had lingered on the periphery of the top forty, signing with EMI supplied the propulsion their ideals and sense of purpose demanded. The view from the number-one spot was their reward. Not that they would smile about it. They wouldn't celebrate – not publicly at least. Instead, they would strive to do, and be, even better.

And better did come. The debut album *Searching for the Young Soul Rebels* landed with some impact and would, over the subsequent decades, be rightly recognised as one of the classic debut albums of British musical history. The accompanying touring was relentless, a foot-down, no-sleep-'til-Bradford tear around the UK. And then continental Europe. And then a whistle-stop jaunt to New York City. Rarely has the word 'intense' been so inadequate as an adjective.

This success, though, wasn't accompanied even by the most modest of financial rewards, at least not for everyone in the band. It transpired that, of the eight, only three of them – the two Kevins and tenor sax player Geoff Blythe – were actually signed to EMI. Despite the supposed common purpose, despite the supposed musketeer-like all-for-one philosophy, there was a two-tier hierarchy in place. A crack became a fissure. That fissure became a void.

In November 1980, just six months after they sat atop the singles chart, five of them (including Geoff Blythe but not trombone player Jimmy Paterson) grabbed their instruments and upped and left, re-emerging in the New Year as the Bureau. Jimmy and the two Kevins remained, and vacancies were rapidly filled.

By January, another position opened up. Kevin Archer was off as well, ground down by the endless gigging and unhappy with Kevin Rowland's increasingly unilateral behaviour. 'Controlling? Yeah,' he explained to *Record Collector* several decades later. 'He was OK at first, but once "Geno" had gone to number one, we were going on stage and he sent an assistant to ask me not to wear my red hat. "Kevin's orders."

'I think he was glad to see the back of me. And I just wanted to form my own band. We seemed to end on good terms, but there was an underlying sense that I had as much right to be in the band as he did.'

Having been tipped off by one-time Dexys manager Bernie Rhodes that folk music was going to be the next big thing, Kevin could see the possibilities of that suggestion and began listening to

'I think he was glad to see the back of me.' Kevin Archer (*right*) catches up with his old bandmate Kevin Rowland around the turn of the millennium. *Dave Tonge/Getty Images*

a lot of what would later be collectively labelled American roots music – Cajun, western swing, black gospel . . .

Enlisting the services of some of his musical associates, including his girlfriend Yasmin Saleh and former Dexys keyboard player Andy Leek, Kevin invited a violin-playing student from the Birmingham School of Music to sit in and play on some demos for this new band, the Blue Ox Babes. Her name was Helen Bevington and she did an excellent job of switching from her classical training to imbue Kevin's songs with plenty of soul.

Kevin Rowland was also privy to Bernie Rhodes's tip, and similarly was wanting to introduce strings into the new version of Dexys, albeit initially plumping for cello and viola. Kevin Archer didn't really take his former bandmate's plans seriously. 'He would talk about blowing up the Houses of Parliament with a straight face!' he later told *Record Collector*. 'I'd had a great time recording the songs. It was a breeze, everybody said they were good. But I needed to get another opinion. Rowland was my old songwriting partner, so no harm, eh? I took a Walkman over to his house. He said, "I can't hear it that well. Can I borrow the tape?"

'Then I never heard from him for about a year. One day, I was in my flat with the group. I happened to switch on the radio and "Come on Eileen" was on. I thought, *We've had it now*. I felt gutted. They'd adopted a similar style to us.' There was no sniff of cello or viola on 'Come on Eileen'. Instead, it was powered along by a violin trio, led by Helen O'Hara, the renamed Helen Bevington, whose phone number Kevin Archer had previously passed on to his former bandmate.

In 1993, Kevin Rowland held up his hands. 'When he left,' he said of Kevin Archer to *Q*, 'we were both experimenting with strings. I wasn't getting what I wanted: he found it and I stole it. As a result, he disbanded his group. Dexys had taken his sound and succeeded with it.'

With 'Come on Eileen' a worldwide hit, Kevin Archer couldn't see a way for the Blue Ox Babes to release their material without – heavy irony alert! – being accused of being copyists. There was a modest offer on the table from Stiff Records, but Kevin declined it. The Blue Ox Babes went their separate ways, no longer a herd.

The following summer, he was actually invited back into the Dexys fold as a co-vocalist but declined this too ('People would have said, "It's Kevin Rowland and who's *that*?"'). Instead, he continued to plough his own furrow. In 1985, Kevin was diagnosed with paranoid schizophrenia, much to his shock. He later attributed it to heavy cannabis use during his Dexys days.

But the medication he was prescribed stabilised him and he reconvened the Blue Ox Babes. This time around, at least on the first demo, the line-up was exclusively taken from Dexys alumni. Joining Kevin were the violin player Steve Shaw (who'd been rebadged as Steve Brennan in his time in Dexys), the bass player Steve Wynne, plus pianist Vincent Crane and drummer Woody Woodmansey, fresh from playing on sessions for the third Dexys album, *Don't Stand Me Down*.

Progress was steady, if not necessarily swift, and by 1988, the Blue Ox Babes were signed to Go! Discs and an album was recorded. Again, the Dexys connections were conspicuous. It was recorded – as *Searching for the Young Soul Rebels* had been – at Chipping Norton Studios in Oxfordshire, with Pete Wingfield again in the producer's chair. Jimmy Paterson and Geoff Blythe played horns on it. And, by now, the Babes were being managed by Kevin Rowland's brother, Pete.

The first single, 'There's No Deceiving You', was an absolute corker, with brass and violin swinging freely, and Kevin and Yasmin's vocals interweaving to great effect. And in the accompanying video, Kevin is beaming away. He looks like a man liberated.

However, the single stalled at number ninety-one. Kevin's previous concerns about the Blue Ox Babes being seen as Dexys imitators

were, a handful of years later, still being borne out. In its review, the
NME couldn't resist the comparison between the two bands, anoint-
ing 'There's No Deceiving You' as 'a thoroughly convincing, impressively precise impersonation of Dexys doing a runner. A neat trick,
but how many times dare they pull it before the clouds of self-doubt
close in on them?'

'You'd never know Kevin Archer had been in Dexys to listen to
the debut album from the Blue Ox Babes,' declared another review.
'It sounds nothing like the Celtic Soul Brothers' swing of "Eileen"
vintage. Well, yes, actually it does.' The review at least went on to
praise how the record was 'fresh, enjoyable and vastly entertaining'.

And when interviewed by Jonathan Romney in the *NME*, reacting
to the observation that 'you can't help noticing an uncanny resem-
blance between Archer's new band and the one he left seven years
ago', Kevin could only protest, 'I can't change the way I write . . .'

Although reviewed in a few places, the album wasn't actually
released. Two subsequent singles failed to make an impression on
the charts, causing those predicted clouds of self-doubt to gather
and internal squabbles to fester. Both Yasmin and Steve Shaw left,
leading to the record label halting the album's pressing as there
was, effectively, no group left to promote it. An eleventh-hour
attempt to save the band, with Kevin writing new songs with the
piano player, failed and, after more than seven on/off years of the
Blue Ox Babes, they dissolved. It would be twenty-one years before
that one album, *Apples & Oranges*, would see light of day.

In 1995, a redemptive Kevin Rowland attempted to make amends
with Kevin Archer, declaring that, from now on, his former bandmate would receive 50 per cent of his royalties from the second Dexys
album, *Too-Rye-Ay*, which obviously included earnings from 'Come
on Eileen', by then a staple of '80s radio stations across the world.
The money allowed Archer to relocate to Hamburg, the change of
scene helping him to come off his medication, which he did for five
years. 'I found when I was in Germany,' he told Everett True, 'I

could wake up and go for a walk and there was nothing – not even a record shop – connected with Dexys.'

After a while, though, Kevin began to hear voices in his head and returned to the UK. Later, as he told *Record Collector* in 2009, 'Rowland phoned up and said that the 50 per cent would now be 5 per cent. He's changed it to 10 per cent now, but he just said, "You've had quite a bit of money." A week later, I started to hear voices again, talking about the devil, and I thought he was out to get me . . . The last thing I heard Rowland say in my head was "I never give up". I'd been in a psychiatric unit for two days, they changed my medication and the voices suddenly stopped. That was in 2007.'

The very belated appearance of *Apples & Oranges* in 2009 – a great record of rootsy pop with Kevin's melodic sensibilities to the fore – sadly didn't create a surge of interest in the Blue Ox Babes. It only sold 1,500 copies on its eventual release. Once again, Kevin Archer didn't receive the plaudits – and sales – that his creations deserved.

Of all the former members of Dexys I speak to over the next few months, not one will have a single bad word to say about him whenever his name crops up in conversation.

'Kevin Archer didn't get enough credit,' says Jimmy Paterson.

'Most of Kevin Rowland's writing was the lyrics,' says Geoff Blythe, 'but I'd say all the really happening music came from Kevin Archer.'

To Steve Shaw, Kevin was 'always incredibly creative, stylish, fun and charismatic'.

'Kevin Archer's songs were brilliant,' says Micky Billingham. 'They were to die for. He was fucking great. A brilliant songwriter.'

In 2019, ten years after the album's eventual release, he was back in the public eye. 'Dexys Midnight Runners founder giving away "lost" album for free,' ran the headline in the *Stourbridge News*. Those who'd missed out on *Apples & Oranges* a decade earlier had an opportunity to belatedly fall in love with it. 'There are twenty-five copies left,' Kevin is quoted as saying, 'free to anyone who is a Dexys fan. Just email me.'

The record remains a testament to his musical nous, his sharp creativity, his unswerving commitment to his art. Those principles have guided him through. Hopefully, at home in Cradley Heath, he still takes great pride in the music he's made, both as a Blue Ox Babe and a Midnight Runner.

'I've still got ideas,' he revealed in one of his most recent interviews, for the online magazine *Outside Left*. 'But it's all or nothing for me.'

Kevin Archer has largely been silent since. The fear that a large number of the rest of the former members of Dexys may share his reluctance to speak is still nagging away at me. I've been unseated at the first hurdle and am hanging from the reins, desperate to avoid the thump of the ground, the ignominious face-plant into the turf.

This was never going to be a straightforward charge to the line, clearing every hurdle confidently and easily, a smooth passage to the winning post. I look down at my wanted list. It's long. There are many, many furlongs to go.

Fortunately, someone helps me straight back into the saddle, back into the race, back on course. The next person on my list, the first member of the band to be recruited by the two Kevins, is happy to talk. A tick goes next to his name. That name is Pete Williams.

2

Pete Williams

Bass, 1978–80

'All we had was each other. We were learning and yearning and striving.'

Life isn't all bowls of M&Ms with the brown ones removed.

Backstage at the Exeter Corn Exchange, here in Dressing Room 2, there are no bowls of M&Ms. There are no bowls of anything, if truth be told, no sustenance on offer at all for tonight's support act. Pete Williams is, alongside his guitarist Andy Wellings, that support act, the turn that'll warm up a Sunday-night crowd of largely well-refreshed, ageing mods who've gathered to hear and see headliners Simon Fowler and Oscar Harrison from Ocean Colour Scene perform a stripped-down set of the band's hits.

To be fair, there is a kettle here in Pete's dressing room, along with Kilner jars of instant coffee and tea bags. There just aren't any mugs.

So, while he waits for his soundcheck slot, Pete and I head out for refreshment, decamping to a café around the corner, seemingly the only such establishment in the city still open on a late Sunday afternoon. He and Andy have just arrived from Portsmouth, the location of last night's gig. Perhaps aware of the absence of a rider here, the pair stopped off for a full-works greasy breakfast at a roadside diner near Dorchester. Then they further broke the journey at Charmouth on the Jurassic Coast, where Pete had a paddle in the sea, soundtracked by the sound of hammer on rock as the Great British Public turned fossil hunters for the day.

Now, over an Americano and a pot of tea, I'm ready to hear about Pete's two-stage tenure within the ranks of Dexys – first as the band's original bass player and then, into a new millennium, a stage-front role as Kevin Rowland's co-vocalist and sparring partner.

First, though, we step into the time machine and set the controls for 1978.

'Back then, I was somebody who'd bought a bass guitar at fourteen and who, by the time I was fifteen or sixteen, had been playing in bands in social clubs with older guys – always older guys – doing the chart hits of the day, picking out the basslines. By the time I was eighteen, in 1978, I was a couple of years into an apprenticeship as a foundry man and pattern-maker in a factory in Oldbury in the Black Country.

'I met Kev Archer when the school I went to became a sixth-form college. He was part of the new intake, a year older than me. We were both music nuts and soon became friends. He was a good "bedroom" guitarist. I got him into a short-lived social-club band I was in and pretty soon after that we formed a punk band called the Negatives, playing at a hundred miles an hour. I remember doing an interview with Kev for the local paper, the *Oldbury News Telephone*. Kev told them, "We're fast. We're faster than the Ramones." When it came out, the quote was "We're faster than the Romans . . ."

'Then there was an advert in the *Birmingham Evening Mail*: "Punk and new wave bands wanted by management." We rang them up, organised a rehearsal and who should come into our rehearsal room, above the Shoulder of Mutton pub in Blackheath, but Kevin Rowland and his brother Pete. "Oh, it's that guy from the Killjoys."

'Pete was looking for bands to manage, but it was also a bit of a ruse as well, as the Killjoys had a few dates coming up with Generation X and Kevin was looking for a guitarist. So Kevin Rowland offered Kevin Archer the position and he left. I was happy about that. I was pleased for him.'

Fast-forward a handful of months and the Killjoys were no more. But the two Kevins were very much a musical item and engaged on a new project that bucked the prevailing trends and tastes of the time. Pete was their first port of call, the first appointment they made for their new-wave soul band. The sleevenotes of *Searching for the Young Soul Rebels* would later paint a romantic portrait of his recruitment: 'A young bass driver by the name of Pete Williams walked into the hide-out carrying his tool under one arm and the complete Stax collection under the other. Disillusioned with new muzak, he put his soul records on the table and shouted, "I want to do something as good these – only better".'

Although a few records by black Americans did get played around the Williams house – Gladys Knight and the Pips by Pete's parents, Stevie Wonder's *Innervisions* and *Talking Book* by his brother – the notion of this new group's fresh-faced teenage bass player being a soul devotee was exaggerated by the sleevenotes-writer's pen.

'None of us were, really. It was the dying embers of punk. There had been bands coming out of the rock thing and swapping their flares for drainpipe trousers and dog collars, but it had become a pastiche by midway through 1978. It was a case of looking around at what was happening. What's the opposite of this? It's black American rhythm and blues and soul music. So we immersed ourselves in soul. It was a concerted effort. "This is what we're going to listen to now." We used to swap records – *Otis Blue*, Booker T, stuff like that. We started to work out what we wanted – the urgency of punk but the polish of the brass.'

With the rest of the crew recruited – and Pete's apprenticeship jacked in – the discipline of a '60s soul band was then applied. 'We worked and worked and worked, rehearsing from ten until six most days. But we squatted places to rehearse. We didn't want to go to a generic rehearsal room. We very, very much kept ourselves to ourselves.'

He takes a sip of his Americano and nods to himself.

'It was a band. All we had was each other. We were learning and yearning and striving, trying to do the best that we possibly could. It was a collective thing, a collective drive. It wasn't dictated. It wasn't that. It was a bunch of us wanting to do the best. And we knew we were good.'

Then, after the intensity of the discipline and dedication of round-the-clock rehearsals, it was time to road-test this new soul vision, to become a live band. And these gigs were no tea dances.

'They were wild but very exciting. At some of the places, there'd still be gobbing. I always hated that. And glass pint pots being thrown. There was a riot at the original Factory club in Hulme in Manchester. Kevin had hit a kid across the nose with his microphone. He was in the centre of a group of loud, pissed-up, relentless hecklers. They all came backstage, broken bottles and everything. We had to fight our way out of there.'

Then came an extended baptism of fire, replacing Madness on one of the Two-Tone tours, opening each show ahead of the Selecter and the Specials. 'When we did the second half of the tour, we had to win that and take no prisoners. Some nights would be infiltrated by the National Front, siegheiling skinheads and all that. There'd be massive fights and stage invasions. It was exciting, uncompromising. We didn't take prisoners. We meant it.'

After such tumultuous gigs, the journey back to the West Midlands would be made in a minibus thick with dope smoke, and with the likes of Augustus Pablo, Iggy Pop or Van Morrison on the stereo. Decompression by whatever means necessary. Bring down the blood pressure, neutralise the adrenaline.

Andrew 'Stoker' Growcott wasn't the first occupant of the drummer's stool, but as soon as he tried out for the band, that position was firmly fixed. Pete had found his true rhythm section partner – and lifelong friend. 'Once Stoker joined the band, we absolutely clicked musically. He could play hard but he also had great swing and groove. He was a funkateer. And when we were locked in, the power and dynamic was great.'

After 'Dance Stance', disappointingly mixed without the band's input, only gently scratched the top forty, even after an appearance on *Top of the Pops*, it was time for Dexys to record their second single, a song that would propel them to the very peak of the charts.

'Kevin Rowland had a poem about going to see Geno Washington that he gave to Kev Archer. The song itself was written in Kev Archer's bedroom. We'd work out the brass lines on a Stylophone and then Geoff Blythe would arrange it. If my memory serves me, I think "Geno" went up the charts, then it went down, then it crept back up and got to number one. It was there for two weeks, I think. Two weeks in May. It was a great feeling.

'People start seeing you in a different light, though. There's that saying, "Remember me when you're famous." Well, remember me if I do happen to be famous, but don't treat me any differently. I was still living with my parents on the estate where I grew up and people who used to bully me at school would come up like they were my best mate. Still, it was great to think that that little tune that was written in Cradley Heath, using the poem that Kevin Rowland had come up with, connected with so many people.'

With a number one under their belt, Dexys then headed south to leafy Oxfordshire to record *Searching for the Young Soul Rebels* under the wing of the avuncular producer Pete Wingfield. The sessions at the residential Chipping Norton studios were intense and productive. Aided by their Beatles-in-Hamburg tightness, and with a clear bunch of songs ready to commit to magnetic tape, the recording was arguably the most straightforward chapter in the band's history. Until a certain heist, that is.

'I try not to talk about that actually,' says Pete, before then revisiting the episode in forensic detail. Once the final mixes were done, the band snatched the master tapes from the studio and fled with them back to the West Midlands, the idea being that they would be held as collateral until EMI renegotiated a more generous royalty agreement. It turns out that Pete, and sax player Steve Spooner, played a pivotal role in the hatching of the plan.

'The original EMI deal that [the management pair of] Bernie Rhodes and Dave Corke had brokered for us wasn't a good deal. Steve and I requested a meeting at EMI with Roger Ames, who later became a very important figure in the music industry. At the time, he was just a guy from Trinidad who believed in us. He was a lovely fella. So Steve and I went to Manchester Square.

'"Listen, we want to renegotiate the deal. It isn't very good. And if you don't, we're going to take possession of the tapes."

'Roger just laughed at us.

'"Boys, you're dealing with EMI. You don't do that. This is a very powerful company and they won't budge, take it from me. They're not going to renegotiate until the term's up. They won't look at it for another year."

'"Well, we're gonna do it."'

The pair returned to Chipping Norton to explain to the band how the meeting went. The heist was now on. With the final mixes complete and Pete Wingfield uncorking the Cava, the choreographed plan was quickly put into action.

'At a given signal, which I think was Steve Spooner coughing, we grabbed the cartons, the master tapes. There was a bit of pushing and shoving. I felt sorry for Pete Wingfield because it was his job as producer to deliver the album and he couldn't do that because we took it. We took our work. He was standing in front of the van trying to stop us, but Trevor the driver just revved his engine, the gates were opened and we were off. The police were called and there were blue lights everywhere, but we managed to get back to Birmingham.

We shared the cartons out among ourselves. I had a carton under my bed at my parents' house and Kev Archer had some.

'It was a result. EMI agreed to upping the deal by a point or a point and a half. Fat lot of good it did me, though. I didn't see any of it. Five of us didn't.'

On its release, *Searching for the Young Soul Rebels* was the punchy statement, and the beautifully realised work of art, that all the band hoped it would be. In the *NME*, Danny Baker couldn't hold back his verdict, blessing it in the very first paragraph of his review: 'Christ, this is a magnificent record.' Baker then went further, declaring that 'those blowsy, arrogant horns are blowing the landscape clean, constructing and urging where everyone else is just leaning on their shovels'.

Others weren't so glowing. Reviewing the album for *The Face*, David Hepworth opened with the suggestion that 'you won't go short of excuses for snickering at Dexys Midnight Runners from behind your hand'; 'lofty self-esteem' was the first crime on the charge sheet. Across the Atlantic, *Rolling Stone* conceded that Dexys 'show themselves capable of becoming the Sex Pistols of soul', before noting that 'it's really too bad that on most of *Searching for the Young Soul Rebels*, the B in Dexys' R&B stands for bullshit'.

Today, Pete admits that, by his self-diagnosis, at the time he suffered from what would become known as imposter syndrome.

'I didn't listen to that album for about ten years after I left Dexys. Possibly more than that. The bass is very forward in the mix on it and I was so insecure about it. I'd got no confidence in what I was doing. When we were at Chipping Norton, I thought, *Any minute now, they're going to say, "Get the kid out. Get a real bass player in. Get a professional who knows what he's doing."* I was insecure because I'd taught myself. When I did finally listen to it again, I thought, *Fucking hell. You did all right there.* Years later, I bumped into Pete Wingfield when I was walking through Camden Town. He said some lovely stuff about my playing. He said it was the heartbeat of the record.

'It was us against the world. All we had was each other and I think that comes across. I'm very proud of that record.'

Even if Pete had shown pride over the album when it came out, that may nonetheless have evaporated shortly after its release when he learned the terms of the EMI deal – that only the so-called nucleus of the two Kevins and Geoff Blythe were signed to the record company.

'My idea of the nucleus was that it was a core of people to do interviews and carry the new soul vision forward. But it turned out that only three people were signed to EMI and that the money wasn't fairly distributed.' The beneficiaries of the slightly improved EMI deal, the reason why the heist had been carried out, were that trio. The other five were left wanting.

'I was the youngest in the band. I'm not using that as an excuse, but I didn't really understand what that meant. I was involved in writing that stuff, but when the record came out, my name was not on any of the writing credits. I said, "What's happened here? Why aren't . . ."' His voice trails off on the air.

The issue of royalties caused a fault line across the band, a shifting of the tectonic plates that forever reconfigured the supposedly so solid crew. 'A fissure is a good way to describe it.' Added to this was a punishing touring schedule that attempted to take full advantage of the leg-up that both 'Geno' and *Searching for the Young Soul Rebels* had given them.

'Fatigue played a big part. The touring was really intense. These were, like, fifty-date tours of the UK and Ireland, a week off, and then a fifty-date tour of mainland Europe and Scandinavia. We were living on top of one another, just working and working with no time to develop where we were going to go. It was "Work the album, work the album".

'But all the shows were blistering. The quality of the music never went. Whenever we hit the stage, it was incredible. I've played plenty of powerful gigs over the years, but with Dexys it was something primordial. I know that sounds pretentious, but on certain nights, it just created its own thing. Even the last show in Zürich – when the original band imploded or however you want to call it – was transcendental. The power was beyond us.'

Despite this ability to create transcendentalism on a nightly basis in municipal venues across the continent, the combination of the EMI deal and the touring fatigue were joined by loud whispers that certain members were imminently to be sacked by Kevin Rowland. 'He isolated himself more and more. I thought that he may have wanted that incarnation of the band to split up. In Zürich, we knew it was the end. The two Kevs took a flight up to Luxembourg to do an interview and we got in the minibus and drove back home through Europe. It was a very quiet, very sombre mood. There was an air of exhaustion. We didn't know what we were going to do.'

The next chapter, though, soon became apparent. Before any P45s could be issued, five of them – Pete, Geoff Blythe, Steve Spooner, Stoker and recently appointed keyboard player Mick Talbot – jumped ship. 'I went up to Kev Archer's and said, "Listen, Kev. We're gonna split." And he just wanted to rest.'

'It wasn't a conspiracy. We knew we didn't own the name. We had no management. We had no label. We had nothing. EMI wouldn't let us in the building. It was a very confusing and unpleasant time. The five of us – what became the Bureau – had to start right from the bottom again, auditioning people and all of that.'

Singer Archie Brown and guitarist Rob Jones were recruited from the ranks of the Upset, one of the support bands on the Intense Emotion Revue, Dexys' most recent UK tour. With Big Jimmy Paterson having decided to stick with Kevin Rowland to co-author Dexys' second coming, another trombonist, Paul Taylor, filled the final Bureau berth. Back to an eight-piece, and retaining that instantly recognisable horn sound, the new band were swiftly signed to WEA for the kind of handsome sum they could only have dreamt of a few months earlier. Six figures, it was. They were WEA's biggest new signing of 1981.

The services of Pete Wingfield were re-engaged to produce their debut single, 'Only for Sheep', another fine slab of new-wave soul. Success, though, proved not to be inevitable. The single failed to make an impression on the UK charts, although it did reach number five in Australia. Not that the record company took advantage of this. Rather than being sent Down Under to maintain their momentum, the Bureau were instead packed off on a tour of North America supporting the Pretenders.

'We never went to Australia,' Pete sighs, more than four decades later. 'When UB40 came back from their first tour there, their keyboard player Mickey Virtue said, "We couldn't get away from that fucking 'Only for Sheep'."' But as their single was seemingly being played on an hourly basis by radio stations from Perth to Brisbane, its creators were on the other side of the world, otherwise engaged.

Ever the positive thinker, Pete could always identify the silver linings. 'What a great experience for a twenty-one-year-old to cross America, to go across the desert in a convoy of three cars. America in '81 was so druggy. Everyone's like "Hey, you like to party? They call me the Quaa Queen. You want some ludes?" All that kind of stuff. "Gee, you sound just like Mick Jagger." I really don't.

'It was an extensive but real budget tour, but the Pretenders were so good to us. They shared their rider, shared their food. But we had to leave our equipment in New York. We didn't go up to Canada because the Pretenders' drummer Martin Chambers broke a bone in his hand and couldn't hold a drumstick. They couldn't do the Canadian leg of the tour, so they flew back home. We were scuppered, stuck in a couple of rooms at the Iroquois Hotel in midtown Manhattan. We pooled the last of the money we had to go to Chicago and explain our position to WEA, the record company, who refused to give us any money for flights. Back home, our manager was nowhere to be seen. We had to leave our gear in hock to get back.

'When we arrived home, we went to the office in Birmingham. We pushed the door open and the floor was covered in brown envelopes.

No VAT had been paid on the record company advance. We were all directors, so we were all liable for bankruptcy. Customs and Excise came after us individually for the VAT on the 100-grand advance. We were furious. We sacked our manager and left our record company.

'We carried on and secured some live dates in Ireland and Europe, but my lung collapsed in Dublin and I got pneumonia.' The writing was on the wall, the steam was running out. And with WEA never having released the Bureau's album in the UK (it only eventually appeared in 2005), there was no momentum to take advantage of. The band just fizzled out. Pete sighs. 'There you go . . .'

It's time for this afternoon's soundcheck, so we saunter back round the corner to the Corn Exchange. The soundcheck, for two men and their guitars, doesn't take long. We're soon back in the dressing room. The story continues, uninterrupted by the kettle's boil. There are still no mugs.

'Eighteen-year-old me would be proud that I stuck with music.' Pete Williams runs through some last-minute checks backstage at the Exeter Corn Exchange.

Post-Bureau – and after two soul-sapping experiences with two major record companies – Pete could be forgiven if he had allowed the capricious ways of the music industry to dent his spirit, to weaken his resolve, especially as he was still yet to see his twenty-second birthday. But he didn't let it.

'I still believed in music, in what it could do, and in the feeling that I got from playing. And I just loved the lifestyle. I loved to travel. I'm from the landlocked edge of the Lion Farm Estate in a little wide spot in the road called Oldbury. Just going to the seaside is still a thrill for me. I went to New York City with Dexys in 1980, a bunch of us mates together in Manhattan when it was dirty and exciting and dangerous. I love to play shows and to travel. I love that part of it.'

A resumption of the apprenticeship at the factory was never on the cards. After helping out his old mate Kev Archer on some demos for the Blue Ox Babes, Pete got together with keyboard player Fred Skidmore and drummer Ian Pettitt to create his own thing. 'Ian was an outstanding drummer and we really clicked as a rhythm section. I was writing my own songs, trying to find my voice. And that became These Tender Virtues, my band through the '80s. It was very much about me wanting to step out from the bass to sing my songs. We did some shows with the Pogues and with the Jesus and Mary Chain. We got a publishing deal, which meant I could buy a Hammond organ, which I loved the sound of.

'At the time, Thatcher was going on about Victorian values. The idea of These Tender Virtues was to turn that onto its head, so we looked like Dickensian urchins in britches. It was so at odds with everything else that was happening. Stock, Aitken & Waterman was just starting up. We wanted to bring back vaudeville and burlesque, and include all kinds of strange things in the set – like trad jazz, but played in an unusual way. It was a very creative time for me.'

Creativity is one thing. Another is having to engage with the world of commerce. But, this time around, Pete's encounter with an unpredictable record industry was decidedly more positive.

'We made a demo and I went down to Charing Cross Road to EMI Music Publishing. I didn't have an appointment. I just walked in in my frock coat and britches and boots. I managed to see a guy called Brian Hopkins, who was the MD. "Come on in. I'll see you." I gave him the cassette and he played it. "I love it. What else have you got?" I played something else on the piano, stumbling about on it.

'"OK, we want you on the label. It's a 7K advance. Here's a list of music industry legal people. Get the contract looked at. We'll pay for it."

'It was completely open. It was the first time somebody in the music industry had been straight with me.'

For the next five years, from 1984 until 1989, These Tender Virtues was Pete's primary musical outlet. Although, like the Bureau, they never recalibrated the musical landscape, they did leave us with the glorious *The Continuing Saga*. . . mini-LP, seven tracks of literate and deeply imaginative art-rock vaudevillism that still sounds sharp more than three decades later. The world just didn't listen hard enough. Pete just wasn't made for those times.

Since the start of the '90s, he's turned his hand to all manner of things to keep the wolf halfway up the garden path. All of them – or almost all of them – have been musical. 'I ain't very good at much else,' he smiles. 'Of course, you could say I'm not very good at this . . .'

He was the house engineer at a community studio in Wolverhampton, he's worked in Brinsford Prison, he's taught at Dudley College, he's worked with excluded kids, he's worked with people with dementia. He's even delivered keyboards to orphanages in Romania. 'That was meaningful. No record to promote, no T-shirts to sell. That was powerful. Music as communication.'

That outward-looking work continues to this day; Pete's taught ukulele for the last eight years, in which time he's tutored more than 300 students in the instrument's ways. The only non-music work he's been forced to undertake was a three-year stint as a delivery postal worker. Even then, it was a job that gave him inspiration for songs. 'You're right up close to the Great British piss-pot public. These were rough estates that I used to deliver to. But I enjoyed it – walking and getting ideas. I'm a very keen walker. It's where I get most of my ideas.'

Then, in 2003, among all this outreach and teaching work, Pete's phone rang. The caller was an unlikely one. It was Kevin Rowland. The call was all the more unexpected bearing in mind comments Kevin had publicly made about Pete a few years earlier, comments the latter describes as 'unnecessary and stupid and wrong'. Nonetheless, he agreed to meet up.

'Kevin wanted to apologise for his past behaviour. I met him at Birmingham New Street station, and it was great. It had been so long that water had gone under the bridge. He looked well. I think he'd been fighting his demons. Meeting me and meeting other people, and apologising for what he did, was part of his recovery. We spoke frankly to one another about what I could have done better and what he could have done better.

'A few months elapsed and he got back in touch. "Pete, I want to put something together. There's a new track I'd like you to put some vocals on." He wanted me to add vocals to a track called "Manhood" at a studio in Highbury Corner in Islington. I went down from Dudley. I was working at the college at the time. He said there was money on the table for a tour so, not long after, we started putting the band together. I suggested Mick Talbot as we'd met just prior to that in Newcastle at a kind of Bureau reunion. And it went from there. The Stop the Burning tour, it was called.'

Previously when sharing a stage with Kevin, Pete had been the bass-playing teenager in the white woolly hat, bouncing up and down on the balls of his feet near the back. Now he was invited into the front row to share singing duties. 'I'm never really comfortable as a frontman,' he confesses. 'I'm always a little nervous. It took some work. It took a lot of work, actually. But our voices, although they're quite different and they have different ranges, kind of gel. It worked. And Kevin was very generous: "This is your line and this is mine." Those shows were very well attended. It was heartening to see that there was so much affection for the band.'

With Mick Talbot as musical director, the tour was a triumph, but no album was forthcoming. Nine or so years elapsed before Kevin made Pete's phone ring again. He needed him in the studio, to play bass on that slow-coming album, 2012's *One Day I'm Going to Soar*. For the subsequent live dates, Pete reprised his role as Kevin's on-stage sparring partner. The string of dates at London's Duke of York's Theatre were captured by the cameras of film-maker Paul Kelly. In the DVD liner notes of the subsequent film *Nowhere Is Home*, Pete's role is shrewdly defined: 'the straight man in the jokes, the sceptic to Kevin's proselytising, the officer investigating the burning'. He's both interrogator and moral compass.

'We worked on that, to get that tension, that area between humour and tragedy. We both like that area of performance. We worked hard on them, tweaking things. We knew what worked and what didn't work. I suggested stuff. What I did wasn't just dictated.'

On this tour, Pete was co-vocalist on several Dexys songs from the band's iterations after his departure in the closing months of 1980, in particular taking Billy Adams' spoken-word parts on 'This is What She's Like' or lustily leading the chorus on 'Come on Eileen'. Was that a strange experience?

'People used to come and stop me in the street. "He was in Dexys. You know, 'Come on Eileen'." "No, not that one, no." I never dined out on it. I don't sign records I didn't play on. Somebody came up to me in Newcastle with a copy of "Show Me". "Sorry, mate, I'm not on that one."'

As it was, revisiting those songs on that tour wasn't an exercise in facsimile. 'Geno', for instance, was retooled as a Colombian merengue. 'It was never about "Get the woolly hats and donkey jackets on again and pretend you're twenty". It was something worthwhile and artful. It was *creative*.

'The last thing I did with Dexys was in 2014, headlining the Acoustic Stage at Glastonbury. Will I ever do anything with them again? I don't know. But I wish Kevin well. When I was eighteen, he was seven years older than me. At that age, it's a big gap. Now it doesn't mean anything. I looked up to him and it was his drive and determination that pulled us along. I don't know what would have happened if mine and Kevin's paths hadn't crossed. I'm glad they did. It was a magical experience. I feel lucky to have been part of it.'

For now, for tonight and for the foreseeable, Pete Williams' main musical preoccupation is as Pete Williams the troubadour. 'I wouldn't say I'm prolific, but I've got three albums out under my own name and I'm very proud of them. They're the best that I could do. I've got no management, I've got no label, I've got no agent. But I'm going to carry on.'

Like its two predecessors, the most recent of those albums, 2018's *H.O.L.L.A.N.D.*, drew plenty of admiring glances. *Classic Rock* magazine likened his art to that of Costello, McCartney and McAloon, notably his 'ability to make magic from the mundane, to find shades of sublimity in the humdrum'. These words can be added to the volume of praise that's come his way in recent years, praise that's earned Pete support slots with the Proclaimers and the Specials. Richard Hawley supplied guitar on the first of those solo albums and sees a kindred spirit in his friend from Oldbury.

'For me,' says Hawley, 'it's all about recognising in another brother or sister that same appreciation, understanding and knowledge, backed up by a feral fucking instinct, that another side of this life exists, a side other than the one we're shown by the greed heads and the businessman and the meaningless, mindless pursuit of money. We can smell each other out. Pete smells good and is a damn fine man and musician.'

Pete has a well-honed sense of smell too. 'I know how not to be a twat, how to get the best out of the people I work with.' He, too, has lived a musical life far from geared towards riches. Monetary riches, that is.

'If, for a second, I felt that what I'm doing – what I did last night, what I'm about to do tonight – was phoney or a bit ridiculous, I would stop immediately. But I haven't got to that yet, thank God. I'm sixty-three now. I remember reading *1984* when I was about twelve, thinking, *I'll be dead by then. I'll be twenty-four and that's ancient.*' Then he remembers that interview he and Kev Archer did for the *Oldbury News Telephone*, back in their Negatives days. 'Kev told them, "People should be banned from being in bands when they're thirty. That's what we believe."

'There's been a certain amount of grind in my life, but eighteen-year-old me would be proud that I stuck with music. I was never really encouraged in my music by my family. This was the Black Country, the industrial Black Country. The secondary school I went to was really fodder for the factories.'

It's nearly showtime now, so Pete swaps his camouflage shirt and shorts for a caramel-brown suit and a black shirt with a generous collar. Even though tonight he's opted against the colourful handkerchief in the top pocket, he remains a dapper fellow. He always was the member of Dexys who carried off the stevedore look with the most style.

He and Andy take to the stage, revisiting the Pete Williams songbook for the burghers of Exeter. The room fills as they play. He hooks them in, all easy charm and heartfelt songs. 'When you play live and can hear a pin drop,' he told me earlier, 'you know you've got them. I'm still winning over audiences. I'm telling my stories and people are moved by some of the songs. And they're not bullshitting me. Why would they?'

After their fifty-minute set, it's a quick dash to press the flesh and sell the back catalogue in the bar during the interval. Exeter's ageing mods, though, feel they're not sufficiently refreshed yet. The queue for the bar is, as it ever was, infinitely longer than the queue for the merch table.

More business would be appreciated. Being the support act on a tour such as this is a lesson in fine margins, certainly once you take into account petrol, roadside breakfasts and hotels that purport to be 'budget' but are anything but.

Tonight's performance marks a little break in the tour, so the pair will make a swift exit back home tonight to the comforts of their native West Midlands, stopping only at Taunton Deane services for a late-night Filet-O-Fish.

Pete, in particular, is anxious to get home to Oldbury. Waiting for him is an audience more precious than this evening's at the Corn Exchange: his first grandchild, two-week-old Loretta, who's visiting for the bank holiday weekend. Tomorrow will mean special time for the baby and her troubadour grandpa.

'She doesn't know it,' he says, that twinkle in his eye shining brighter than ever, his heart still full of optimism, 'but she's the centre of our world.'

3

Pete Saunders

Keyboards, 1978–79, 1980

'Imagine if you wanted to go to the moon, but you'd been there
by the time you were nineteen.'

Between 1978 and 1985, Dexys Midnight Runners had many
keyboard players. But before Andy Leek, before Mick Talbot, before Micky Billingham, before Bob Noble, before Vince
Crane, before Mick Burton and before saxophonist Nick Gatfield
sometimes doubled up on keys, there was Pete Saunders.

And here he is now, forty-five years after he first signed up with
Dexys, sat behind the piano in a cellar bar in Edinburgh. Shaven-
headed but wearing a fine and full white beard, his hands glide
effortlessly across the keys, rolling notes filling the room. That it's
August in the Scottish capital, and that it's two o'clock on a weekday
afternoon, means one thing: this is one of the many thousands of
events that form the city's fringe festival.

This afternoon's free show is part of a month-long residency Pete
has here in Fingers Piano Bar, an hour-long revisit of his two-part
time in Dexys. Like Pete Williams, he's keen for the public to know
his time in the band ended in 1980. The show is called Not On Eileen.

'I'm going to tell you about myself,' he explains to the audience
in his opening remarks, 'because it's cheaper than therapy.' For

the next sixty minutes, he regales all-comers with tales from the first iteration of the band, while also performing a handful of songs from *Searching for the Young Soul Rebels*. Pete has plenty of grit and gravel in his singing voice. He puts this down to the ongoing effects of long COVID, but it acts as a boon to this particular piano man. With playing that's florid and flowing, he sounds like Dr John doing Dexys' first album. This is no bad thing. In fact, it's a very satisfying thing indeed. At three o'clock, the punters leave happy.

Rewind a couple of hours and Pete and I are sitting upstairs in Greenwoods, the café directly above the piano bar. He orders the Breakfast Stack Pancakes, a teetering pile of pancakes, eggs, bacon, sausage, hash brown, tomato, soured cream and maple syrup. He adds a portion of black pudding for good measure, all washed down by strength-giving coffee. Pete's in need of sustenance. He's performing in multiple shows at the festival. After this afternoon's solo turn, later on he'll be hosting his nightly Blues and Burlesque show across town at the Voodoo Rooms, an evening spent providing piano accompaniment to burlesque performer Belle de Beauvoir.

After that's over, Pete will be on the last bus to Musselburgh. Not for him a month of bank-busting lodgings in the city. For the entirety of August, home is a campsite a few miles east of Edinburgh. He's under canvas for the whole month, although thankfully his tent is large enough to stand up in. Or, at least, to sit up in. He has a piano set up inside it, on which he presumably serenades his fellow campers every morning.

My first question is about this solo show, about Not On Eileen. It's the first public exploration of his time as a teenager in Dexys. Why now?

'I'd never done a one-man show before. I thought, maybe at the age of sixty-three, I'd start standing on my own two feet. I'm a bit of a late deliverer. I don't have a lot of self-belief. I was forty before

I started my own band. Maybe I had a bit too much too young. It all happened suddenly, rather than a gradual build-up. So I just wanted to be able to sit down and tell the stories. Why not reclaim it? We're all on limited time.'

When he was recruited into Dexys' ranks in 1978 at the age of eighteen, Pete was already something of a seasoned performer. 'My family moved to Birmingham when I was fourteen and I found myself at the posh grammar school called King Edward's. I got involved in a theatre group when I was sixteen and I used to hang around the Cannon Hill Arts Centre. I got to know some people who were doing theatre shows in pubs, so I ended up writing songs for those at the age of sixteen or seventeen.'

This experience included making his Edinburgh Fringe debut in 1977. 'In those days, there was a Fringe Club for everybody in the Fringe. Just one club on the Royal Mile. It was before comedy was the new rock 'n' roll.' That show was based around King Kong. 'It was a revue show. To be honest, what I'm doing now isn't a million miles away from what I was doing then – a bunch of fairly silly cabaret songs in different styles. But it had a wondrous climax which I can't reveal because I want to revive it one day.'

A pause.

'But it did involve a four-foot girl dressed in a gorilla costume with everyone throwing paper aeroplanes at her.'

The following summer, a week after Pete had sat his A-levels, he saw an ad in the *Birmingham Evening Mail*: 'Keyboard player. New wave band.' The words 'new' and 'wave' particularly struck the young Saunders.

'I was on a very open track musically at that stage. I never could afford many records, but I remember one day I bought "Motorbikin'" by Chris Spedding, "Is This Love?" by Bob Marley, "Roadrunner" by Jonathan Richman and a Charlie Parker/Miles Davis album. So I was a bit all over the place. I also loved Steve Nieve's playing on the Elvis Costello albums, and the Stranglers had a keyboard player. Those were the bands I thought of as new wave.

'I had a place at university and was thinking, *What am I going to do? Well, for now, I want to be in a band.* And, yes, new wave was the thing that was going on. All that Stiff Records stuff was starting to happen.'

Pete called the number on the ad and an audition was duly arranged. But then there was the small matter of getting his instrument across Birmingham to Oldbury from his home in Moseley.

'I had to pay a man with a Transit van to drive my Hammond organ to Kevin Rowland's house. Kevin was twenty-five or so by then. He'd been a Vidal Sassoon hairdresser and made a bit of money doing that. The audition was in a tiny bedroom. He and Kevin Archer sat on the bed playing guitar. They weren't even plugged into the amps. I played along to "Hold On, I'm Coming" and then they played one of their own songs to me, "Tell Me When My Light Turns Green". They played it full-on. I was knocked out by it, by the power and the commitment. I thought, *There's something about these guys. Something's going to happen.*'

Pete passed the audition, but the man with the Transit van had done a disappearing act. There was no ride back to Moseley for Pete and his organ. Added to this logistical issue was the fact that he was just about to start a temporary job in Bristol. 'My dad was in the exhibition business and he got me this job working at the World Wine Fair for a month. It was good money, so I told the two Kevins I couldn't start until after that was over. So I left my Hammond in a strange house with two people I'd never met before . . .'

Once the four-week Bristol job was finished, Pete threw himself into the band, helping to recruit musicians for the remaining positions. These auditions took place in a garage in suburban Birmingham, where Kevin Rowland explained the working arrangements to the hopeful candidates. 'He told them, "We need you to give up whatever job you're doing. We'll be practising every day – nine 'til one, two 'til five." Not many people wanted to do that. There wasn't any money, so it wasn't a gig for jobbing musicians.

'Kevin was the dominant character because he *is* a dominant character. He was older, but he was also naturally like that. I remember one bloke who turned up. He had a beard. Kevin said, "You'd have to shave that off." He said, "I can't do that. I've got some quite bad scars." Kevin said, "That'd be great!" Looking back now, his vision doesn't seem so crazy. It's about how to make a pop group look interesting rather than just being a bunch of boring musicians.

'I picked Jimmy Paterson up from New Street station at six in the morning because I had a Ford Anglia. He'd got an overnight train from Portsoy in the Highlands. I gave him a cup of coffee back where I lived, then took him out magic mushroom picking in Cannon Hill Park. It was about seven-thirty in the morning. He'd just arrived in a new city and was taken out by this middle-class boy to pick magic mushrooms. We didn't take any before the audition, but I did have a couple of weeks where I got severely into them and was encouraging anyone I met to do the same.

'Geoff Blythe had been playing with Geno Washington and was a hell of a player. He could write parts too. Both he and Jimmy had studied music at college, but both were willing to commit. For Jimmy, it was a way of not being in Portsoy, or playing in a cabaret band or an orchestra. Then there was Steve Spooner, a sweet bloke who played alto and who was willing to fit in between the two of them.

'Somehow we believed. Kevin exuded this energy and drive. He got me into things. It wasn't his fault I got convicted of shoplifting, but I would never have got into it otherwise. I became a compulsive shoplifter. I couldn't go into a shop without stealing something. At one time, I was working in a head shop in Kensington Market, selling drug gear. The woman running the place asked me to go over to Woolworths to buy some batteries. I nicked the batteries but then had to go back in because I didn't get a receipt. So I went and bought a pork pie for the same value in order to get a receipt. How insane is that?'

The freezing winter of '78–'79 tested the resolve of the band, both in whatever unheated rehearsal space they were currently squatting and out on the road, skidding around the motorway network, doing gigs. As he harpoons another piece of black pudding with his fork, Pete shivers slightly at the thought. 'It was crazily cold. The pavements were covered in ice until about March. I can remember going to a gig in Sheffield and there were snowdrifts on either side of the road.'

The weather was harsh enough, but the reception the band often got was equally frosty. 'No one wanted to know us. It was "What sort of rock band are you?"; "Where's your lead guitarist?"; "With this horn section, are you a cabaret band?" And Kevin didn't really like talking to audiences in the early days, so he used to do recordings on a cassette to introduce the next song, like train announcements. "The band on this platform is Dexys Midnight Runners and the next song will be . . ."'

Dexys were then picked up by manager Dave Corke ('a used-car salesman who gave used-car salesmen a bad rep'), who secured them a residency at the Midland Hotel in the centre of Birmingham. He had connections to Bernie Rhodes, the former Clash manager who helped make London aware of these eight likely lads from the West Midlands.

'Bernie got us our first London gig, on a Rough Trade show at the Electric Ballroom. It was supposed to be the Raincoats, Kleenex, Spizzenergi and Subway Sect. But he pulled Subway Sect and put us on instead, without telling anyone that we weren't them. They realised after the soundcheck. Bernie just said something like "They're the new Subway Sect", so they said, "OK, you can have half an hour."

'We blew the roof off the place, but we over-ran, so they switched off the PA. But we carried on with horns and drums. As we came off the stage, we just saw all our gear literally being thrown into this courtyard. It worked, though. It got us noticed in the way we wanted to be noticed.

'Bernie got us to change our clothes because Kevin had the idea of this weird New Romantic concept before New Romantics had been invented. He had a pink hat with black netting over his whole hair, while I was dressed like some sort of 19th-century fencer in this big white buttoned shirt.' That wasn't the extent of it. At that point, the band had a trumpet player by the name of Geoff Kent, who opted to wear a white lab coat. Arguably the most striking, though, was Geoff Blythe, who was dressed like a Latin American general in a big jacket with a sash across it; he set the look off with jodhpurs and the kind of asymmetrical haircut that the Human League would soon favour.

'Bernie was the one who said we needed to go and see *Mean Streets*. So we went on the train from Birmingham to London, to the Screen on the Green in Islington to watch the film. That's what you did back then. You didn't just download it. You had to go all the way to London to see it.' Suitably impressed, the band stuck their proto-New Romantic clothes in the wardrobe and invested in more proletarian streetwear instead.

With the recording of first single 'Dance Stance' in the can, the autumn of '79 saw Dexys replacing Madness for that spot on the Two-Tone tour, the success of Suggs and co. by then having rendered them too big a draw for a package tour. Pete, though, had just taken up his place at the University of East Anglia in Norwich, having deferred for a year while the band shaped up. 'I was doing English and American Literature and History, and I couldn't defer my place any longer. Then suddenly this tour came up and, of course, there was no way I wasn't going to do that. So I was on this tour for the first few weeks of university.'

Pete's tutors seemed to be relaxed about the absences from academic life that his dual Dexys existence necessitated. 'I gave one of my English teachers a copy of "Dance Stance" when it came out and she gave me a B because of its references to Irish literature. Ah, those days of unscrutinised marking and unashamed political bias. May they long survive . . .'

The Two-Tone tour was an adventure, although far from always positive. 'It was very hard work being in Dexys because we were such a miserable bunch of cunts. We weren't nice to anyone. That was the rule. No smiling, even on a bus with the nice Specials people, the people who put you on their tour. You couldn't be seen to be friendly.

'I remember one night when all the band had been dropped off in Birmingham after a gig. Being a student in Norwich, I had nowhere to go. I stayed on the bus. The Specials got off later to visit a chippy. I was like a little boy lost, looking through the window at the people in the chippy. Then Terry Hall, who I'd never spoken to, got back on the bus and gave me a meat pie: "I thought you might be hungry." How sweet was that?

'I remember Jerry Dammers put me up one night too. When we did stay in hotels, the money we got paid only covered two hotel rooms and the sound man insisted on having his own.' That left the entire band squeezing into the other room. Surely eight into one doesn't go. 'It does if you take the mattresses off the beds and make it look like a massive gay orgy . . .

'We had no money. I can remember being at Rehearsal Rehearsals, Bernie Rhodes' place in Camden. We'd been there for three days, rehearsing. We said, "Look, look. We haven't eaten today. We need to." Bernie and Dave Corke turned around and said, "Don't worry. Tomorrow we eat." Not "Oh, I'll go and get you some food". It was "*Tomorrow* we eat"!'

After the tour, Pete headed back to East Anglia, but before the Christmas of '79 he'd made his unscheduled first exit from

Dexys. 'I'd gone back to college but we were still doing some gigs. And those were still good. But the one that killed me off was in Newtown in mid-Wales. I drove from Norwich to Newtown in my Renault 6 with my organ in the back. After the gig, I ran out of petrol. I managed to roll into a petrol station that was shut and I spent the night in the car. When I woke up, the car was covered in snow and I was shivering. I managed to fill up before driving back to Norwich and then on to London at the end of term. I was ill for two weeks. So I didn't mean to leave as such. It wasn't a conscious leaving. It was just that I couldn't cope any more. I might as well study *Beowulf* instead.'

Between shows at the Edinburgh Fringe, Pete Saunders lingers outside the watering-hole made famous by Ian Rankin's hard-drinking detective John Rebus.

Pete's position as keyboard player was filled by Andy Leek, previously known as the singer with Willenhall outfit the Wailing Cocks. As well as the thirty-eight-date Straight to the Heart tour that January, Andy also played on the recording of 'Geno'. That spring, after that slow ascent up the charts, it reached number one, much to student Pete's consternation.

'My Easter job was working at the CBS distribution warehouse in Barlby Road in North Kensington. I joke that it was my first entry into the music business – I was driving a petrol-powered vacuum cleaner around the car park, as well as feeding warped records into a compactor, records like PiL's *Metal Box* and Michael Jackson's *Off the Wall* that had been returned. That was my job. And each week on the Tuesday lunchtime chart countdown on Radio 1, I'm hearing "Geno" going up the charts.'

He was back in Norwich when it hit top spot. 'A few weeks ago, I went for a drink with some old friends from university. One of them said, "Oh Pete, I'll never forget that time, that Tuesday lunchtime, with your head in your hands in the students' union when 'Geno' got to number one, saying, 'What have I done?'"'

Within a week, though, it was announced that Andy Leek had left the band. Pete instantly put his hat into the ring to fill the vacancy. He called Pete Williams: 'I'm available if you want me.'

Before he received a reply, he had to go to London to pay EMI Publishing a visit. 'EMI wanted to publish the songs that I'd written, like the B-side of "Dance Stance", which I'd written the tune for. So I was driving the Renault down the M11 with my girlfriend when I had a blow-out. The car went up the verge and rolled over three times. We were completely unscathed, but it was fairly dramatic. So this lump of scrap metal got towed to my mum and dad's house in Chiswick. I can remember my dad's face, looking at the car thinking, *What am I supposed to do with that outside the house?*, but also relieved that we were alive.

'Then the phone rang. It was Pete Williams: "Why don't you come up on Monday?" That was quite a day.'

The conditions within Dexys had somewhat improved. Having a number-one single can do that. With those memories of Terry Hall's generosity still only six months old, Pete was part of the caravan decamping to Chipping Norton to record *Searching for the Young Soul Rebels*. 'I suddenly had a Cotswold cottage to myself in the heart of the town. Everything was there. People cooked whatever breakfast you wanted each morning and there were these barrels of Hook Norton beer around the place to help yourself to.

'And Pete Wingfield's a brilliant bloke, a really nice guy. As it happened, he had one of the world's biggest collections of soul records. He'd been around the States in the 1960s, collecting them. He'd visited the Stax studio in around '67, '68. You knew you were in the hands of someone who knew the source material. And he brought a massive pile of these albums down. So I was sitting in my little cottage, basically pirating his soul music collection.

'He was a brilliant player, too. It's his playing on things like "I Couldn't Help If I Tried". He played the piano on that. I think he pretty much did it on one take. To tell the truth, I was lucky he let me anywhere near it, lucky that he let me get a credit on the album. He worked really fast and that suited us. We knew our stuff. He didn't try to fine-tune the live outfit. He said, "Let's chuck it down. Get the energy on the record." I think it was done in two weeks.'

Nonetheless, Pete apportions a light helping of the blame for the stealing of the master tapes to Wingfield. 'He was the one who, when he heard how bad our deal was, said we needed to do something about it. I just don't think he realised Kevin's flexible attitude towards law, order and property . . .' (Indeed, the *NME* reported that Wingfield believed that 'Dexys did deserve a better shakedown but was well outraged at the method they used to achieve it'.)

Despite his shoplifting pedigree, Pete's part in the heist was underwhelming. 'I let the side down. I was at the back of the van where some of these reels of tape were. Pete Wingfield came running out and grabbed one of them. I remember thinking, *What am I supposed to do?* I kind of got castigated for not whacking him or stopping him taking it. But I'd just been working with the guy for two weeks. It wasn't in me. I'm glad I didn't hit him, but I was considered a weak link.'

Throughout June and July 1980, Dexys zigzagged across the country on the Intense Emotion Revue tour, topping a package that included the Upset, the Black Arabs and comedian/MC Keith Allen. 'Absolutely amazing gigs,' Pete smiles. 'Landmark gigs.'

The band's first US shows, at Hurrahs on the west side of Manhattan, swiftly followed in August, but by then Pete had begun to fear the worst. 'I had very bad feelings about things. I guess they'd already decided to sack me. No one was talking to me, no one was hanging out with me. They were all going off and doing other things.'

Was this a legacy of that passive part in the heist a few months earlier?

'I was nineteen, so I was a less cautious version of this sixty-three-year-old who's carefully choosing his words right now. At the time, it was reported to the rest of the band that I'd said something suggesting that maybe we should give the tapes back to EMI to get the album out. Time was moving on and the album wasn't being released. But apparently that was a thought-crime. Even just speculating on it was. I wasn't in a position to *insist* on anything, anyway. I wasn't on a contract and was being paid just fifty quid a week, just about enough to live on. That and all the donkey jackets I could wear . . .

'When we got back, Dave Corke invited me for lunch, which wasn't a good sign. He basically said, "You're out of this." I phoned up Geoff Blythe to have it confirmed. I got 200 quid to go and that was it.

'I didn't feel like going back to university. I wish I had, but I went back to my parents in west London instead and got a job as a van driver. I was still only nineteen. A has-been at nineteen. It did fuck me up a bit, because I'd done the thing I wanted to do. Imagine if you wanted to go to the moon, but you'd been there by the time you were nineteen. I'd been in the best band in the country, so I didn't want to be in another band. They were all shit. Other bands all wanted to get drunk and not practise. They didn't try, they didn't work. They didn't do all the things I'd just seen in Dexys. It took me an awful long time to get past any of that. And it made me completely unsuitable for trying to get back into the music business. I now knew it was really rotten, full of nasty people.'

But being back at his parents' home in Chiswick put Pete in touching distance of the west London punk scene. He played for a while in Jake Burns' post-Stiff Little Fingers band the Big Wheel, as well as undertaking a short period of service with the Damned; Rat Scabies lived just around the corner from Pete's folks.

'They were doing a gig at the Lyceum. I never met them before the gig. I had to go to Croydon to learn the songs with Captain Sensible's girlfriend, who just played me recordings. They introduced me onstage at the Lyceum: "Pete Saunders – he used to play with a band called Dexys Midnight Runners. Weren't they a load of shit?" I didn't like working with them. They were a bit too rock 'n' roll for me. I'd gone from the kind of Stalinist/Puritan Dexys thing to a band that made the Who look like amateurs. Serious sex, drugs and rock 'n' roll. Very testosterone.'

More civilised were Pete's contributions to Carmel's 1984 album *The Drum is Everything*. While Steve Nieve was on Hammond duty on the record's biggest song, 'Bad Day', Pete wrote and played the chunky organ that leads the trio's other top-twenty hit, 'More More

More'. He played on a couple of other album tracks – 'Willow Weep for Me' and a cover of Smokey Robinson's 'Tracks of My Tears'.

At the same time, Pete was also playing with Serious Drinking, a band formed by mates of his from Norwich. 'That was so much fun. It was really nice being in a band that had almost no chance of being successful in the charts. We toured Germany, but we were doing gigs largely for laughs. It felt very real. We didn't have a tour manager. We were reading our own maps. We weren't being treated like idiots. There's far more autonomy. That's the trouble with the pop world. You become infantilised because there's someone who does everything for you.'

By the mid-'80s, though, came a screeching career change. 'I started to have enough of the whole thing. I realised I didn't actually even like pop or rock music. My girlfriend at the time saw a job for holiday reps. They wanted a couple to run a villa in Rhodes. It was completely different. It was in the sun. I learned to windsurf and water ski.'

Once that job was over, it was time to find a new vocation back in the UK. 'My girlfriend's brother had a little decorating business. Actually it was quite lucrative as it was in the middle of a property boom. So I became a decorator. At one stage, I had about a dozen people working for me. But nothing lasts, does it?'

What did for Pete's trade was the 1988 budget, as delivered by chancellor of the exchequer Nigel Lawson, which announced that the double mortgage tax relief enjoyed by couples would shortly be withdrawn. Cue a frenzy of home-buying, followed by the inevitable market crash. 'Suddenly no one was getting decorating done and I lost the whole business. I just about survived, working on my own or with one other person.

'I got into a slough of despond after the financial crash, but I then joined the Jive Aces as their piano player. That got me out of a hole. I did an audition in Ilford and a week later I found myself off to

Bochum and Essen in Germany. Then I started doing duo gigs with female jazz singers. Through that, I started to sing more, whether doing backing vocals or singing one or two of the songs myself. So, bit by bit, I started doing what I do now.'

Then, in 2003, Pete Williams was ringing him again. A version of Dexys had been reformed and they needed Pete's piano skills in the studio. 'I was living in Islington and they were recording at Mike Hedges' studio nearby. It was all very weird. I had hardly any time to prepare. I'd only been given the recordings of what was going to happen a day or two before, and these recordings already had keyboards on them. It was a really nice day though – lots of joking and laughing. But I don't think they used anything that I played in the studio. You kind of know they're just going to dump everything you've done when they say, "Oh, don't worry. We'll fix it in Pro Tools . . ."'

Then, a couple of years later, came the move into the saucy world of burlesque.

'In 2005, I did some gigs with an American blues singer called Corliss Randall. We ended up playing a cabaret venue called Volupte. Soon I found myself regularly playing piano there and put together a cabaret package and called it Blues and Burlesque. It was burlesque with live music – no one else was doing it at the time. And the musicians seemed surprisingly enthusiastic! As one of them said, it made a change from entertaining woodwork teachers on the blues circuit. It was a match made in heaven: dirty old musicians and fresh young burlesque dancers.'

Pete's since taken the concept to arts festivals in Australia. This month's run in Edinburgh has provided sell-out show after sell-out show. 'Belle de Beauvoir is from Birmingham too. She went to the same school as me – just a hundred years later. She sings, she dances, she can do comedy. And she takes her clothes off to "Come on Eileen" . . .'

Whether in the one-man show or as a single-song highlight of the burlesque events, Pete's Dexys heritage continues to leave its mark. Dominating the first few years of adulthood, it was a formative time that understandably left an indelible imprint. Tumultuous gigs, inspiring recording sessions, car crashes, sackings – they've all shaped and coloured his musical life since.

A closing question. From those action-packed twenty-four or so months as an on/off member of Dexys, is there a single anecdote that encapsulates his time in the gang?

'Oh God . . .'

A lengthy silence. The first silence of the past hour.

'I'd need some preparation to answer that.'

OK, the most fun moment then?

'Fun?!'

Pete Williams said it was fun.

'He's got a more positive attitude than me.' Piano man Pete pushes his knife and fork together and wipes his mouth with a napkin. 'He was probably the most optimistic of all those eight sociopaths . . .'

Reminisce #2

Broad Street, Birmingham

In search of the Apollonia. In search of Dexys Midnight Runners' favourite caff, their HQ. In search of a meeting house long gone.

The Gentleman & Scholar pub and bistro, part of the Hyatt Regency hotel on Broad Street in downtown Birmingham, now stands where the Apollonia lived and died. There are no squeezy ketchup-dispensing plastic tomatoes here. There's no jukebox. There's no sporadically functioning payphone for which the band saved up their two-pence pieces in order to call potential promoters. No bacon butties, no egg rolls. Far from it. The bistro's dry-aged beef fillet, at £36.50, is comfortably double what a week's dole money was in 1978. You can't even get a mug of tea here. Those eight young men would hate it.

The view out of the window isn't what it once was either. Across the street now, blocking out the blue sky, is the hulking mass of the Symphony Hall, its glass and quartz and metal shining in the late afternoon sun.

The Apollonia might have been crushed to dust, but a couple of hundred yards down the street, a certain brick building is still standing. This is the Brasshouse, a portion of which the band appropriated for a rehearsal space, with Kevin Archer using his electrician training to hook their amps up to the mains. Like the rest of Broad Street, like much of the city centre, the Brasshouse is somewhat more upmarket these days. Swanky, in fact. This afternoon, on one of its outside tables, an empty bottle of champagne sits, upturned and discarded, in a silver bucket.

Next to the Brasshouse is the Black Sabbath Bridge, carrying traffic over the canal. On the bridge is a bench, complete with cut-outs of the four members of one of Birmingham's most successful musical exports – Ozzy and Geezer and Tony and Bill. The eight original members of Dexys – West Midlands boys bar the Scotsman Jimmy Paterson, and a band whose musical evolution was devised and honed just yards away – have yet to have a bridge, or even a bench, named in their honour.

On the pavement is the second city's Walk of Stars, a Hollywood-style salute to the region's finest who've made their stamp on the wider world. Sabbath are included here too, alongside such luminaries as Chris Tarrant, Toyah Willcox, Jasper Carrott, Noddy Holder, Jeff Lynne and the 1982 European Cup-winning Aston Villa side. Even the Trinidadian cricketer Brian Lara, who once scored 501 not out down the road at Edgbaston, gets a star.

Once again, Dexys are ignored. The invisibles, the forgotten.

4

Geoff Blythe

Tenor sax, 1978–80

'Just when I thought we'd got everything as tight as it could possibly be,
we'd still do it another five thousand times.'

When I set off in search of Geoff Blythe, the tenor sax player and horn arranger in the original Dexys line-up, my email was bound, I believed, for New York City. That's where Geoff has lived since the mid-'80s, initially with his first wife and their daughters in Little Italy in Lower Manhattan, and then with his second wife on Long Island.

I'm diligent in my detective work and like to think my methods maximise the chance of getting a positive result. So I send my email at 12.30 p.m. Greenwich Mean Time, presuming that it will coincide with Geoff – five hours behind – sitting down to his breakfast, to his bagels and coffee. The thinking is that the first incoming email of the day will get the closest attention. The opening request before the avalanche.

My aim appears to be true. Just thirty-two minutes later, Geoff's reply hits my inbox: 'I could consider this, sure.' But the reply hasn't travelled across the Atlantic. Geoff tells me he's been living in Cornwall for the last couple of years. We're in the same time zone and he's presumably just sitting down for his lunch, not breakfast.

47

Initially annoyed that my sleuthing isn't taking me over the water to Gotham, I'm also relieved that I'll be saving on a transatlantic air fare. Instead, it'll just be a couple of hours' sprint down the A30.

And that's what happens three weeks later – although the hare's sprint turns into a tortoise's crawl the closer that the A30 gets to St Ives, its single carriageway clogged by gallery-visiting holiday-makers. Geoff and his American wife Clare live further south, in a small village a handful of miles outside Penzance. There's a warm welcome for me when I arrive at their bungalow, which is bordered by an ivy-clad stone wall and set in a generously sized English country garden. It's a long way from the tight, unsleeping streets of Little Italy.

Plus, there's no airport check-in, no jet lag. Instead, a pot of tea is rustled up and Clare brings through the orange and cardamom cake she's baked specially for my visit. The service is even better than if I were flying club class.

'It was always the plan to come here when Clare could retire,' explains Geoff, pouring the tea. 'We'd been coming to Cornwall on holiday for fifteen years or so. We'd spend a month here at a time, sometimes two if Clare had stacked her annual leave up. She was a respiratory therapist and had worked there long enough to have earned very good holiday entitlement. Then COVID happened, so she took early retirement, a couple of years before it was due. I don't know if you realise how hard New York was hit by COVID. They were bringing in trailers for the dead bodies. Trump had lied about it and the hospitals weren't prepared. Medical staff would be given a single mask that they had to make last for an entire week, and the Javits Convention Center was opened up to house crash beds. So we got out a little earlier than expected and spent half a year in Delaware before coming to Cornwall.'

All those years in and around New York City are only occasionally discernible in Geoff's voice – just the odd 'going to' that becomes 'gonna', 'want to' that becomes 'wanna'. Otherwise, he's just the older version of the sax-mad young man.

'I always knew I wanted to be a sax player. Improvising was my thing. But I loved classical music and I wanted to be classically trained, to have two years of playing that music. The thing about going to a small, unknown music college in Coventry is that I was playing concerts all the time, as well as teaching while I was there. I was the principal clarinet. Friends of mine who'd gone to the Royal College of Music in London would moan that they weren't playing because London is full of professional musicians. Coventry isn't. So I was playing in the Coventry Symphony Orchestra, I was playing in the Coventry Wind Players . . . I was doing concerts all the time.

'But I didn't want to become a professional classical musician. And I've never particularly wanted to be a jazz player. People think that's weird if you're a sax player, but it's no weirder to be playing sax in a rock band than to be a jazz guitarist. I always intended to be a sax player in some sort of pop/rock outfit.

'The fusion thing was very big for me – Soft Machine, Weather Report, that kind of stuff. After college, I went down to London with a bunch of friends to form a fusion band. Total failure. We all came back to the Midlands with our tails between our legs. For a few months, I got a job counting screws in a factory in Tyseley on the outskirts of Birmingham. Literally counting screws. That was my job – stock auditor. It was a factory that made auto parts and there were cartons of different-sized screws and washers and nuts and bolts. I would go around every day to see how much of every-thing they needed to order. By about four o'clock every afternoon, I was ready to throw myself out of the window. That only lasted for a couple of months, thank God.'

Spiritual intervention came in the form of a certain American soul singer. Through one of his mates from the failed fusion band, Geoff learned that Geno Washington, the former US airman now living in the UK, needed a sax player for his band. Screw-counter Geoff jumped at the opportunity and joined the ranks, chugging up and down the motorway network, playing the pubs and clubs.

'That job really gave me the intro into soul. It was only for a few months because that was when Geno decided to pack up and go back to America to try his luck there. That's where I was when I met Dexys. That's *how* I met Dexys. They put an ad in the *Birmingham Evening Mail*: "Musicians wanted to form new post-punk/soul band. Influences: Geno Washington."'

Geoff's most recent employment must have deeply impressed this embryonic band when he called them up. Cue a speedy audition. 'They thought I was a shoo-in. They said they couldn't believe it. I was – unlike now – this little skinny guy and I blew the windows out of the room.'

Geoff was immediately offered the tenor sax berth, but he set a condition before he agreed to join. 'They already had a sax player. I said, "Listen, I'll do this, but you gotta let him go. He can't play. And he's not going to be able to. He's not gonna make it." So they did.'

Fortunately, also walking up the front path for an audition that same day was another sax player, Steve Spooner. He was offered the other spot, playing alto. 'I didn't hear Steve audition, but I did talk to him outside. He was a few years younger than me, but we bonded. We became room-mates on the road and really close friends. We still are.

'I couldn't be certain that the whole thing was gonna work, but I thought it really could because it was raw and unformed enough. It was very, very rough, but I knew the potential was there because there wasn't anything there yet, except for the songs. I hadn't walked into a situation that was together. We were starting from the bottom. There wasn't a plan per se. It wasn't "This has to sound like this. This has to sound like that." But it was a very original concept, with soul as the root, and the way it ended up sounding was really natural.'

What soon became apparent was that the horns would effectively be the lead guitars, with Geoff and Steve – soon to be joined by trombone player Jimmy Paterson – right at the front and extremely energetic when it came to their stagecraft. He agrees with the lead guitar analogy.

'That's exactly how I thought of my job. That was the interest for me. It wasn't two guys with horns stood at the back. And what I didn't get in terms of improvisation and soloing was made up by me doing all the arranging for the horns, designing the sound. That came from me doing composing while I was at music college. The arrangements were done in more of a classical way than a rock/ soul way. Steve played the high sax while I played the lower sax. He played alto, I played tenor. But, as the lead sax, I had to play over him a lot of the time. You don't normally have a tenor playing over an alto, and then the trombone on the bottom.'

When Jimmy turned up for that rehearsal, trombone in hand – and his fingers presumably still carrying the odour of his early-morning fungi forage – Geoff instantly knew that the classically trained Scotsman was the real deal. 'Yeah, yeah. Right off the bat. The minute we started playing with him, we just knew.'

With Jimmy signed up, the horn section was actually four-strong at that point. Completing the quartet was a trumpet player, Geoff Kent, who later moved to the suburbs of New Orleans, where he still teaches trumpet today. 'He left after a little while because he didn't want to do it any more. I convinced the band to keep the section just the three of us. I wanted to have this reedy, down-low sort of dirty sound. You put a trumpet in a four-piece horn section and primarily all you hear is the trumpet. I didn't want that.'

With the crew largely recruited ('We had a problem with drummers. That was our weak spot. I think we went through half a dozen of them'), that legendary Dexys discipline was adopted. 'It was the two Kevins' decision that we all had to sign on to the programme. It was really serious, like being in a gang. You had to be there and together all the time. If we weren't rehearsing, if we weren't playing, we still had to hang together.

'The Apollonia was our hang-out because they didn't bother us there. You could buy a cup of tea and sit there for five hours and they really didn't care. I think a lot of their trade was take-out early in the morning – construction workers and the like. Much of our talk was about the approach, about what we would do. And the rehearsing was ridiculous. It was non-stop for months and months and months and months. Just when I thought we'd got everything as tight as it could possibly be, we'd still do it another five thousand times. This is why we were such a great band on stage. We were certainly prepared enough.'

Geoff pauses for breath. And a forkful of cake. And then he's off again, recalling the Two-Tone tour that Dexys were co-opted onto halfway through its dates.

'Doing that tour was what really started it going for us. Two-Tone wanted to sign us to the label actually, which we didn't do because we didn't want to be totally locked in with their scene – basically, forever being second fiddle to the Specials. But it was great to do the tour, even though we were totally broke. We were on the dole – or, as we used to call it, state-sponsored practice. Sometimes we'd be in a hotel and would sign a meal to a room, just making up a room number.'

Declining to be just another band on the Two-Tone roster would prove to be a wise move. Another idea to set themselves distinct from the rest of the pack was approaching Van Morrison to be their producer. 'Kevin Rowland thought it would be great. He's a big Van Morrison fan. By this time, we had a residency at the Cedar Club in Birmingham, playing there every couple of weeks. We were packing it out and they were happy with us, so they let us use the place. The approach had been made to Van Morrison and he was going to come down and see us there. So, one afternoon, we were in the empty Cedar Club, just us on stage. We wanted to make an impression – we wanted to be blasting away when he walked in, so we had look-outs out on the street. We were blowing away when the door to the street opened. The sunlight was so bright, really blinding, and I just saw three silhouettes – a little guy and these two huge guys either side of him, presumably his bouncers. They walked in, stood there for literally about two seconds, turned around and walked back out. Then the door shut and that was that. It was the funniest thing. It was like a cowboy movie. I guess he just hated us. A lot of people, when they first heard us, hated us too.'

Certainly, second single 'Geno' – saluting Geoff's former employer – didn't automatically chime with everyone's ears. *Record Mirror*'s review described 'a turgid eulogy with few redeeming features'. *Sounds* went even further: 'the most boring band of 1979 burst forth again with this erratic and timeless tribute to their hero Geno Washington, who would probably keep his earplugs in if he heard it'.

The record company didn't get it at first either. 'They didn't want us to release "Geno" as a single. We had a big fight. They said, "It isn't going to chart. It won't work because of all the time changes in it." But we insisted. And look what happened . . .'

With Van Morrison having rejected them so abruptly, Pete Wingfield took the rudder, first on 'Geno' and then on *Searching for the Young Soul Rebels*. 'He was heaven sent,' nods Geoff. 'Heaven sent. He did a brilliant job. And Barry Hammond the engineer too. He was superb.

'It was a magical time in Chipping Norton. Going into a residential studio was the best thing we could have done. It was brilliant. We were taken away from the world and all we thought about was making this record. All the stars aligned and Pete Wingfield was very much part of that. Thank God we got him and not Van Morrison. Pete put the polish on it.'

Not that Pete was a laidback, passive producer, gently marshalling these eight characters. If he felt something was awry, he made his feelings known – as he did about the song 'Keep It', declaring that Kevin Rowland's words didn't fit the music. Instead, Geoff took himself away and came up with the lyrics. 'I don't think Kevin ever liked a song going out where he didn't write the lyrics on it. That was the only one. He didn't like it, but Wingfield refused to do it.'

After the heist involving the master tapes ('It was like an Ealing comedy') and the album's subsequent release, Geoff felt that the only way was up, that the band were buoyant, riding a wave, reaping the rewards of all that graft. Kevin Rowland appeared to see it differently.

'I thought that we'd made this great album and so we'd make another ten great albums,' says Geoff. 'Obviously not the same – as a band we'd progress. But he wasn't going to do that. Instead of going from A to B, then B to C, and C to D, we were going to go back to A, then to B again, then back to A. He was going to fire most of the band, so we had this idea: why don't the band just leave *him*? Get someone else in and keep going in the direction that we all wanted to go in. That was the idea. We had hoped that person was going to be Kevin Archer. He didn't stay with Kevin, but went his own way. He did his own thing.'

The irony is that the supposed sense of solidarity instilled within the band showed itself most readily in five of the band departing en masse. 'I bought into this – all for one, one for all. Everybody else bought into it too. Then I realised the one person who didn't really believe in the whole ethos was him.'

The five of them carried the ethos across with them to the Bureau. Jimmy Paterson had wavered over whether to turn five into six, but ultimately chose to remain to help recruit and reshape the new Dexys. Meanwhile, the Bureau found things moving quickly for them – and not always in a good way.

'The Bureau was a great band, but it had its problems too. We signed to Warners for more money than they'd signed anybody in a long time. On the week that the first single, "Only For Sheep", was to be released, the BBC cut all Warners' records off its playlists because the record company had been done for hyping. It was the American acts they'd been hyping. They'd been getting shit from the parent company in the States because they weren't selling the American acts well enough. So the BBC took Warners' records off their playlists for the next three months or something like that. We were screwed.

'The next thing is we're playing a gig at Dingwalls in Camden Town. We were just about to go on stage and our A&R guy comes in: "I've got something to tell you, fellas. I've just come from my office. There was a handwritten note on my desk. It said, 'From five o'clock this evening, you no longer work for this company.'"

'So the new management that came in just cut us out. They didn't fire us, but they stopped all support. Then we were on the Pretenders tour in the States when "Only for Sheep" became a hit in Australia. We should have been going to Australia, not being the warm-up on the Pretenders tour.' Like Pete Williams's recollection, one of Geoff's abiding memories of that tour was the generosity of the headliners. 'The Pretenders looked after us. Chrissie said we could eat with their crew. Otherwise, we'd have starved. And their crew crewed for us. Their drum tech did us for free. We'd have been dead without them.'

Stranded in the States by the record company, Geoff didn't need a magnifying glass to read the writing on the wall. 'Dexys had had an alignment of the stars with *Searching for the Young Soul Rebels*. It was the complete freaking opposite for the Bureau. It was obviously not meant to be.

'One of the most depressing times of my entire life was on the train after the end of the Pretenders tour – a packed train coming from London up to Birmingham to go home, drizzle hitting the window, knowing it was all over.'

On a sunny day in his English country garden, adopted Cornishman
Geoff Blythe dusts off the very sax that led the famous riff of 'Geno'.

Geoff found work wherever he could get it, which fortunately
didn't include a return to his screw-counting heritage. He was
commissioned to undertake some soundtrack work, supplying
music for a three-part series of short TV programmes aimed at
first-time voters, explaining what each of the three main political
parties stood for ahead of the forthcoming 1983 general election.

'It was very, very low budget. I did it in my living room at home.
Then I was on my way down to London to mix it and I bumped
into Jimmy on the train. I was walking down the corridor to go and
get a drink at the bar and he was walking the other way.

"'Geoff, how are you? Would you be interested in doing an album with Elvis Costello? I'd love you to do it, but you'd have to play alto.'"

Geoff's response was immediate and affirmative. 'So, after that depressing earlier train journey, it was a brilliant ride going in the opposite direction, going back to London. Absolutely brilliant.'

He had been recruited into a three-piece freelance horn section that would become known as the TKO Horns – as christened by Costello, after his song 'TKO (Boxing Day)' from his soon-to-be-recorded album *Punch the Clock*, on which the three horn players would feature heavily.

Jimmy had formed the horn section with Brian Brummitt and Paul Speare, his colleagues from Dexys Mk II. The three had jumped ship – Brian and Jim first, then Paul not long after – before *Too-Rye-Ay* had reached the nation's record racks. After the trio secured the odd job, most notably touring with the Paul Young-fronted Q-Tips, Brummitt resigned and returned to his native Newcastle. Paul had replaced Geoff as Dexys' tenor sax player, but playing alto wasn't a problem for the new recruit. A trumpet player, Dave Plews, was also added, creating the four-part horn section that Geoff had very deliberately avoided with Dexys.

Once *Punch the Clock* was in the can, the TKO Horns joined Costello and the Attractions for scores of gigs throughout the rest of 1983, including a particularly long haul across the US, starting in Allentown, Pennsylvania, and ending in San Francisco nearly two months later.

The TKO Horns were no shrinking violets on stage. They might have been the hired help, and they might not have stood upfront next to Elvis in the way they used to be positioned alongside Kevin Rowland, but they were far more energetic than the Attractions. Geoff was a restless, whirling dervish in the back line. Jimmy and Paul were equally lively. Dave was a little more reserved.

'That was a year's gig basically, because that's what Elvis does – start the year by recording the album, then you tour it for the rest of the year. I think our last gig with them was at Christmas and then it was over. But we knew it was going to be, that he'd go and do something else next that didn't need a horn section. So that was that.

'After the TKO Horns, I had a sax quartet for a while. We played in New York, having got a free flight over on Virgin in return for providing entertainment on the plane. It was a jumbo jet, so we had to play for ten minutes in one cabin, then ten minutes in the next and so on. It was an experiment they did – and people hated it. Can you imagine a sax bell in your face when you're trying to sleep? But at least it got us over to New York to play a few shows there.'

This was the point at which Geoff became a Manhattanite – which wasn't without logistical problems. Mario, the manager of Pete Williams' These Tender Virtues, wanted to recruit Geoff for another band he looked after. They were called the Neighbourhood. And that he now lived on the opposite side of the Atlantic wasn't seen as a barrier to his membership. 'Mario said, "I'll fly you back and forth", so I was living in New York but had joined a band in London. I got Jimmy involved with it too. It was fast funk stuff, not like the soul thing. Like Dexys, we also got signed to EMI. We made one album, a great album, but it was a complete flop. Again, just nothing happened.'

Living in Manhattan wasn't supposed to be a long-term thing, but Geoff ended up getting married and having two daughters. 'A lot of my time was taken up being a father, making their lunches, taking them to school, going on the school trips.' His sax playing was thus curtailed somewhat, largely limited to jamming in bars. Until, that is, a nascent Celtic rock band called Black 47 came calling. Geoff would be a member of that particular outfit for the next quarter of a century.

'My first wife knew the lead singer Larry Kirwan, who was just starting to put this together. He was a huge fan of the Bureau. He'd seen us in Ireland, where he was from. There were just two of them at that point – him and the uillean pipes player Chris Byrne, who was also a cop – and a drum machine. What was good about Larry was that, sort of like in the early stages of Dexys, he didn't preordain how the thing was absolutely going to sound. But he knew he wanted it to be political, very socialist. That was his big thing.

'Larry wrote a lot of rock stuff, but much of it was based on traditional Irish tunes. He said, "Come and jam with us. We're doing an open street festival in Far Rockaway." So I went and was standing there with a tenor sax hanging around my neck. "What the fuck am I going to do with this?!" What I did was get out my soprano sax, which I'd never played before in any of these outfits, and invited Chris the pipes player around one afternoon and learned all the traditional tunes. Then I played all the rock stuff on the tenor.

'We developed into a better and better band. Again, I got signed to EMI, the third time with three different bands. We were a very hot commodity. Joe Strummer was a big fan. Whenever he was in town, he'd come and hang out at our gigs. Brooke Shields would come down. We did a movie called *The Saint of Fort Washington* with Danny Glover and Matt Dillon. Matt was a fan. He came to watch us all the time. Kiefer Sutherland came in a few times. We definitely started a scene. There wouldn't have been the Dropkick Murphys or Flogging Molly if it weren't for Black 47. The scene became big on our back.

'We closed down Hoboken in 1994. We played a street festival there and it was mobbed. The cars couldn't move. It was an afternoon thing and when we were done, everybody just went into the bars. Then the cops went round Hoboken, threw everybody out the bars and closed the entire city down. The following year, we played at Shea Stadium. After the ball game, they would sometimes have a band play on a flatbed truck on the field. We did that three times. The first time was thirty years to the day after the Beatles played there.'

Black 47 put out around twenty albums, but Geoff didn't really regard it as a recording project. 'I never thought we made very good records. It was a live band. That's what it was.' While Black 47 was still a going concern, in 2012 Geoff put out an album of his own, under the name G.I. Blythe. 'Where I was going with that was where Dexys should have gone. I got Jim involved, and Archie, the singer from the Bureau. I had a couple of people from New York on there, but it was mainly people from England flying over. I sank money into that record. It didn't get anywhere, but I really wanted to make it. I *had* to make that record. It was unfinished business.'

Spool forward to now, to his retreat to Cornwall. His daughters still live in the States – Alice, his youngest, is in New York, while her older sister Charlotte is based in Seattle, where she's the singer with death-rock outfit Nox Novacula. Geoff's musical appetite hasn't retreated either, although what he's working on is somewhat more delicate than Charlotte's music making.

Most recently he's been composing, setting some W.B. Yeats poems to music for voice and string quartet. 'I just need to find someone to play them now. There's a very strong classical music scene down here. It's very rich for chamber music. It's not a cultural cul-de-sac by any means. We're supposed to be retired, but every day we have to get ready and go out somewhere.'

And what of those golden saxes? Are they mummified under a layer of dust?

'I haven't played for a couple of years, really. I've been really concentrating on composing. But I do intend to pick up the saxes and start playing again.'

Geoff actually picks up his sax quicker than he thinks. I ask if I can take a few photos of him and he scurries off into another room in the bungalow. I can hear a case clicking open. He returns cradling his precious tenor sax, the one that played such a part in defining the sound of *Searching for the Young Soul Rebels*. The lead guitar.

We head outside into that English country garden where the light is better. Geoff takes his position for a few shots, arching his back and pointing his sax towards the heavens, towards the blue. He might now be more than forty years older than when he skipped away from Dexys, but he still strikes the same pose. It comes naturally to him, the soul rebel forever.

5

Steve Spooner

Alto sax, 1978–80

*'That record was everything we'd rehearsed, everything we'd built up to.
It wasn't just a collection of songs. It was us.'*

I'm staying in Cornwall. There's no need to leave just yet. The A30 will still be flooded with summer-holiday traffic. And I need to make a visit to an ice cream factory.

Twenty miles east of Geoff Blythe's bungalow lies the village of St Keverne. It is the home of Roskilly's, the county's premier purveyors of frozen refreshment. It is also the home of Geoff's sax-toting buddy, Steve Spooner. Not at all by design, the thick-as-thieves pair – divided by the Atlantic Ocean for several decades – have ended up living just half an hour apart at the far tip of this sceptred isle.

Roskilly's isn't just an ice cream factory. It's also a farm that invites visitors to admire its various goats and pigs and turkeys and chickens and cows, as well as sample its wares in its courtyard café/ restaurant. Once parked up, I pause at the gate into the courtyard. There's a sign on it, listing the live entertainment that can be found here for the rest of the summer. At the bottom of the list, under the dates for folk acts, swing bands, singer-songwriters and puppet shows, the season ends with a performance by the St Keverne

Brass Band. Bearing in mind the population of the village is in the hundreds rather than the thousands, and bearing in mind Steve's horn-blowing heritage, there's surely a high chance that he keeps his art sharpened by playing among their number.

I soon find out that this is not the case. Steve has appeared right behind me. 'No, nothing to do with me, Nige.' I'll find out later why I'm wide of the mark.

We take the furthest table in the courtyard. It's late afternoon and the café is quietening down. Squealing, ice cream-fuelled kids are being led away by their parents, back to their cars, back to their holiday cottages and campsites. Our conversation will only be punctuated by the chirping sparrows in the eaves of the farm buildings and by the music playing over the café's PA. Currently it's Herb Alpert's 'Spanish Flea'. A cow in an adjacent field appears to be joining in on trombone.

Steve and I have chosen to meet here because it's where he works. And it's where he's worked for nearly twenty years. He's just finished his shift. Most days he can be found zipping along Cornwall's narrow lanes delivering ice cream to outlets across the county, making him a man who knows exactly how to swerve those queues on the A30. Today, though, he's been working in the warehouse, in the big freezer.

Yesterday was the forty-third anniversary of the release of *Searching for the Young Soul Rebels* ('Was it indeed? Fuck, I'm not that old!'), so it's an entirely apposite time for Steve to reel in the years, to pull back the curtain on what ended up – certainly compared to his bandmates – to be a short, sharp musical career.

Unlike Geoff, Steve didn't see, let alone answer, that ad in the *Birmingham Evening Mail*. He wasn't actively looking to join a band. 'I was just a happy little kid who enjoyed playing his sax in the evening.' A band, though, was actively looking for him.

'I had just turned nineteen and I was – let's call it – an amateur musician. I'd learnt at school. The sax teacher there was a jazz player during the war, so he played dance band and all that sort of stuff. He was giving me private lessons as an individual teacher, but he also started running the school band and he turned that into a little dance band – Glenn Miller and all that. Once I left school, I did want to pursue music, but I was a bit too thick to go to music college. I didn't have enough exam results. I even almost joined the army at one stage after some grown-up told me about this place called Kneller Hall, the army music college. But I didn't do that in the end. But I was playing in the Midland Youth Jazz Orchestra, which used to rehearse at the arts centre at Cannon Hill Park.

'One evening, I was having a cup of tea in the break and this bunch of three or four roughnecks turned up. The two Kevs were there, so was Pete Williams, and I think Pete Saunders was with them. They came over to my table. "We've just been watching you play. Do you want to come to a rehearsal? We're forming a band." They also already had the original drummer, John Jay. Now they were trying to find some brass players. They said they wanted a brass *section*, which is probably why I was interested. I've always been a section player.

'When you're a schoolkid, you're playing in school bands and daydreaming. Back in the '70s, there weren't many bands with brass sections. It was every instrument-playing kid's dream to be playing in a pop band, not in a dance band or an orchestra.

'I said, "Yeah, I'll come and rehearse."

'So I caught the bus over to Pete Rowland's house in Northfield, where the rehearsal was. He was a cracking bloke, Pete was. I was walking up the path to knock on the door and another geezer with a sax was also walking up the path. It was Geoff. We looked at each other. "Oh, right." That bonded us straight away. And we both got recruited.'

Despite Steve's self-described amateurism going toe to toe with college-educated Geoff and his professional experience, the teenager wasn't fazed or intimidated. 'I didn't look at it like that, I really didn't. I was a nineteen-year-old innocent kid. Call it the confidence of youth.'

The older Geoff took him under his wing and, invariably standing stage-left, the pair became the visual focus of the band, emitting great energy and power in every performance. Steve smiles. 'Oh, yeah. From day one, the whole idea was that the brass section was going to be the lead guitar.' Why have one lead guitarist when you can have three?

Pete Williams had bounced his apprenticeship into the long grass, and Pete Saunders had pressed the pause button on his academic career. Steve didn't need any persuading to throw his all in with the band. 'I'd done quite a few jobs by then. At the time I was working for Rank Xerox at their photocopying bureau in the middle of town. I was there, learning all about printing blah blah blah. But once the band came together, we all decided we were all committed. Forget trying to do it part-time.

'And then we spent – and you'll have heard this a thousand times – the next six months rehearsing. But not just rehearsing. Learning about each other too. We didn't really know what we were doing. We just knew how we wanted to be. We wanted to be different. We didn't want to associate ourselves with anybody else. We went out of our way to be belligerent. Looking back at the history of it all, it feels like there was always a master plan, but there wasn't really one at all. The first six months, the first twelve months, all grew organically and naturally. If you put a bunch of eight lads together for six months in close proximity, you're either going to all punch each other up or you're going to turn into a tight, solid little unit.'

While the precise details sometimes elude him ('I'm notoriously bad with names'), Steve speaks carefully, with clear-eyed insight and wisdom. He makes astute assessments of times past, of triumphs and mistakes, the elapsed years allowing him to set Dexys' high adventures into context. He can, though, recall all their earliest gigs, including one at the school where Pete Rowland was a teacher. 'We played to a bunch of schoolkids one evening in an assembly sort of thing.' It was a case of whatever it took to get match-fit, 'playing obscure places to see if we could actually stand there and do it'.

As I speak to the various members of the original line-up, there are differing accounts of what was Dexys' first proper gig, the one where the eight of them were confident enough to replicate the intensity of rehearsals while looking into the whites of an audience's eyes. For Steve, it was at the Barrel Organ in Digbeth, in downtown Birmingham. 'That was a cracking little venue, right next to the coach station. We put the gig on and put in a proper sound system. Terry the sound guy stayed with us all the way through our career. There was a bond with him as well. We'd always use him.'

Then came a residency at the Imperial Hotel on Needless Alley in the city centre. 'We played there a lot, a little cellar-type bar called Mr Sam's. We played there every week or every fortnight for a little while. We had UB40 as support for pretty much all those gigs.

'I think the biggest local gig we did was at a club called the Romulus on the Hagley Road. We had Joy Division supporting us. That was August 1979, a few months before the Two-Tone tour. Boy George was in the audience. He was still George O'Dowd then, but he stood out like a sore thumb. I've got these memories of him looking like he hadn't yet learned how to put on the slap properly. It's funny the things you remember, isn't it?'

The courtyard here at Roskilly's is much quieter now. And the cow has stopped blowing that trombone. We can hear the PA more clearly. Whoever's selected the music has fine taste. The unmistakable voice and sax of Fela Kuti is now audible.

'Then it was on to the Specials tour. That was the first time we'd all been away for weeks on end. It was a proper tour. It was absolutely massive for us. The halls were absolutely packed and we were going down a storm. Those audiences were up for it. They weren't just there for the Specials. It was a real learning curve for us. That's when we became a proper, proper band. Right from day one we thought we were the best, but we proved it to ourselves on that tour.'

Before the Two-Tone tour, the band had already been gazing longingly beyond the boundaries of Birmingham and the Black Country. 'We made demos and started tripping down to London, walking around record companies. We'd always go en masse. And the legendary tales are the reality, the truth. We'd always bunk the train. We were on the dole and didn't have two pennies to rub together. We'd find ways of getting ourselves into record companies. We always ended up seeing somebody. But nothing really came of it.'

Then Bernie Rhodes came on the scene. 'Whether he approached Kevin or Kevin approached him, I can't remember. However it happened, we got involved with him for a little while. Just a short period of time. Maybe six months.

'We went down to Rehearsal Rehearsals, his studios in Camden, for a couple of weeks. This also turned out to be legendary, but you didn't know it at the time when you were in this grotty hole. That was where we'd sleep. It was a proper shithole. The Clash's merchandise was all over the place. We'd use it as bedding. Half a dozen Clash T-shirts would be your pillow.'

While in Camden, 'Dance Stance' was recorded in a studio behind the nearby Monarch pub, the first recorded Dexys offering to the world. 'We thought it was great, but then Bernie and his mate mixed it and we didn't like it at all. I think that's what severed the contact with Bernie. When you listen back to it now, it actually sounds pretty good. But it wasn't the Dexys sound. It wasn't right.'

What did sound right were the subsequent recording sessions overseen by Pete Wingfield, first of 'Geno' and then of *Searching for the Young Soul Rebels*. Steve allows himself a smile at the thought of the results.

'"Geno" was at number one when I turned twenty-one on 6 May 1980. By then, we'd all indoctrinated each other. By the time we were on *Top of the Pops*, we knew we deserved to be. And we were ready for it. You know, youthful arrogance. I don't think I gave anything a second thought. I was just living in the moment.

'Mind you, we were all pretty shocked at how the album sounded. Yeah, we thought we were great, but I don't think any of us expected it to sound quite as professional as that. Pete Wingfield's hand was all over it. That's what made it sound so good. That record was everything we'd rehearsed, everything we'd built up to. We knew exactly what we were doing. It wasn't just a collection of songs. It was us.'

As Steve recalls though, there had been a danger that *Searching for the Young Soul Rebels* might have become the album that never was – all thanks to the stealing of the master tapes. 'It was a coordinated plan. We'd done it cleverly enough to know we needed two vehicles, one of which was going to be a dummy. My memory is hazy, but I know the police were involved because they ended up chasing the other car.

'And, as a tool with which to negotiate with the record company, it worked. Then it was time to return the tapes to EMI. We jumped on the tube and somebody suddenly said, "What about the magnetism?" We had this moment: "Fuck, have we just blanked all the tapes by doing something daft?" Fortunately, it didn't happen. But imagine if it had. Just imagine that.'

What did happen, little more than three months later, was that the fissure in the band grew to become insurmountable. Steve remains sanguine about it, no matter how bitter the taste at the time.

'That band was an eight-man effort. There's no question about that. But Kevin was definitely the firm leader. It was his inspiration to start with. I don't want to speak ill of anybody because I don't feel ill towards any of them – and certainly not towards Kevin. But he'd been patted on the back a lot and was starting to buy it. He was starting to want to dominate everything, whereas we'd spent those two years bonding as a unit. But, again, now you look back years later, that was the right move for Kevin. We couldn't have carried on as the same band. He wanted it to be different every time.'

If Steve is sanguine about Dexys, there is definitely regret in his voice when it comes to talking about the Bureau.

'As far as I'm concerned, we were fools to ourselves with the Bureau. That band had such big potential. It really did. With Dexys, it was "Nobody's having it. We're controlling everything. You're not messing with us. We know exactly what we're doing." With the Bureau, it was more of a sigh of relief: "Right, let's just do the band then. Let's enjoy ourselves." We hadn't got a master plan. We were just writing music and seeing where it went. And we let the management do the managing – which was ultimately the end of the band. I think that was our mistake. We laid back too much. We took our foot off the pedal – which, of course, was perfectly understandable because Dexys had been such an intense affair. If we'd clung on a bit tighter, if we'd taken our time, the Bureau really would have had a chance.

'It was definitely too soon to have done the Bureau album. But, again, we were youngsters being given the opportunity. Of course you're going to do it. And then that album didn't get released in the UK. There is a version of it out now, but it must have been remixed or re-engineered. It's the tinniest, horrible sound that you've ever heard.'

'We didn't really know what we were doing. We just knew what we wanted to be.' Steve Spooner sets the time machine back to 1978.

Dexys had split in two and the Bureau had faded away. But Steve was still in his early twenties. Did he feel, like Pete Saunders did, that he'd climbed all the mountains already, that the only way was down?

'I don't think my head told me "Right, the band's finished, I'm finished too". I don't think it worked like that for any of us because the Bureau didn't even officially split up. We just fizzled out. Before I knew it, I was back home in Shirley in Birmingham, messing about, not really thinking about the future, not really thinking about anything.

'I found myself needing work. And I wasn't without ego. I didn't want to play the sax again, particularly in bands. I was thinking, *Well, am I going to advertise to see if any wee band wants a sax player?* That thought of playing in a poxy pub again. "Look at him. He was number one a year ago." There was a bit of that in me.

'I'd never looked to be in a band. Had they not found me in 1978, I'd probably still be playing in amateur dance bands of some description as a hobby. So, yes, I didn't have any great desire to keep playing. And, again, Geoff and Jimmy were proper, proper players. I was an enthusiastic amateur. I was good enough. I had to be good enough and you can hear that on the records. But I wasn't hot like they were.'

Having joined Dexys on the same day, Steve and Geoff shared the same close-quarters position on stage. They roomed together. And they left Dexys on the same day. They then repeated the entire process with the Bureau. But when Geoff's career continued its course for a few more decades, Steve put his sax into metaphorical storage, calling time on his musical life.

'You blink and another few months have gone by and you're working and you've settled down. You're gradually getting embroiled back into your home life. Years go by. And before you blink again, forty-three of them have gone . . .'

Steve's throaty chuckle rides the air, where it meets Al Green singing 'Take Me to the River' over the PA. After both Dexys and the Bureau were tossed about on choppy waters, it turns out that finding his land legs wasn't an easy task.

'I did all sorts of jobs but none worth talking about. The truth is, once the bands had finished, it took me a good ten years to come back down to normality. I did jobs, I breezed through them, but I never really felt part of them, part of society. That five-year period was such a novel thing. And then I felt like an alien in real society. I could never take a job seriously. One time, I started work at this warehouse place in Birmingham as a shelf-stacker. Within twelve months I was floor manager. I obviously had the capabilities to have done whatever I wanted, but I always felt I was turning into the job, so I'd be off.'

Steve moved to Cornwall with his then girlfriend, but after they split up, he found himself homeless. So, with a little money in his pocket, he travelled to India with a couple of Cornish friends. 'We hadn't gone there to find ourselves. We just went to have a look. They came back after only a few weeks. They found it excessive. But I loved it. It was another adventure, just like Dexys had been. I ended up staying there for around four months. I came back completely skint and with nowhere to go. I arrived at Heathrow with an open-ended bus ticket. "What am I going to do? Am I going back to Birmingham or am I going back to Cornwall?"'

Steve headed south.

'It probably took me a couple more years to establish myself. I was homeless and jobless. I dossed around with mates. But eventually I pulled it together. I suppose I was around thirty-five or thirty-six before I started feeling normal again, by which time I'd met a local girl, Mae, whom I'm now married to. She sorted me out really. Generally, it's the other way round. People get to their forties and say, "Oh, I wish I'd done this, I wish I'd done that." But I look back and I'm very satisfied I got such a lot out of my system in my twenties.

'Meeting Mae was a good thing. I've got a stepson, Kirk. He was five when I turned up. He's thirty-six now. That was probably the first conscious decision I made about life. "If I'm going to take Mae on, I've got to take Kirk on. I've got to do this properly."'

But the musical story wasn't over – not completely. Fast-forward to the early 2000s. 'When the Bureau split up, I lost touch with everybody completely. I spent twenty years not knowing anything about anybody from the band. Then, out of the blue, I had a phone call from my mother. She said there was an advert in the *Birmingham Evening Mail*: "Searching for Steve Spooner. Phone this number." So she sent it to me down in Cornwall. At first, I thought, *Am I going to phone this number? Did I get someone pregnant or something? Am I going to hear about a secret son or daughter?*

'Anyway, I rang it and it was this guy called Ian Jennings. He was a massive Dexys fan and he'd heard that Kevin wanted to do another Dexys tour. The upshot of that was that I got back in touch with Pete Williams, who was involved with it. I met him at New Street station and we drove down to London together to see Kevin, a few hours in the car, having a proper catch-up and a proper reminisce. I think we both ended up in tears. I met Kevin and we did a little rehearsal. Over this twenty-year period, I'd not actually played any sax. It was still in the loft, gathering dust, so I had to learn to play it again. In the end, though, nothing came of it. He did the tour without horns. It was all done electronically.'

But the partial musical renaissance didn't end there. 'Out of the blue, Geoff came over from the States on holiday and happened to come down to Cornwall. I met up with him and it was wonderful. Various chats later, by 2005, we'd all decided it might be a clever idea to try to have a Bureau reunion. Warners finally agreed to release the album and that got us all back together. We ended up doing two gigs – one in Birmingham, one in London. If I'm honest, I shit my pants after twenty years of not playing live. But I was so pleased with myself for actually standing up and doing it.

'We also went into the studio and recorded a couple of tracks. They came out on another Bureau album called *And Another Thing*. The whole affair kind of got me daydreaming and I think I let myself run with it a little bit. "Oh God, is this going to go somewhere again?" Of course, it didn't. But it was still fantastic. I'm so glad it happened.'

Since then, the saxophone has fallen silent again – mostly. 'I get it out once in a blue moon, just to dust it off. We've got a granddaughter now, Ruby. She comes and stays with us fairly regularly. The sax happened to be in the spare room, which is her bedroom. She spotted it one day, so I played it to show her what it sounds like. But I had to put it away quickly. She thought it was too noisy.'

'I don't suppose I'll ever get round to joining another group,' Steve concludes, rising up from his seat. 'But one of these days I might meet up with a bunch of oldies and start playing a bit of Glenn Miller again. You never know . . .'

We wander out of the courtyard, but as I start heading towards the visitors' car park, Steve beckons me towards his own car, parked up in the farmyard. On the passenger seat is a supermarket carrier bag. He reaches inside. It holds long-forgotten treasure: a good few handfuls of Dexys memorabilia. Its survival, though, is in no way due to Steve faithfully gathering and preserving all ephemera that came his way. Instead, his mum can take the credit.

Every time he came back from tour, back to her house in Shirley on Birmingham's southern outskirts, she'd empty his bags of dirty washing and set aside any items that wouldn't survive the high-speed revolutions of the washing machine. After storing these bits and pieces away, she handed them over to Steve years later, since when they've been in storage, neglected and forgotten. Maybe one day a Dexys museum might open its doors and display them in glass cabinets. Or, as today proves, more likely a visit from an author prompts Steve to go searching in cupboards, to go reaching under beds.

There's some real treasure in this carrier bag for the Dexys nerd. Badges, stickers, tour programmes . . . One such programme, for that aptly named Intense Emotion Revue tour of mid-1980, finds each member given a dedicated page. A photo of each youthful, cherubic face takes up much of the space, accompanied by two lines of copy referencing their particular likes and dislikes. Steve expresses a penchant for 'staying awake all night', while the turn-of-the-'80s Geoff Blythe salutes British Rail. Stoker the drummer apparently hates drummers.

But the most fascinating item is a thick wad of photocopied pages. This was the tour manager's dossier for the entire forty-date jaunt, containing all the information required to keep the show on the road. There are several hand-drawn maps. One shows where Huddersfield lies in relation to Manchester and Leeds, along with all the adjacent motorways and trunk roads, to ensure the van doesn't get lost crossing the Pennines. There are floor plans of all the venues on the tour, detailing the best entrances for load-ins and load-outs, each venue's capacity, the dimensions of each stage, the locations of all power sockets, and the route from each dressing room to each stage to avoid a recreation of *that* Spinal Tap moment . . .

There are also copies of contracts to avoid any post-gig disagreements between band and promoter. And there are tour itineraries, detailing whether a modest hotel or B&B would be provided for the night. Playing in Coventry, Shrewsbury or Malvern? Then the band were straight back to their own beds in Birmingham. Even playing Liverpool meant a small-hours return to their home city that same night.

If accommodation were needed, this dossier contains details and prices of local hotels and B&Bs. When playing Sheffield, for instance, the Harley Hotel on Glossop Road ('Thirty bedrooms, writing room, colour TV lounge') offered single rooms for £6.90 from Monday to Thursday, but the rate decreased to the decidedly irregular £6.04 come the weekend. Meanwhile, for the Newcastle date of the tour, the establishment run by Mrs M Batty of Queens Road in Jesmond could provide five cheaper rooms: a fiver for a single, a tenner for a double, including breakfast.

Mrs Batty didn't have a telly, mind.

Reminisce #3

Needless Alley, Birmingham

The ghosthunter stands still and silent on the pavement again, imagining another expectant queue of pre-gig punters.

It's rush-hour in downtown Birmingham, its pedestrianised streets thick with human traffic in the remains of the day, much of it flowing from office block to New Street station, a centipede of marching commuters. The ghosthunter loiters with intent as the world rushes past, a stationary obstacle for the peloton of food-delivering cyclists, with other people's dinners on their backs, to weave around.

He stares at the rear of the old Imperial Hotel, now divided up into offices, boasting distinctly 21st-century amenities like a podcast studio, e-parking bays and a contemplation room. It's a language that back in 1979, in a small club under the Imperial Hotel, a small club called Mr Sam's, filled with wide-eyed young punters hungry for a good time, would never have been understood.

Several future members of Dexys would have seen them play here in their weekly residency, intrigued by their vision and energy, and envious of those already aboard the juggernaut, already part of the city's sharpest young band. Beginning to outgrow their hometown, they wouldn't be a fixture at Mr Sam's for very long. Get them while you can. Get them while they're hot.

The shows are full-on. In your face. Intense. If you want quiet contemplation, come back in forty-five years' time. There'll be a special room here for just that by then.

6

Andy Leek

Keyboards, 1979–80

*'I've always been more of a lone wolf – a solo artist rather than
a band member. I don't like people telling me what to do.'*

'When you're in the music business, you have to take every opportunity as it comes. You can't let the way you're feeling, or anything
else, stop you from doing stuff or you'd get nowhere.'

At home in his bungalow in Willenhall, the Black Country town
where he grew up and to where he returned later in life, Andy Leek
is explaining the source of his persistence with a music career that's
known more than its fair share of knock-backs. Specifically, he's
referring to joining Dexys as its new keyboard player following the
demise of his previous band, the Wailing Cocks, after their guitarist,
Alan Boyle, was killed in a car crash.

'His death was a huge shock. He was my greatest musical friend
and the first person I really knew who'd died.' The Wailing Cocks –
also featuring another future Dexys conscript, the drummer Stoker,
then known as plain old Andrew Growcott – were at the time more
established than Dexys. With Andy as their frontman, they already
had sessions for John Peel's show under their belts and had released
three singles. Although Andy was very influenced by the Clash and
the Sex Pistols, the other Cocks had less punky credentials and so 'the
music we made wasn't really in keeping with the punk philosophy as

we really could play our instruments. The wild spirit of that period still invested our performances, though.'

Between the end of the Wailing Cocks and his recruitment into Dexys' ranks, Andy made an unlikely – and highly distressing – diversion into alternative employment. 'I decided I really had to get a job as I was totally broke and couldn't afford to do anything. I managed to get a job in the A&E department of the local hospital as a porter. Friday nights were pretty gruesome. I lost count of how many druggies' stomachs I helped pump and how many faces I saw stitched after drunken fights. It awoke me to quite a few of the real horrors of the world and I realised just how protected I'd been.

'A cynical, world-weary overtone slowly crept into my demeanour and I swore to escape the job and all the bad images and nightmares it gave me. Unfortunately, it was about to get worse. I was called into the boss's office, where I was complimented on my work and told that there was another job I could have which paid more money for fewer hours. I would only have to do four shifts a week. I immediately said yes and signed the form accepting the new job. I didn't realise what it was . . .

'I started as a night mortuary attendant the following Monday. I was required to undress the dead bodies as they came in from road accidents or home or hospital deaths, put the identifier around the big toe and put them in the fridge. I was really disturbed by some of the experiences it brought. Here again was death staring me in the face. I determined to hand in my resignation.'

Salvation from the mortuary came in the form of a certain eight-piece new-wave soul band. Or, rather, as they were on the hunt for a new member, a certain *seven*-piece new-wave soul band. A West Midlands agent called Roy Williams, on whom the Wailing Cocks had made an enduring impression, told Andy that 'a band in the charts were looking for a good, young keyboard player. They were called Dexys Midnight Runners.'

Pete Saunders' decision to return to Norwich and his studies of the great literary texts had created a vacancy that Andy was decidedly keen to fill. Anything to rescue him from spending four nights a week in the company of a room of cadavers.

'My manager had told me to dress smart for the audition, so I wore a mac and dressed all posh and everything. Then I arrived and looked completely out of place. Kevin Rowland said to me, "What have you come as?" Everyone had a strange image that resembled New York dockers. Or, if you want to get specific, Kevin Rowland was like Jake LaMotta in *Raging Bull* and Big Jimmy was like the character Alex in *A Clockwork Orange*, but neither Kevin nor Jimmy were so violent or offensive. Kevin Archer reminded me of Robert De Niro from *Taxi Driver*. In fact, their harder shell belied a softer belly of intellect and kindness, albeit of an intense variety.

'Thanks to my experience with the Wailing Cocks, I flew through the audition and I then rehearsed with them at the Lafayette in Birmingham for a few weeks. Then we started gigging and our first single "Dance Stance" made its way up to number forty in the UK charts. This had been recorded before I was recruited, but I appeared on TV shows to promote it. It was really quite exciting.

'During these early days, there was a real obsession with portraying the right image. This basically meant a short haircut – provided free by Kevin Rowland himself – and a donkey jacket, crew-neck top, boots or brogues, and black, baggy trousers. I had no problem with this as I was really into playing the part, but a few band members often turned up in their civvies. This frustrated Kevin. He had an idea about how we should look and some members didn't take him seriously, so he would send them back home to get changed. People didn't like to be told, but their protests cut no ice with Kevin. It was this single-minded determination that resulted in our success.

'He used to complain to me privately that most of the group were hippies and brown ricers. At least I had previously been a punk like him and that gave me a little more cred. The only thing that got me about the image is that it was so manufactured and, in fact, largely phoney. None of us were, or had been, New York dockers or had lived on "mean streets". Our image was as made up and false as that of Dollar . . .'

Having joined towards the end of 1979, and having also rec-ommended his school pal and former Wailing Cocks bandmate Andrew Growcott for the vacant drummer's stool, 1980 would open with a blast for Andy and Dexys. The first fortnight of the year brought several engagements in London. After a gig at the Marquee and demoing a hefty number of songs at EMI's in-house studio, the band then recorded their debut Radio 1 session. The four tracks, for David 'Kid' Jensen's show, showed what a good fit Andy was – and what a smooth transition he'd made into the ranks. His backing vocals on 'Geno', 'Dance Stance' and 'Respect' were luminous and bell-clear, while his organ playing on 'The Teams that Meet in Caffs' revealed a musician of taste and restraint.

That same month, Dexys' *Top of the Pops* bow, with 'Dance Stance' drifting to the edge of the top forty, confirmed Andy looked the part too. He was one of the most energetic on stage, giving it as much bounce as Pete Williams and Jim Paterson, and offering echoes of Jerry Dammers behind his organ. The new boy's confidence was high. Possibly too high. Having met Suggs backstage and enjoyed a long chat with Chrissie Hynde, Andy then had 'a small contretemps with Simon Bates. It was my fault. I was too arrogant.'

With EMI's adoption of them, it was time to turn the promise of those demos into the next single. 'We finally decided it would be "Geno", backed on the B-side by "Breaking Down the Walls of Heartache". This was good for me. I had an organ solo on it and you could hear my backing vocals on both tracks. The band were pretty keen on it, but I think they liked "Tell Me When My Light Turns Green" more.

'When we were recording "Geno", the producer, Pete Wingfield, turned to Kevin and asked him if he really wanted the brass so loud. "Yes, I do. And then some." I didn't think it was good enough to go to number one, but it obviously did and I was wrong. As it climbed the charts, we went from being nobodies to somebodies.

'My favourite moment in Dexys was when we were recording the "Geno" video. On the second day, Kevin Rowland and I were filmed jumping over the gates at Birmingham New Street station. It was where true life meets art. Because we hated travelling in the van with all the other members, Kevin and I would take the train to each gig. He taught me how to hide behind the toilet door so that, even if the ticket inspector opened it, he still didn't catch you. We also used to get out at a station, walk down the platform to the other end of the train and get on again as the ticket inspector had already covered that section of the train.'

As 'Geno' climbed the charts, as Dexys turned into those somebodies, Andy admitted to being uncomfortable with how this was changing the perception of the band. And his ambitions for fame wasn't as one of eight, telling *Sounds* that he 'wanted respect for myself, not just because of being in a "star" band'.

'It was strange the way people suddenly started asking for things. I guess that's just a symbol of success, but it made me feel quite cynical, the way people's attitudes changed towards us as we got famous. Fame came very quickly with "Geno". Kevin told me this much one day, saying something like, "This wasn't really the way I wanted to become famous. I'd rather have had some experience of slowly reaching number one, not to suddenly be there."

'I'd never been less than ready to go back out front. I'd been ready to be out front from when I was a kid. One day at school, I was in assembly with my harmonica around my neck in a holder, playing along to the hymns. The teacher said, "Who's making that racket? Is that you, Leek? Would you like to come to the front and play for the whole school?" I thought about it for a few seconds. I said yes and marched up to the stage.

'I've always been more of a lone wolf – a solo artist, rather than a band member. I don't like people telling me what to do.'

Andy's departure from the band, less than six months after joining, gained immediate press coverage, with stories appearing near-instantly in a range of publications. 'After leaving, the *Sun*, the *Daily Mirror*, *Record Mirror*, *Sounds* and the local *Express & Star* all called me and did phone interviews about why I'd left. They sensationalised my replies and wrote many things that embarrassed me and that anyone who knows me knows I would never say. Unfortunately, many Dexys fans still hold it against me that I left. I would never

'I didn't think "Geno" was good enough to go to number one, but it obviously did and I was wrong.' Andy Leek's short time in Dexys still included playing on a chart-topping single.

have left if it hadn't been for the violence inflicted on me.' A physical altercation with his old pal Stoker, in the back of manager Dave Corke's car, had signalled the point of no return.

Shortly after leaving, just ahead of 'Geno' reaching the summit of the charts, Andy's debut solo single was released. 'The owner of Bird's Nest Records, Clive Selwood, came to me saying he had a deal with Beggars Banquet for me to release "Move On (In Your Maserati)". The song wasn't about Dexys, as people assumed. I'd written and recorded it before the Wailing Cocks. Anyway, I went along with the release because it was so welcoming to be promoting my own material. Unfortunately, it looked like I was cashing in on Dexys' fame and I spoke to both Kevin Rowland and Kev Archer to explain what was happening. I think they understood. But it was early days in their careers and they didn't like anything distracting from their own group. But what was I supposed to do? Disappear for their convenience?'

Aside from being named as single of the week in *Sounds*, 'Move On (In Your Maserati)' failed to leave an impression. 'I was disappointed,' says Andy. 'I thought it was better than Dexys' stuff.' By 1981, after Kev Archer had also jumped ship, Andy hooked up again with his former bandmate, who was just sketching out his plans for the Blue Ox Babes.

'I had made a very strong connection with him in Dexys – and a personal one, not just musical. I liked him as a person. I still do. I'd wasted about a year or so doing nothing and then he called me, telling me he was starting a new band playing folk music. Since I'd always got on well with him and was willing to try something new, we met up again in the summer of '81.

'He was rehearsing his new songs with his girlfriend Yasmin on melodica and vocals. The group had no name and the songs were still developing. I quickly became very into the group and even adopted the strange image they had – folksy loose tops and furry boots. Yasmin cut my hair in their style, which I loved, and she became like a sister to me. Yasmin and Kevin were fantastic and I really admired their partnership. We become closer friends than we ever were in Dexys. The expanding group became like a family, which I was touched to be a part of.

'The Dexys experience had left us scarred and bruised, and we needed a safe haven in which to enjoy our talents. A whole philosophy developed around the group and it became a big influence on me. Although I still had hopes for my solo career, I was much happier in the Blue Ox Babes than any group I'd ever been in. We rehearsed above a barber's shop in Dudley and soon consisted of drums, bass, keyboards, melodica, guitar and vocals. The most inspiring things about the group were the new songs and Kevin's vocals. He adopted a sort of Marc Bolan-esque approach, which suited him. We were so completely different to anything else around.'

The Blue Ox Babes sound still required a little more filling-out and finesse, and their successful search for this additional depth would later have great significance. Kev Archer and Andy paid a visit to the Birmingham School of Music in search of a violinist. And they found one: Helen Bevington.

'When we first played with Helen,' Andy recalls, 'because she was classically trained, it became my job to interpret Kevin's ideas to her and teach her the solos and riffs. I'd been through the classical stuff as a child, so I spoke her language. She very soon got totally into it, although she was from another musical world.

'We recorded four tracks at Phil Savage's Outlaw studio. I played a really old piano and a harmonium that Kevin had found in a pawn shop. That was new to me. I had to pump it with my feet as I played, which gave a breathing-type effect, which you can hear on the track "Four Golden Tongues". I also started playing harmonica on a couple of tracks and sang harmonies. I felt, more than ever, part of something that was going to be unique and popular. We had a lot of ace cards on our side. We were so filled with hope that summer.'

Then came Kev Archer's sharing of the Blue Ox Babes demo tape with Kevin Rowland, and all the fall-out that that entailed. Andy shakes his head. 'Exactly how he had the heart to destroy someone who had been his best friend by stealing those ideas, I will never know. He later apologised to Kevin Archer and I believe gave him some royalties from the *Too-Rye-Ay* album, but by that time the Blue Ox Babes' time had come and gone. Also, what about me? I had something precious taken away from me too, and not for the first time did I receive no compensation or apology.'

Distressed and distraught, Andy retreated to Glasgow with his girlfriend. Then the clouds parted, letting a chunk of golden light in. An A&R man from Beggars Banquet, Steve Webbon, managed to track the phone-less Andy down via his friends and offered him a recording contract. Such a break sounds unlikely for someone who'd gone to ground to make sense of a tumultuous couple of years. It turned out that Andy's mum was responsible, having sent the label a collection of her son's songs on tape. An album was recorded but not released at the time. Indeed, it would be more than two decades later that the LP, *Midnight Music*, would officially come out.

The path of Andy's solo career was proving turbulent and decidedly uneven, the peaks and troughs making rapid, alternating appearances. One of those peaks came in 1984 when a friend of his, one Kirsty MacColl, got in touch. She was writing some songs for a solo album by Frida from Abba.

'She'd played Frida my album *Midnight Music* and Frida loved the song "Twist in the Dark" and wanted to record it. I was overjoyed and was invited to Paris to meet Frida and Kirsty's husband, Steve Lillywhite, who was producing it. Unfortunately, on the train to Paris, I decided to grab a coffee and a sandwich, and while I was gone, someone stole my suitcase. I was always too trusting and optimistic. When I got to Paris, Steve lent me some of his clothes. We were the same size, but they were so completely different to mine that I felt like I'd stepped into someone else's life. My manager got me a £5,000 advance for "Twist in the Dark". We felt like it was all beginning. I went out for an Indian and bought some new clothes.'

It wasn't Andy's only encounter with Abba that year. In the meantime, billed as Andde Leek, he'd released a single, a cover of 'Dancing Queen', produced by Tony Visconti. 'It was quite a coup for me, but I really couldn't stand it myself. I realised I'd just lost my way. I really wanted out. Then the writers, Benny and Björn, wouldn't let me use my own lyrics which I'd written, which gave it a lot more credibility and a poetic, modern relevance. They insisted that I use their lyrics, which were trite and ordinary, in my not-so-humble opinion. This stole the magic out of the song for me.'

Peaks and troughs, troughs and peaks.

One particular upswing came towards the end of the '80s when Atlantic Records offered Andy a contract, which he speedily signed. Would this provide the breakthrough for which he had desperately been searching for the best part of a decade?

'My manager asked me who I'd like to produce the album. I never have taken much notice of who produces what, so I hadn't got a clue who to say. He pushed further.

'"Who's your favourite band?"

'"The Beatles."

'"Well, we can't really ask George Martin. You'll be lucky to even get a reply from him."

'With the idea of what incredible coup it would be to get George Martin involved, I put together a tape of seven songs, which we sent him. Three weeks later, I was sitting in my manager's office, talking about the future when the phone rang.

'"Hi, this is George Martin. I've been listening to the tape of Andy Leek's songs and I think they're superb. Let's get together and schedule some time for recording."

'I was on cloud nine. We met in a small Italian café in Soho and hit it off immediately. I'd been listening to the Beatles all my life and spoke the same language as him. I didn't feel overwhelmed in the slightest. I trusted him from the off. He had a nurturing character, which brought out the best in me. He became like a father figure during the recording sessions, and often shared Beatles anecdotes down the pub while he enjoyed a sausage and a pint. He was a thoroughly decent man – a rare thing in the music business.'

George thought much of Andy too. The man who had produced *Revolver*, *The White Album*, *Abbey Road* et al. told the reporter from *BBC Breakfast Time* that the subsequent LP, *Say Something*, was 'one of the best albums I think I've ever made'. He then went on to declare that Andy had 'the same kind of talent that Elton had when he was just starting'. Nonetheless, the avuncular hand of one of the most famous producers in the world couldn't turn Andy into a star. Solo success continued to elude him. 'I was so down at the album's failure to set the world alight. My balladeering orchestral pop didn't fit in with fashion. I just wanted to hide away, to forget all about Andy Leek the artist.

'In 1989, after a few months of feeling very thin and depressed, I went back home to my mum to rest, get well, lick my considerable wounds and re-evaluate my situation. I was feeling vulnerable and broken inside, but I had a few ideas of what I wanted to do. I decided to become a lawyer and work in the music business helping people like me. I took on a law access course at a local college and fell in love with a student there. Deborah became my absolute saviour and the true love of my life. We're still together now.'

Andy would record a couple more albums, as well as enrolling at Cardiff University to study music composition. But one day, strolling down New Street in Birmingham, 'slightly the worse for wear', he had some kind of epiphany.

'I saw a sign that said "Piano Bar". I walked in and saw a beautiful Steinway grand piano. It was immaculate. I asked the bartender if I could play a few songs on it. "No, we only allow professionals to play it." I spoke to the manager, told him about my history and said, "Just let me play one song." I played "Let It Be" and the twelve people in the bar applauded.' He became a regular turn there.

'I had boundless energy during this period and just enjoyed having somewhere to play where I could express myself. It was a relief to play music with no pressure. I had so many fabulous times there.' The pleasure to play without great expectation, without chasing the fickle flame of stardom, led him to form Andy Leek and the Blue Angels, a band for hire that played all manner of parties, weddings, charity balls and the like.

But then, in 2008, his world flipped on its axis. Andy was diagnosed with young-onset Parkinson's. He was just forty-nine.

'I was diagnosed following years of becoming increasingly, desperately ill. My doctor didn't take me seriously and even accused me of malingering. It was unbelievable.

'I spent years seeing different consultants and specialists, but it was only when my chiropractor referred me for a brain scan that things started to happen. We really didn't believe anything serious was wrong and that this was nothing more than the requisite path of differential diagnosis – successively ruling out the big guns until you land on what is wrong. Only that isn't how it played out.

'I remember Deborah and I standing in the hospital car park, crying and holding on to each other. Then the heavens opened. We were soaked to the bone and shocked to the core. We drove home, got changed and headed back out to our favourite café for breakfast, as if this act of normality could restore the universe to its rightful place.

'After three days, we declared "Fuck this". My consultant had made the devastating prognosis that I would either be dead or in a home within three to five years. Fifteen years on and I'm still here, still standing. It's amazing what love, music and a hefty dose of positive defiance can achieve.

'Rest assured, I can still sing and play. Parkinson's is a weird condition with more than forty different symptoms, but fortunately for me, researchers have found that recruiting the singing parts of the brain can help with speech. It's using one neural network in the brain to support the other. The hard part is that you have to do it consciously, so it takes constant effort and is really tiring. Parkinson's is essentially a breakdown of the automatic functions of the body. It's as if the autopilot no longer works, so you have to do everything manually.'

Both professionally and personally, the road hasn't been the smoothest for Andy Leek, but moments of despair have been leavened by moments of life-affirming positivity. He has saved one of the best examples of this to the end.

'I received a phone call from a prominent DJ in Lebanon. He called himself DJ Beavis but his real name was Khalill. He told me that he would like to remix the title track from the *Say Something* album. No one had ever offered to remix a track of mine before, so I was pleasantly surprised. I asked him what made him want to remix it.

'"I was hoping it could be number one again."

'"What do you mean *again*?"

'He then explained that, back in 1989, "Say Something" had been number one in Lebanon during the civil war. I was totally astounded. I had tears in my eyes at the thought that the song had done so much without any promotion. I had never known I'd had a number one.

'I found out later that the song had become an anthem during the war and was played up to twenty times a day on the radio. That means more to me than any royalty cheque ever could.

'I only wish George had known this before he died.'

7

Andrew 'Stoker' Growcott

Drums, 1979–80

'My dad marched into the room: "Andrew! Sting's on the phone!"
I think that's when he realised that I was doing all right.'

'I have to admit I was clueless at nineteen. I've been very lucky. I appreciate what the gods of rock 'n' roll have given me.'

A late October lunchtime in the northern suburbs of Fresno, California. The sky is unfailing blue, the temperature a very agreeable seventy degrees and the Sierra Nevada mountains frame the horizon to the east. Andrew Growcott – the man known as Stoker – is in his backyard in his shorts, standing on a lawn of fake grass. The digging paws of his eleven-year-old Australian labradoodle have taken care of the yard's natural grass, hence the substitute. Plus, residents get a rebate if they 'plant' an artificial lawn. It helps with the Californian droughts.

'For nine months of the year, there are no clouds here,' explains this native of the Black Country town of Willenhall. 'Every day is the same. I'd give anything for a wet, miserable English summer. I'd be as happy as a pig in shit.'

Stoker's been Stateside since the mid-'80s, first in and around Philadelphia before 'driving to California on the back of my first divorce'. He's lived in the Golden State ever since, first in

Los Angeles, but now in Fresno, the hometown of his second wife. Despite his grumbles about the predictability of the weather, life here is good. And has been for decades. 'Mosquitos, flies and blue skies,' he shrugs. 'That's what I'm dealing with.'

It's a long, long way from a Boys' Brigade hut in Willenhall at the tail end of the 1960s. As the brigade's leader Mr Mayo was giving a sermon on the stage to a hall of prepubescent lads, nine-year-old Andrew Growcott had other ideas. Underneath the stage, he'd arranged all the bass and tenor drums played by the young musicians before embarking on the first drum solo of his life, drowning out Mr Mayo's speech. Very shortly afterwards, Andrew Growcott was ejected from this particular branch of the Boys' Brigade.

So began a life spent with drumsticks in hand. And, then, a life in recording studios. Over the next hour, Stoker will trace the arc of his musical existence – one which has been populated by the likes of Sting and Prince and Ice Cube and even William Shatner, and one which also includes a sideline in music for television and advertising. He's been a busy boy.

It properly starts in the house of his childhood best friend and future Dexys bandmate, Andy Leek. 'His dad was a window cleaner, but they'd bought a doctor's house that also contained a surgery, which they'd converted into a kind of rehearsal room. From the age of eleven, we'd jam and write songs. As soon as school was finished, I'd be round there. We'd play until seven or eight o'clock when I'd go home for my tea.

'We both started out playing in working men's clubs. We were in separate bands. I got a job in a band called Benny and the Jets.' Andy went on to form the Wailing Cocks, a band that Stoker was deeply envious of. 'They supported the Boomtown Rats and I went to watch the show. That's when I desperately wanted to be in them, with my best friend. So I replaced their drummer, who took my job in Benny and the Jets. I gave him my fluorescent blue suit with black lapels. It fitted him perfectly.'

In November 1978, the same month that Dexys were making their live debut, the Wailing Cocks were already further down the road, gaining their first national exposure. Yet to put a single out, they nonetheless found themselves recording a session for John Peel. Their introduction to the nation came via Peel's observation that 'with such a name, they should be a reggae band from the East End of London'. But they weren't. They were a progressive punk outfit from the Black Country.

'That Peel session was heaven-sent. It was great prep. Andy was a great songwriter and his voice was like a lovely church bell. He really meant what he was singing, so it didn't surprise me that we got that session. But I always thought that Kevin and Kev had way more of an idea of what they wanted to do than the Wailing Cocks ever had. I think it was a happy circumstance that the Wailing Cocks got some traction. But I could see why Dexys immediately jumped off. Rowland's idea of what he wanted was very defined. He knew exactly.'

By late 1979, with the Wailing Cocks having dissolved after Alan Boyle's tragically premature death, Andy had joined Dexys, with Stoker auditioning shortly after. It wasn't his first flirtation with the idea of joining their ranks. 'About six months before, I got this call from Geoff Blythe. They were still looking for a drummer and he managed to get my number. He was trying to explain what they were doing and what they wanted to do. I said, "What do you look like?" He said, "Well, we kind of dress up as doctors and judges and policemen." Huh? What? I never called him back.'

Half a year later, Dexys might just have got their man, the final piece in the jigsaw after working with a series of ill-fitting drummers. 'I got dragged along to Club Lafayette in Wolverhampton for an audition, where Kevin Rowland tried to teach me "Geno".

'You know the break? That's a pretty complicated little riff for a guitarist to play. It's all downstrokes. And Kevin was just breaking strings left, right and centre on this dodgy blue guitar – a semi-acoustic piece of shit. I couldn't figure out what he was trying to show me. So Kev Archer had a go and proceeded to break a bunch of strings and cut his finger. Then Pete Williams came over and went, da-da-da-da-da-da-da-da-da-da-da-da-da-da-da-da-da. And that was it. They called me back the following day and said, "Yeah, yeah. Come on." After that, me and Pete were inseparable – glued together, stitched together. We were fast friends. We still are. I spoke to him just yesterday for an hour.

'Other than that earlier phone call from Geoff, I hadn't been aware of Dexys. As soon as I put the phone down on him, I had forgotten about them completely. I was getting a lot of calls from people at that point – "Do you want to be in our band?" I got a job in a heavy metal band, which I hated. I never listened to hard rock. I never listened to bands like Status Quo and Thin Lizzy. I was a northern soul kid. I used to go up to the soul discos in Wigan. I was really into soul music and I think Dexys figured that out pretty quick. I could do a funk shuffle and I think a lot of their drummers up until that point couldn't even do that.'

Stoker accepted their offer, relieved that the doctor/judge/policeman look had been jettisoned. 'They must have reconsidered their look because none of that existed when I actually joined. Everybody was in jeans and T-shirts and woolly hats. I turned up in a pair of bright blue Levi's, Beatles boots and a brown mohair jumper, thinking that was what I should look like to join Dexys, but that wasn't the case. I remember Kev Archer was very dismissive of the outfit that I was wearing: "What do you look like?!"'

Despite his attire, Dexys had solved their drumming conundrum, filling the vacancy that had appeared after Stoker's predecessor, Bobby 'Jnr' Ward, formerly of Subway Sect, had reportedly sold his kit to buy heroin. Stoker was only too pleased to throw his lot in with the band, which of course meant jacking in his job to live as a member of Dexys 24/7.

'I remember the day perfectly. I was working with my dad. He'd given up being a travelling salesman – I guess all the driving was making him crazy – and had got a job at a company in Cannock. They made push bikes for kids, and boat trailers. When Andy Leek called me about the audition, I took it very seriously. I said, "Dad, give me your keys", and I left. When I got back later, he said, "Where the bloody hell did you go?"

'"I've got a job in a band. We've got a record deal so I'm done here, thanks Dad." I gave it all up immediately. I didn't think twice.

'I think part of the catalyst for me was that Dexys gave me this look that I loved. I looked good – donkey jacket and Dr Martens. I felt good putting that on and seeing everybody looking like me. It was more than a band in that sense. It was the thing that gelled what I thought we should be.'

The band, with Bobby Jnr, had already recorded 'Dance Stance', but it had yet to be released as a single. This meant that, when it very gently punctured the top forty, Stoker had a near-immediate *Top of the Pops* appearance on his CV. 'It was maybe three weeks after I'd quit my job. Everybody from the factory watched it. My dad was pleased as punch. He couldn't believe it.

'It was a whirlwind time. As far as I remember, before we were even on *Top of the Pops*, we'd already recorded "Geno". Within a week or two of me joining, we were in this recording studio in London. It was weird. I'd never seen a studio like it. The tiny drum room was all mirrors. I was just staring at myself.'

With Pete Wingfield at the controls, the magic was made. 'I promised I'd have a number one before I was twenty-one,' Stoker chuckles, 'and I actually did it. I had no clue how I'd do it, but I did.'

While 'Geno' was lingering around the lower reaches of the chart, planning its assault on the upper slopes of the top ten, the band were preparing to decamp to Chipping Norton to record the album. And they'd been preparing hard.

'We used to rehearse for eight hours a day, but I think we should have toured more, doing a bunch of gigs before recording *Searching for the Young Soul Rebels*. Kevin was a great sergeant-major, keeping us on our toes. He was a very driven taskmaster, but I didn't mind. We all looked to him for guidance. I learned so much about discipline from him.

'If you were late for rehearsals, he'd be fucking pissed off. And musicians are usually late. Once, I was on the platform at Wolverhampton to get the train to Birmingham and a couple of guys took offence at me. I must have glanced at them wrongly as they then decided to beat the shit out of me on the train to Birmingham. They just pounced on me. But I was still on time for rehearsal. Of course, the band all saw me with my bloody nose, so rehearsals were cancelled, but I actually made it there on time with a busted lip and bruised face and busted eyelid.'

Once the sessions in Chipping Norton were underway, Kevin largely demurred to Pete Wingfield – certainly where the rhythm tracks were concerned. 'He wasn't involved in those. He knew from rehearsals that he'd gotten us to a point where he didn't need to be in the room. Plus, in my experience, he wasn't very musical. He could sing his ass off and his vocals were amazing, but when it came to telling us what he wanted musically, I don't think he really had much of a clue back then. His strength was knowing that vision of "Let's be disciplined. Let's be like a regiment. Let's be so on it."

'Having a guy like Pete Wingfield come in and really understand what we were trying to do made the recording of the record pretty easy. I don't think it took more than four days for Pete and I to record our parts. But at the same time that we were putting our hearts and souls into this, we were still having a blast. It was a lot of fun while also being something purposeful.

'Chipping Norton was a step up from what I'd previously experienced and that gave me and Pete, especially, a reality check. But Pete Wingfield was good at conducting us in the room. He didn't just sit behind the console. He came in the room and hung out. He danced. He loved it. I always thought that was a pretty genius move.'

It turns out that the experience of those weeks in April 1980 – and the conduct and manner of the record's producer – would have a lasting effect on Stoker. When he later went into production himself, he realised Pete Wingfield had made an impression that was hard to erase, hard to ignore. Not that he wanted to.

'I channel him every moment. I spent last week recording an eighteen-year-old drummer called Jimmy. He's an amazing drummer and I just wanted to encourage the kid. The last thing a producer should say is no. And you don't say no to an eighteen-year-old kid. You have to find what's going on inside and you pull that out. You don't say "No, don't do it like that. Do it like this." You've taken that kid out of his comfort zone and that's what Pete Wingfield did for us. Every answer he gave was encouragement. Nothing negative. I thought that was a great lesson. I hark back to that every time I go in the studio. Pete Wingfield never said no.'

There was, though, one occasion when Pete Wingfield did say no: when the band executed their plan to use the master tapes as a bargaining chip. 'There was a lot of discussion about it. Being the youngest member – well, the shortest-serving member – I was like "What? We want more points? What does that mean? I haven't got a clue what that means." I was told that, to get a better deal with EMI, we needed to hold the tapes to ransom. Steve

Spooner turned off the power to the building, someone who was more careful than me managed to get the tapes off before the power went off, and then we did a runner. I remember hiding behind hedges in Chipping Norton and police cars flying by. It never occurred to me that we could get arrested and put in prison. Roger Ames at EMI, the white guy with the Trinidadian accent, was so pissed off. "Man, you took me tapes." I loved Roger. He was such a beautiful man.

'But it was the perfect legend for that band, wasn't it?'

'I'd give anything for a wet, miserable English summer.' Stoker at home in cloudless Fresno, California, with a picture of his trombone-playing daughter on the wall behind.

After the deal had been partially renegotiated and the tapes returned, Stoker unwittingly found himself centre stage on the album's artwork and promotional materials, namely a full-length shot of him from behind, walking away from the camera, holdall in hand. It appears on the back sleeve of *Searching for the Young Soul Rebels* and became a symbol of both the album and that particular moment in Dexys history. He was the poster boy.

'It never occurred to me that I'd been singled out as the face of that particular record, nor that it was wrong or weird to have been. It was flattering, but I was quite surprised. I think Rowland used his assets wisely and I looked good in a woolly hat. It didn't affect me. I just thought it was part of the job. Me walking up and down the street was just part of the shoot. I've still got the poster on my wall.'

Here on a wall in Fresno, that portrait of the artist as a young man is like a wedding photo, seen daily by Stoker's daughters, a visual record of Dad in a past life. He says they're indifferent to its charms. 'They don't give a damn about it. They grew up with me making records and talking about Dexys and punk bands and hip hop.'

Despite Stoker's selection as the album's poster boy, cracks in the band were showing. 'If you want to know the truth, me and Rowland really didn't get on. There was definite antipathy between us. It started to show when we were playing live. He'd come over and smash my cymbal with his mic. It must have made a terrible sound out front. He'd start banging my cymbals and denting them. I've still got the cymbal from the last show. I used it on a recording just last week, but it's still dented from back then. I think I was on the verge of getting the sack because I apologised to somebody at *Melody Maker* about what Kevin had said in the press. I got cornered into apologising and he got really upset about it. And I could see his point. That caused a rift between me and him. Then I just started getting madder and madder at him and we'd get into punch-ups.

I was one of the biggest blokes in the group and Rowland didn't intimidate me physically.

'Somehow the energy got misdirected. There should have been more control but, because we were touring so much, there was no rest for the wicked. The power that drove us at the beginning of the record was the stuff that tore us apart at the end. Plus, there was a lot of dissatisfaction from the five guys who weren't the nucleus. Kevin, Kev and Geoff were the ones who dealt with the record company and were the ones who were signed. I didn't make much money from Dexys. But it wasn't an issue. I didn't care, as long as I got to eat what I needed to eat and had a bed to sleep in. I was just happy being in my gang. I didn't care that I was only making thirty quid a week. I was getting paid to be on *Top of the Pops*. And I was getting laid. I was nineteen, for Christ's sake.

'But there were guys in the band who were pissed off about the money and all that energy went into dissatisfaction. I remember Steve Spooner and Kevin Rowland really going at it in Zürich. Steve had the mental capacity to understand what was going on. At the time, I didn't have a clue. All I knew was that something bad was happening.'

The famous five escaped and their adventures very rapidly continued as the Bureau. 'The Bureau was a marriage of convenience as we wanted to move ahead really quickly. There was an element of feeling trapped within soul music. Obviously we couldn't go out and sound like Dexys, so we decided to do this kind of rock/funk blue-eyed soul thing. We were pissed off, but that anger got redirected into what we were doing next. And I've always been a bit like that. "What's next?" I knew we had to keep moving forward. I learned that from young Kevin too.'

After being stranded in the US on the Pretenders tour with the rest of the Bureau, Stoker returned to the West Midlands to assess his options. He did a short stint with the synth-heavy new-wave Birmingham band Fashïon before hooking up with Stephen Duffy, the original singer of Duran Duran, UB40's original producer Bob Lamb and a couple of members of Fashiøn. Signed to WEA, the band – Tin Tin – released a single, 'Kiss Me', which failed to chart. When later remixed by the celebrated French DJ François Kevorkian and re-released as a Stephen Duffy solo single, it made a decent impression, topping the Billboard dance chart in the States. It was a second number one for Stoker.

'After working with Duffy, I ended up playing with pretty much every band in Birmingham. I was the drummer of choice.' He was soon headhunted to join General Public, the new outfit being formed by Dave Wakeling and Ranking Roger in the aftermath of the Beat splitting up. It was something of a supergroup. Horace Panter, freshly out of the employ of the Specials, was on bass, while Mick Jones, recently released by the Clash, became its guitarist. On keyboards was another Dexys alumni, Micky Billingham. He and Stoker's paths hadn't crossed before; their respective tenures hadn't overlapped.

'I walked in the room and there was one of the Specials. My jaw just dropped. They hadn't told me. And Horace and I just gelled. I think he was pleased he had a drummer who was willing to sit down with him for hours at a time, working on grooves. And I didn't know Micky Billingham had been in Dexys. I hadn't paid any attention to them after I left. Both Horace and Micky had joined General Public before me. They'd been working with drum machines up until then.

'We were in Rockfield Studios in Monmouthshire for a week. There was a song called "Anxious", which had the weirdest drum groove you've ever heard in your life. Roger had designed it on a drum machine. But I think that's the reason I got the job: because I could actually play it.' It was a repeat of the situation with 'Geno' at Stoker's Dexys audition. He instantly proved no groove or no break was too hard.

General Public earned more praise and attention in the US than in the UK. 'It was great being on these huge stages and actually being received pretty well. The record company really got behind us on the tours. We had roadies! The tour with Hall & Oates was huge for us. And then we did a world tour with Queen. We couldn't go to South Africa because of apartheid. Roger couldn't be on the same bus as us. That's when we quit the tour.'

After he left General Public ('me and Dave didn't really get on – I don't know what it is about drummers and lead singers'), and after a failed attempt to join Big Audio Dynamite ('I tried calling Don Letts: "Give me a job! Give me a job!"'), Stoker made his move to the US. When he rolled up in California in the late '80s, freshly divorced and looking for his next musical move, he found he'd reached the promised land. A life as a studio engineer and producer beckoned.

'It was just impossible not to work. I got a job at Paramount Recording Studios and never looked back. I worked there for six years, after which I went freelance but just kept working at Paramount because I knew all the rooms.' One of the biggest albums he worked on was Ice Cube's *Death Certificate*. 'West Coast hip hop was in its really early stages. It was just like the punk movement in England when I was a kid and I couldn't get enough of it. Plus, I was the only engineer at Paramount who was willing to sit with a bunch of black blokes with guns.

'I worked with Aretha Franklin while I was there. She was wonderful. I said, "You know, I used to be in a group called Dexys Midnight Runners and we used to play 'Respect'." She said, "Oh, you guys rocked." The studio time had finished, but we chatted for about four hours. We ended up talking about recipes for apple pie, that kind of shit. It was brilliant. I was just sat there in awe.'

One of his more surreal clients was William Shatner.

'This was the mid-'90s when video games were fairly embryonic. They were doing the *Star Trek* video game and he came in to do the voiceover. He was very nice to me, but I was just the grunt in the room, recording him. I felt very sorry for the producer, who was about the same age as me. Shatner went absolutely livid that this kid was telling him what to do. He turned purple. Somewhere, on an old, broken DAT cassette, I've got William Shatner going batshit. Oh man, that's what the internet is for, isn't it? I never put it out, though. I never had the wherewithal. Plus, I didn't want to risk the wrath of Shatner . . .'

Stoker wasn't always the grunt. He often occupied the producer's chair. His highest-profile charge was almost certainly Sting.

'We did the title track to *Demolition Man*, the movie with Sylvester Stallone and Wesley Snipes. I did the demo and sent it to A&M. Then I happened to be back in England, in my parents' home on Lichfeld Road. The phone started ringing and my dad answered it.

'"Bloxwich 76333."

'"Hello, Mr Growcott. This is Sting."

'My dad marched into the room, like he was still in the army.

'"Andrew! Sting's on the phone!"

'I think that's when he realised that I was doing all right.

'The funniest thing I remember about Sting happened at Paisley Park, Prince's studio in Minneapolis, recording the vocals to "Demolition Man". It was nine o'clock at night and the A&R guy, Mark Mazzetti, offered to make some tea, to which Sting announced he liked his tea served in china cups. So Mark Mazzetti then had to go and find a china tea service at nine o'clock at night somewhere in Minneapolis. And he did come back with one. Once Mazzetti had left the room, Sting said, "I was just fucking with him."'

That time in Minneapolis was a surreal one for the boy from Willenhall. 'Prince and Sting would be talking to each other just in front of me. I couldn't believe what the fuck I was seeing. And there's me, in charge . . .'

Stoker's biggest hit as a producer was surely Pato Banton's version of the Equals' 'Baby Come Back', which Pato covered in the company of Ali and Robin Campbell from UB40. The single topped the charts in the UK – another number one of sorts for Stoker. And it was even more significant than that. 'The proceeds of "Baby Come Back", the royalties from that record, bought this house,' he announces proudly.

'We could have bought a house in LA, but I didn't want to raise my kids there. It was an easier lifestyle here in Fresno.' It's also his wife's hometown. 'She was born here. Her great-great-grandfather was a slave, and one of her grandfathers was an SS officer. I've always thought that was an interesting dichotomy.'

Stoker and his family have lived in this house since 1998, around the same time that his career as a producer was being curtailed by external forces. 'The music business in LA was huge. It was on the same scale as the movie business. But the bottom dropped out because of MP3s. So many people were fired.' Stoker needed a new career, a new source of income, a new chapter.

He picked up his drumsticks again and moved into providing music for TV and advertising.

Teaming up with a guy called Tim Moser, best known as the guitarist of the hard rock band Junkyard, the pair started writing and recording music to order – often for clients with deep pockets. 'I had just been doing my thing at Paramount and he called me to do a Cornetto advert for South America. Tim's a schmoozer and he got us this job. It was exorbitant money for three days' work. We then came on leaps and bounds. We did all these punk rock tracks for Toyota commercials. It was a blast. That's the biggest gig you can get, a Toyota commercial that's played nationally every five minutes. We made fortunes – enough to live on for a year from one commercial.

'At the beginning of my advertising and television music career, I did 300,000 miles in my Toyota 4Runner driving backwards and forwards from here to Los Angeles. Once the internet kicked in, it was a lot easier. Last weekend was actually the first time I'd seen Tim in person for six years. We can do everything online. And we have a very business-like relationship. We don't necessarily socialise or talk on the phone about football scores. We don't do any of that. It's strictly about music and how to make it better. And we're very productive. Our sense of what he needs from me and what I need from him is pretty defined. We have a shorthand.'

It's not just the advertising buck they've chased. They've also been keen to apply their creativity to TV shows. One of the first pitches they made was for the signature tune for the US version of *The Office*. 'They wanted something that sounded like "Mr Blue Sky". Not necessarily a knock-off, but something that had the same rhythmic wistfulness. So we wrote and recorded this song and reached the final two. Then someone else licensed "Mr Blue Sky" for their show, so we didn't get the job.

'But we knew the line producer for Craig Ferguson's chat show. They were looking for a theme tune, so we gave him the track. He told Craig that I was the drummer in Dexys and General Public, and that was enough to get us a meeting. Tim and Craig sat down and worked out the lyrics, then Craig came into Paramount to record it. He sang it just once. Craig Ferguson can sing. He's a good singer. And he loves the way I played my drums. We then worked pretty exclusively on his show for ten years. Every piece of music you hear on any of the Craig Ferguson shows, we wrote.'

From the Boys' Brigade to Hollywood, via the Wailing Cocks, Dexys and much more, it's been a hell of a ride for Stoker. At every stage, he's heeded one particular gem of advice from Kevin Rowland: always move forward. He's never been someone to let the grass grow under his feet – not that his hole-digging dog would allow it to grow anyway.

'I love that I have almost a diary of my life in the music that I've worked on.'

He runs a hand through an enviably thick head of hair. A smile of contentment plays on his face. The sky is still blue.

'I wouldn't change a thing.'

Reminisce #4

New Street, Chipping Norton

At dusk, as the market town slips into deeper and darker shades of blue, the schoolchildren of Chipping Norton skip happily down the hill. Most of them, anyway. A brother and sister are being diverted by a grandparent through the door of Damira Dental Studios. The heavy mosquito buzz of the dentist's drill possibly awaits.

In decades past, more pleasant sounds would have come wafting from 28 New Street. For twenty-eight years, from the early '70s until the eve of the millennium, this handsome Cotswold stone building, once a school, was home to the unimaginatively named Chipping Norton Recording Studios. As such, it welcomed an endless trail of musicians and bands to sample the delights of one of the country's first residential studios. The blue plaque on the wall tells us the likes of Radiohead, Status Quo, XTC, Duran Duran, Steve Winwood and Beverley Craven have recorded albums here. The sax solo to Gerry Rafferty's 'Baker Street' was played in what is now the dental surgery's reception area.

This is also where Searching for the Young Soul Rebels *was born – and thus, by definition, where it was kidnapped from too, up and away in a fury and a flurry of urgent shouts and revving engines.*

Crime is low in these parts, and memories appear to be long. Dexys have been left off the blue plaque, the involvement of Thames Valley Police during their time here seemingly disqualifying them from any due recognition.

8

Seb Shelton

Drums, 1980–84

'The sound was so hard and we achieved that by pushing players way beyond what they thought they could achieve.'

Seb Shelton is a man rarely interviewed, his voice seldom heard.

One of the first new recruits after the famous five buggered off and rebadged themselves as the Bureau, Seb took over the Dexys drum stool, having been lured across from the mod-revival quartet Secret Affair. He came with experience, having already graced both the *Top of the Pops* studio and the cover of *Smash Hits* before the end of the '70s. Indeed, Jerry Dammers had already scouted him for the original line-up of the Specials.

Dexys' move towards a public image of exercise and fitness, of personal restraint and discipline, suited Seb down to a tee; he may even have been the co-architect of the new approach. After he'd announced to Secret Affair that he was departing, the band's singer Ian Page observed that 'he never drank or smoked and he was always very keen on keeping fit, so I'm sure he's very happy there'. He and new guitarist Billy Adams were both devotees of martial arts and joined a kung fu club together. 'He was the first person who ever said to me, with a straight face, "My body is a temple",' says Billy. On tour, while the horn players in particular let off post-gig steam by sinking a few pints, Seb instigated the Tea Club, decompressing with nothing stronger than an innocent cuppa. Helen O'Hara and Billy were regular members.

Seb became more than just the drummer in Dexys. He was the musician charged with knocking new recruits into shape if needed, the one to push them, to test their commitment. Patient but firm appeared to be his way. In an extremely rare public-facing appearance – an interview for the BBC *Young Guns* documentary about Dexys at the turn of the millennium – Seb explained that 'when we were rehearsing new sax players, they'd be asked to play louder and harder, and so they'd reach for the volume control, but would be told "No, that isn't what's required". You'd have good players coming away with bleeding lips because they were having to blow so much harder than they'd ever thought that they could do.'

And positive results were forthcoming. 'The sound was so hard and we achieved that by pushing players way beyond what they thought they could achieve.' Kevin was surely thrilled to have someone very much on the same hymn sheet.

Nonetheless, their relationship appears to have been tetchy. One conspicuous example of this is the shoot for the 'Come on Eileen' video, eighteen months into his tenure in the band. In the scenes shot in daylight outside that corner shop in south London, Seb is a committed performer, offering spirited backing vocals while beating a drum held under his arm. However, in the scenes shot after sundown, he's nowhere to be seen. A disagreement with Kevin had occurred during the time in between. Seb had walked off set and gone home, returning to the fold three days later.

A more fundamental, more fatal, fissure opened up a further eighteen months after, at the start of 1984. Seb and his partner Kate, Helen O'Hara's sister, visited Helen and Kevin at their flat in Birmingham. The two men went out for a walk to discuss a business matter. Seb left the band shortly after. 'He explained to me that he had been finding rehearsals and demos tortuous,' Helen later wrote, 'that Kevin was unpredictable and increasingly difficult to work with . . . but the final straw was about his future record royalties.'

Known for his commercial nous, Seb hung up his drumsticks and turned to artist management. He had some notable charges to steer, among them Julian Cope, Adrian Sherwood, Tackhead and the Woodentops. It was with the latter that he last appeared publicly behind a drum kit, on the video for their 1985 single 'Move Me', behind a pair of shades and with his hair now touching his collar. The following year, he was listed on the credits of their album *Giant*, an acknowledgement of his 'coordination and business acumen'.

At some point, Seb retreated from the music industry and settled for apparent retirement in the peace of the Norfolk countryside. A very keen angler, the most recent clue as to his day-to-day existence is a sixteen-second YouTube video of him reeling in a pike while stood in a boat on Chew Valley Lake in Somerset. I have designs on spending the afternoon with him on a riverbank somewhere in the Norfolk Broads, fishing rod in the water and waiting for a bite, while one of Dexys' most enigmatic former members explains all about his three years in the band and his life since.

But an enigma he shall remain.

I manage to track down a physical address for Seb and send him a good old-fashioned letter outlining my proposal, together with a copy of a previous book to bolster my credentials, to offer some reassurance. I leave it a few weeks, regularly checking my spam folder, but no reply comes. I even take the liberty of asking Helen if she could gently nudge her brother-in-law. Again, no reply from him. I can take a hint. I leave him in peace.

The angler didn't take the bait. He avoided the hook. The one that got away.

Dexys Midnight Runners, July 1981. (l–r) Kev 'Billy' Adams, Kevin Rowland, Steve Wynne, Jimmy Paterson, Paul Speare, Micky Billingham, Seb Shelton and Brian Brummitt (aka Brian Maurice). *Fin Costello/Getty Images*

9

Micky Billingham

Keyboards and accordion, 1980–82

'I didn't mind the pay cut. I was doing exactly what I wanted to do.'

It's lunchtime in drizzly Dudley and the chairlift designed to take visitors up the steep hill of the town's zoo is travelling empty. It loops up, around and back down again in the service of precisely no one.

The nearby Malt Shovel pub is empty too, the students from the college across the road choosing not to opt for a liquid lunch. The pub has no patrons, except for the man in the corner nursing a freshly poured glass of Madri. He's a man ready to tell his story. He is Micky Billingham, the formerly flaxen-haired player of Dexys' organ, piano and accordion between December 1980 and December 1982. The flaxen hair has gone: his head is shaven, but the golden sleepers in both ears remain.

Micky's first public appearance with the band was on the Christmas edition of *Top of the Pops* in 1980, one of five new members reprising 'Geno' as a salute to one of the year's landmark singles. Back then, he stood before his organ in headband and hoodie and boxer boots, the new Dexys look. His last outing with the band was precisely two years later, also on the Christmas edition of *Top of the Pops*. This time, in dungarees and espadrilles, he had an accordion strapped across his shoulders as the band revisited 'Come on Eileen'.

In between those two visits to BBC Television Centre in Shepherd's Bush were twenty-four months of tumult and triumph. But his tenure could have started earlier, and lasted longer, as Micky, taking a sip of his beer, explains.

'When he was first getting Dexys together in 1978, Kevin watched me play in a pub. I had a Hammond organ. Afterwards he asked me if I was interested in playing for him. It was a no from me. I'd heard some terrible stories about him. I'd heard about him apparently locking some other band in the studio at break time and not letting them go to the pub. But then, when I saw them on *Top of the Pops* doing "Dance Stance", I could have kicked myself. And then, of course, came "Geno".

'I started in bands when I was fifteen. I was self-taught on the piano. The final band I was in before Dexys was a rock outfit called Cryer. It was a big set-up. Pyrotechnics at the gigs, you know. But they never seemed to be going anywhere, so I applied to join Squeeze as Jools Holland's replacement, but Paul Carrack got the job instead.

'At that point, I was working in a builders' merchants. I was the sales manager. I'd been in that trade for years. Kevin phoned me up at work one day and asked me to go and meet him in a café. There he told me what had happened with the band, how more than half of them had left.'

Did that not sound the same alarm bells that had rung in your head a couple of years earlier?

'Yeah, a bit, but I was ready for a slice of the action by then. I'd seen Dexys play a few times and I didn't think anybody could touch them. Ever since I bought *Searching for the Young Soul Rebels*, I hadn't stopped playing it. I loved that record. I still love it now. I thought it was fantastic, so to be playing with the band that brought that out would have sent me over the moon. I asked him what songs to learn for the audition. I think they were "I'm Just Looking", "There, There My Dear" and possibly "Geno". I hadn't got any keyboards at the time so I had to keep listening to the records. Fortunately, I've got perfect pitch so I learned all the parts in my head. I got them dead right when I went to play there. I knew the songs inside out. I was determined that I would join them at some point and my persistence paid off in the finish. I made sure Kevin didn't forget me.

'I'd packed a job in once before to go on tour with a band because I'd used all my holiday entitlement up. When my dad found out, he kicked me out of the house, so I had something to prove. When I finished at the builders' merchants, I was on about ninety pounds a week. When I joined Dexys, it was down to sixty pounds. And that was if you could find the manager to pay you. There was no guaranteed amount of money put into your account at the end of the month. Sometimes we wouldn't have anything. In fairness, though, if Kevin thought you were struggling, he'd get you to meet him in Birmingham and would usually slip you a couple of quid. He was quite good like that. But I didn't mind the pay cut. I was doing exactly what I wanted to do.'

From having greatly admired Dexys from the outside looking in, Micky now discovered the intensity of life on the inside. He found it was the kind of experience he'd not encountered in any of his previous bands.

'It actually didn't feel like a band at all. It was quite clinical and you could never tell what Kevin was thinking. He always held his cards really close to his chest. The manager sat us down one day and told us to remember that this was Kevin's band. And that's what it was from day one. Sometimes at rehearsals, you'd walk in and, after about five minutes, you'd know who he'd got it in for that day. You were really on your guard all the time.

'I had no idea how intense it could get. Kevin could be charming one minute but change so quickly. You never really knew where you stood with him. And that was absolutely deliberate.

'From what Pete Williams and Jimmy Paterson have told me, there was a lot of drug-taking going on in the first line-up of the band. This was completely banned in our line-up. You couldn't even take a couple of tins to rehearsals. No drinking at rehearsals, no drinking before shows, and definitely no smoking dope or taking drugs. So I never smoked dope while I was with him. If I had a joint, somebody having a go at me when I was stoned wouldn't be very nice – especially not him.'

Nonetheless, Micky found kindred spirits among the horn section. 'When we were let off the leash, there was Paul, Brian, Jimmy and myself. We could drink. We could really drink.'

Once into the swing of rehearsals, the discipline of which had been carried over from the original line-up ('Ten o'clock 'til five o'clock, Monday to Friday. We put the work in'), that first *Top of the Pops* appearance came calling. For Micky, reassurance had rapidly arrived, confirmation that he'd made the right choice to jack in his job, ignoring the whispered concerns of his immediate family. 'It was so tempting to rub my dad's nose in it, but I never did. But he was one of those people. He used to boast to all his friends about me, but he'd never turn around and say well done. He was always right, I was always wrong. I know he was dead proud, though. He just never admitted it to me.'

Further near-immediate satisfaction with his career choice came when Dexys were booked into a certain legendary studio in January 1981 in order to record the single 'Plan B', the first with the new line-up. That month, the five new members were joined – following Kevin Archer's retreat from the band – by a sixth, the fresh-faced guitarist Kev Adams, who was promptly christened 'Billy'. The youngest in the band, he was often also referred to as 'The Boy'.

Micky's eyes dance at the memory of that first recording session. 'That was another great opportunity. Abbey Road, of all places. It was amazing.'

But there wasn't unanimity over the release of 'Plan B' as the next single. EMI ploughed ahead, despite voices within the band declaring their opposition, unhappy that the recording didn't quite do the rebooted band full justice and suffered from a fractious relationship between Kevin Rowland and producer Alan Shacklock. The reviews weren't the kindest; *Smash Hits* believed the song did 'have its moments' and that there were 'steps in the right direction', but was ultimately underwhelmed by this first calling-card of Dexys Mk II. On the Radio 1 review programme *Roundtable*, guest Malcolm McLaren wondered what had happened to Plan A.

On its first week of release, the single entered the chart at number sixty-five. The following week, it limped to number fifty-eight. It rose no higher. Not helped by Kevin's refusal to interact with the music press, it was a boxing boot in the teeth for the band's new sound and recalibrated vision – especially as, in that week's top ten, and thus massively outstripping the sales of 'Plan B', were such rear-view retrograde efforts as Shakin' Stevens' 'This Ole House' and Coast to Coast's '(Do) The Hucklebuck'.

The relationship with EMI was moribund, but their eagle-eyed manager, by now a Geordie called Paul 'Basher' Burton, found a way of extricating the band from its contract. The record company had failed to take up their option. And, despite EMI's protestations, the courts found in Dexys' favour. The eight of them hurriedly crawled through the escape tunnel to freedom.

However, now without the backing of a record company, and without the chart positions that guaranteed bums on seats, the scheduled Projected Passion Revue tour, with dates pencilled in for theatres across the country, was severely curtailed. Just three shows survived: Birmingham, Chelmsford and the Dominion Theatre in London. The latter was a full-house triumph, with many Dexys devotees still agreeing that, despite the shortness of the tour, it represents the band's zenith as a live band. Micky's then partner came to see one of the shows: 'Afterwards he said it felt like a gospel meeting.'

The spiritual occasion that Kevin Rowland had been aiming for had arrived. The tour programme showed his workings: a list of songs that had 'provided inspiration during the preparation of the Projected Passion Revue', which included Aretha Franklin's 'I Say a Little Prayer', the Edwin Hawkins Singers' 'Oh Happy Day' and the Commodores' 'I Feel Sanctified'.

Also in the programme was a message of welcome which outlined the nature of that evening's show. 'We decided quite a while ago to try and steer away from the usual rock concert routine, where anonymous support groups try to hold the attention of uninterested audiences. Instead, we want to present a varied evening's entertainment with three physically different, though spiritually in tune acts coming together to make one complete show. You'll see the result tonight.' The other two acts were the comedy pair of Peter Richardson and Nigel Planer, billed as the Outer Limits, and the dance troupe Torque.

Dexys were soon scooped up by Phonogram, where they were reunited with Roger Ames, the man who'd counselled the original line-up against stealing the debut album's master tapes. The first release under the new arrangement was 'Show Me', a song that had already been recorded independently with Tony Visconti in the producer's chair. And it was a song that delivered Dexys back into the top twenty.

'We played some good festivals abroad,' says Micky. 'I remember us playing in Portugal and it was sponsored by the Portuguese Communist Party. It was the time that Bobby Sands was on hunger strike and there was a big banner in front of us that said "Viva IRA, Viva Dexys". And I think we had to give 10 per cent of the earnings to the Portuguese Communist Party. The leader gave a speech, which seemed to last a couple of hours, and it was so hot that people were fainting in the audience. The stage was at the bottom of a hill, and as night-time came, all you could see for miles and miles were lights in the forest. There were a quarter of a million people there. Everybody abroad absolutely adored us. It was nice that we were treated like that. Nobody seemed to notice it was a different line-up, or that we were now dressed differently.'

Then came Kevin's experiments with the strings, first getting the reluctant horn section – Jimmy Paterson, Paul Speare and Brian Brummitt (also known as Brian Maurice) – to attempt to rapidly learn cello and viola, before the arrival of the violins of the three-strong Emerald Express. Whatever the strings added to the mix, 'Kevin didn't want it to sound like the Electric Light Orchestra,' says Micky. Dexys were regenerating, moving into their third phase, their third incarnation. That white-hot second coming, the 1981 line-up, never got the chance to make an LP, cruelly denied the opportunity to create their own classic album. 'I've heard Kevin refer to us as the lost line-up of Dexys. He said it was the best one ever.'

A roll of the eyes. 'Not that you would have known about it at the time from the way he used to treat people . . .'

'I've had no regrets at all. I really haven't looked back.' Micky Billingham on holiday in Ross-on-Wye with his husband Alan.

With the new sound came the new look. Out came the denim. Micky shakes his head. 'Those dungarees weren't snug. I could get three people in mine. Kevin would walk through Birmingham dressed in his, but none of the rest of us would. People had looked at us when we had the wrestling boots and the hoodies on because we stuck out. But I didn't mind that. I thought that they must think we're pretty cool.'

At the same time came a renewed desire on Micky's part to play a larger role in the songs' composition. 'I wanted to get involved in the writing and "The Celtic Soul Brothers" was the first time for that. A lot of the time, some of my keyboard parts would end up as violin lines and things like that. I'd be like "That means that I've written . . ." Of course, I never used to get anything for it. I really thought that "The Celtic Soul Brothers" would have been a hit, if not quite a big hit, as there was still nothing out there like that.'

On its first release, the single stalled at number forty-five, a few places off a chart position that was likely to have gifted Dexys a return to that *Top of the Pops* studio. Still, it was an improvement on the previous single 'Liars A to E', which failed to make even the slightest of inroads into the top seventy-five. 'That was a dreadful single, that was. It was awful. The production didn't go anywhere close to how it was supposed to sound. The only good thing was that the piano I played was the one that was used on "Hey Jude".'

And then came 'Come on Eileen', the soundtrack to Dexys' occupation of the last-chance saloon. Initially lingering in the lower reaches of the charts, the single rose and rose and rose, eventually giving Rowland, the only original member now left, his second number one. Alongside the fiddles and banjos, Micky and his accordion became a fixture of television screens all summer long, from chat shows to specialist music programmes and Saturday-morning kids' shows.

But all was not well in the camp. Brian and Jimmy had already jumped ship before the single's release, unhappy with the horns' relegation at the hands of the strings. Second fiddle and all that. Paul followed suit shortly after *Too-Rye-Ay* was completed. Micky, already not the happiest camper, had lost his drinking buddies. Bass player Giorgio Kilkenny had said arrivederci too.

'I was wondering whether I wanted to leave or not. It wasn't any fun any more. They all came round to my flat and I told them I was thinking of knocking it on the head. Paul Burton asked me if I could do the European and UK tours. I could name my price. So I did those two last tours, but they were weird because I didn't know the brass section. It felt very fragmented. I got to know the new bass player, John Edwards, but there was only me, Billy, Seb, Kevin and Helen. The rest were proper session players from London. We all got on in the end and had some good laughs, but it wasn't the same.

'We did the Christmas *Top of the Pops* and that was that. They asked if I was interested in going to America with them, but that was the last thing I could ever imagine doing. I'm glad I didn't because it was a complete flop. They were playing to half-empty houses. It was a real shame.'

Micky made a clean break. Unlike Steve Spooner, he has no carrier bag of Dexys memorabilia and ephemera stashed away, waiting to be handled again, to be sifted through. 'I wish I'd kept some of the clothes now, especially the hoodies. Not the dungarees, though. After I left, I didn't want any reminders around me. It had been my life for two years, so it was all still a bit raw.'

He disappears out the back of the pub for a cigarette and I get his glass refilled. There are more stories to be told. Those post-Dexys years need fleshing out.

'I had no options at that point,' he explains on his return to our table. 'I vividly remember waking up on a Sunday morning in my flat and wondering whether Adam and the Ants, who were always obsessed with Dexys, needed a keyboard player. But I didn't follow up on it. I didn't know what to do. I just wanted some time off from it. It had consumed all of my time, all of my life. I'd lost a few relationships. I'd had a few break-ups because of it. Dexys had come first every time. It was a way of life.'

Having briefly come up for air, Micky found music soon came calling again. And has called ever since. He's written down his CV on a slip of paper, not just for my use but also as an aide memoire for himself. It details his various musical roles since Dexys. First on the list is the three-year spell he did as a member of General Public, having been headhunted by the post-Beat Dave Wakeling and Ranking Roger.

'Being in Dexys did my reputation wonders and I didn't have to wait long. The guy who lived next door to me was big friends with Dave. He told me Dave wanted a word. I knew that the Beat had split up, so I went to see him over in Handsworth. He explained how they'd listened to *Too-Rye-Ay* a lot when they were on tour and liked the keyboards on it. He made a recording into a Walkman, whistling some ideas. "See what you can do with that," he said, before he went on holiday to Greece. The first thing I had a go at was "Tenderness", putting some meat on its bones. I recorded an arrangement of that and played it to him when he came back from holiday. And I was in.

'We started writing the songs together then. Dave, Roger and I went to a farmhouse in Ross-on-Wye. I'd got my four-track Portastudio and the three of us wrote the songs together. I'd never done it like that before. Then we demoed all those songs at Rockfield in Monmouthshire. It was a much more convivial atmosphere. It was how creating stuff should be.'

The rest of the band were then recruited, turning the outfit into that supergroup by signing up Mick Jones, Horace Panter and drummer boy Stoker. 'The first tour we did was small gigs. We played a few pubs around Birmingham and then played to three people at the Haçienda in Manchester. Three people! That was a disappointment. Then we played at Glastonbury, on the Pyramid Stage. While our gear was being set up, a few of us went out into the festival and started sampling fudge and that kind of thing. When I came off stage later, it felt like I'd had a religious experience, I was that stoned.

'But General Public didn't seem to be a big deal in this country, which I was surprised about. I think people here are always a bit wary of so-called supergroups. We did better in America, where the first LP was a hit and was played all over college radio. We'd sold all these copies and all the gigs were sold out. People were screaming at us when we walked into the auditorium and were waiting for us outside when we came out.

'I realised then that I made the right move by not going to America with Dexys, though. I just didn't like it there. I'd stay in the hotel and not go out in the daytime. I started drinking a hell of a lot too. I was drinking Jim Beam. And I went to a really dark place. I went to San Francisco and smoked so much draw one night that I couldn't get to sleep as I was waiting for an earth-quake to start.'

General Public's success in the US certainly wasn't hindered by them becoming a favourite of directors of teen comedies. One of their songs, 'Taking the Day Off', was used on the soundtrack to *Ferris Bueller's Day Off*, while 'Tenderness' – the song that Micky had worked on before officially joining the band – appeared in both *Weird Science* and, later, *Clueless*. Such exposure helped record sales; 'Tenderness' made the top thirty in both the US and Canada. 'For two years running, we had the number-one dancefloor track in New York, first with "Tenderness" and then with a song called "Hot You're Cool". Then we got Arthur Baker to remix a few tunes as well.'

The second album, 1986's *Hand to Mouth*, didn't replicate the debut's success. 'The audiences were lukewarm for the new material, but as soon as we'd play songs from the first album, they loved it. And, by then, I think Dave had already got it into his head that he wanted to go solo.'

With General Public dissolved, Micky then assisted Dave on that first solo LP, moving out to California. 'I lived in West Hollywood for a couple of years. I remember we were getting $117 a fortnight from IRS, the record company. They were paying all our bills at the apartment we had but, still, $117 in Los Angeles wouldn't even last you a good night.' The recording went over budget and IRS wouldn't fund its completion any further. 'They said, "If you want to finish it, you've got to pay for it yourself."'

'I'd given up everything in England to be out there, so I came home that Christmas, 1988. I went back to nothing. I'd got nothing. I had a bit of a nervous breakdown because I wondered what I was going to do. But I had to do something because I'd got no money. That's when I got into the pub trade.' He takes a sip of his beer. 'Something close to my heart . . .'

But a few years as landlord of a handful of pubs around the Black Country couldn't dilute a particular passion that had carried on simmering. 'I got the bug for music again. There was a band in Birmingham called the International Beat. Everett Morton from the Beat was their drummer. Ranking Roger was producing their album for Blue Beat Records, Buster Bloodvessel's label, but nobody had given him his advance so he backed out. They asked me to step in, so I produced the second half of the album. I ended up playing guest keyboards on it and then we went to America to promote it, playing gigs all over. But that came to an end because nothing happened. The record company didn't promote the LP very well and there was a limit to how many times we could go around playing the same stuff.

'Some people who my partner worked with were in a musical theatre company based in the Black Country and they needed a new musical director. I did that for a fair few years. We did all the usual musicals – *Calamity Jane* and all that. Then, one night, one of the singers told me they were looking for a singing teacher down at Dudley College. I'd never taught before and I had no qualifications, but I still went down for an interview. I mentioned about playing with Dexys and the interviewer gave me the job there and then, just because of my background.'

Micky glances down at the slip of paper between us, checking dates.

'I did that from 2000, right up until 2010. In the meantime, I studied for a BA in music at Wolverhampton University as I couldn't get a full-time teaching job at Dudley unless I had a degree. So I graduated and then, that summer, instead of getting a timetable from the college through the post, I got my P45. The new principal had decided they had to cut down on certain costs, so they got rid of all the visiting lecturers and gave all their hours to the full-time staff. I was a visiting lecturer, so I was one of the first to go. No "Thank you for the past ten years". Not even a compliment slip. Just a P45 and I was finished. Out of it again.

'Armed with my degree, I applied for other teaching jobs but my age was against me. I'd have been about fifty-five by then. I was too old. That's what I heard back every time.'

At the same time that he'd been lecturing, Micky had been playing keyboards in Ranking Roger's version of the Beat. 'I'd been playing with them for a couple of years before I got the push from the college. But then he decided that he didn't want keyboards any more. He wanted another guitarist instead, so I was out. Everett had been in the band as well, but he'd had an accident and broken his knee, so he couldn't play the drums and was retired off.

'As Everett and I were out on our ears, we joined forces, along with the guitarist from the Beat, Neil Deathridge. We came up with the name Beat Goes Bang. It was another version of the Beat, but with the idea that we were going to write our own stuff, which we started doing. But, unfortunately, an LP of new songs never came to fruition because Everett died of cancer in 2021. Neil decided he'd had enough of it, but I kept the band going, right up until now.'

I don't immediately register the significance of the 'now' that Micky's just uttered. He carries on and I'm soon up to speed.

'I don't like it when people aren't committed enough to be able to turn up on time at rehearsals, which has happened a few times. It happened again the other night. I sat there waiting for forty minutes for people to turn up. I thought, *Right, if they can't be bothered, I can't be bothered*. I'm off home to bed. So I'm retiring from the whole lot. I've had enough. That's it.'

This decision was made on Tuesday night. Today is Thursday. Micky Billingham retired from music less than forty-eight hours ago.

There are other reasons for Micky's retreat, aside from tardy, less-than-dedicated bandmates.

'I've really damaged my hand. I got out of bed in the middle of the night to go to the toilet and went flying over my shoes. I broke the fifth metacarpal, so I've got deformity in my hand. And, as a result of the trauma, I've got arthritis in my fingers. I can still play with the other hand, but I can't put any pressure on this one. It's like needles.

'I'm sixty-six now, so I've reached retirement age. I've nothing to complain about because I've still got my studio and I can still play the piano for my own amusement once my fingers are healed. It's a shame because the band was great. I'll miss it.'

A couple of hours ago, Micky seemed reserved, a little cautious, slightly guarded. That seems to have dissolved since. 'This has been cathartic,' he says, rising from his seat and giving me a hug. The post-Dexys years have been mixed for him professionally, but any wrong turns are never looked upon ruefully. Even if the dice rarely rolled a double six, Micky remains sanguine – grateful, even – about how those dice did actually land.

'Since that fateful day when Kevin Rowland phoned me up at the builders' merchants, I've had no regrets at all. I really haven't looked back. And I've been lucky. I've been virtually all over the world and didn't have to pay for it.'

He returns his glass to the bar.

'And all I had to do was play some keyboards.'

10

Steve Wynne and Mick 'Giorgio Kilkenny' Galic

Bass, 1980–81 / bass, 1981–82

'Steve was so laid-back. He wasn't taking it as seriously as everybody else.' –
Micky Billingham

The hunt is on for Steve Wynne, the second bass player for Dexys. There are several potential leads, but most of these can be discounted without a need to make door-to-door enquiries.

He's not Steve Wynne, strawberry-blond CEO of Strawberry Blond TV and director of numerous shows on the Disney Channel.

He's not Steve Wynne, retired professional rugby league player who made a modest number of appearances for Widnes and Salford.

He's not Steve Wynne, founder of Sports Motorcycles racing team.

And nor is he Dr Steven Wynne, senior lecturer at Manchester Metropolitan University business school.

However, he could well be Steve Hope Wynne – an actor who's appeared in Tim Burton's *Charlie and the Chocolate Factory* and who supplied the voice of Lara Croft's father in the *Tomb Raider* video game. A message is pinged off. Hopes are high.

Hopes are quickly dashed.

'I am afraid you may have misidentified me,' comes his response. 'Regretfully, I am not Steve Wynne the bass player and have not

worked with the Blue Ox Babes. However, as part of the Kidz Next
Door [a band with very close connections to Sham 69], I did enjoy
the privilege of supporting Dexys Midnight Runners on a few of
their early dates.

'I am so sorry not to be of any value or help.'

As I pause for a moment to consider the chances of two men with
near-identical names having such close links with Dexys, it's apparent
that my options are slimming down. But the search isn't quite done.

There's a Steve Wynne on Facebook who lists 'musical performance' and 'making music' as his vocations of choice. His profile
picture shows a man in his early sixties with shoulder-length silver
hair and a silver goatee. There's also a Steve Wynne on Soundcloud
who's posted lots of compositions on the site, which he describes as
double bass-led 'fake jazz cat lounge'. The thumbnail pic accompanying one of the tunes is of the same guy with the same shoulder-
length silver hair and the same silver goatee. Have I found our man?

I find an email address and send off a message. 'Are you the Steve
Wynne who was in Dexys Midnight Runners? Please get if touch if
so.' I wait a week or two. I send another email. I wait some more.

Then, late on a Sunday afternoon, just as I'm heading out of
the door to give the dog his final constitutional of the weekend, an
email pings into my inbox. It's an email that will put a skip in my
stride as I head to the woods.

'It's me, guilty.'

Over a subsequent email conversation, my happiness in successfully hunting down Steve Wynne is somewhat tempered. I send
across a sample of the kind of questions I want to ask him. 'Good
questions,' he initially replies. But, after a few days of contemplation, Steve is reluctant to go into the past in too much depth. 'I'm
stuck in the now,' he explains.

He does, though, offer a brief overview of his early bass-playing
days around Coventry. It starts with Transposed Men, the band

he was in with future Specials drummer John Bradbury and future Selecter guitarist Neol Davies. Indeed, before the Selecter took 'On My Radio' into the charts, it was a fixture of the Transposed Men's set.

When the band went their separate, high-flying ways, Steve became part of another Two-Tone outfit, the Swinging Cats. Described by the *NME* as being 'not so much plain old ska and punk as incidental music – the John Barry t'ing – and '60s pop', they included guitarist John Shipley (later of the Special AKA) and future Colourfield member Toby Lyons. Their time in the sun was short; Two-Tone released just one Swinging Cats' single. And the sun didn't shine hard upon it. Despite retailing for 50p, 'Mantovani' died a quick death. The band lasted not much longer.

The Swinging Cats' implosion inadvertently timed itself well, as the bass-playing berth in Dexys had become available after Bureau-bound Pete Williams had left. Steve was a fixture of the band from the last few weeks of 1980 until the following September. He's there on the Christmas *Top of the Pops*, the reprise of 'Geno' adorned by his distinctive, melodic style of playing. He's there on the recording of 'Plan B' at Abbey Road, his throbbing bassline the backbone of the song. And he's there on the earlier shows on the Projected Passion Revue tour, running in tandem with guitarist Billy Adams to the front of the stage to clamber onto the monitors.

Steve's departure that autumn suggests he wasn't the most committed member. 'He got the sack,' Micky Billingham tells me. 'He was always late for rehearsals and he was really half-hearted about the whole thing. He was so laidback. He wasn't taking it as seriously as everybody else.'

No hard feelings were clearly harboured on either side, though; Steve would be invited to be part of the early sessions and demos for what became the third album, *Don't Stand Me Down*. Indeed, he has a writing credit on 'Knowledge of Beauty', retitled as 'My National Pride' when the LP was reissued by Creation in 1997.

Around that point in the mid-'80s, Steve also did time in the service of the new bands of a couple of former Dexys members. First was a call-up from Pete Williams to play in These Tender Virtues. Then, after he 'kept on bumping into Kevin Archer on the Hagley Road', came a prolonged spell with the Blue Ox Babes, during which time he played bass on the *Apples & Oranges* album.

Much of the '90s was spent collecting arts degrees – initially a BA from Nottingham Trent University and then a Masters in strategic management for the creative arts from the University of the Arts London. Steve has since worked in both film and photography, but music has always been the constant. He's never stopped composing, as well as having been a freelance recording engineer for many years. There has also been consultancy work with a number of disabled charities.

Steve's first tenure with Dexys might have been comparatively short, but he offers a succinct appraisal of this nine-month spell, this blur of rehearsals, touring, recording and TV appearances. It's one that confirms Micky Billingham's description of him as not being remotely uptight and bitter.

'Good times were had!'

*

In September 1981, Steve Wynne was replaced in Dexys by another bass player from Coventry, one who came from another of the city's ska-flavoured bands, Team 23.

His name was Mick Galic – although that doesn't appear on any sleeves of any Dexys records. Shortly after joining the fold, Mick was rechristened Giorgio Kilkenny by Kevin Rowland, a name that not so much hinted but shouted out loud about a manufactured Irish-Italian heritage.

As well as playing on all of *Too-Rye-Ay*, Mick is there in the 'Come on Eileen' video, playing a tea-chest bass and looking like he must be a close relative of future comedian Noel Fielding. He's also there playing live on the Saturday morning kids' show *Number 73*, this time playing an electric bass. The following month, though, with '. . . Eileen' still riding high in the charts, Mick left, to be replaced on the upcoming tour by John Edwards.

In her memoir, *What's She Like*, Helen O'Hara remembers Mick as 'quiet with a hint of a smile', a man who 'didn't have any of the exuberance of Italians I had met, but he looked Italian with his jet-black hair'. But what does he look like now? I ask almost all the past Dexys members I meet, regardless of when they were part of the band, whether they know of his whereabouts. To a person, no one appears to have stayed in touch with him. No one's been in contact with him since long before the days of email and mobile phones.

My search isn't helped by there being dual spellings of Mick's surname. Sometimes he's referred to as 'Galic', occasionally as 'Gallick'. There's a Mick Galic on LinkedIn who's a company director of a 'managed document solutions' company in Hemel Hempstead. It might be him. I send him a message. I get no reply. Either it's not him or he wants to be left alone.

A Mick Gallick apparently toured with the Australian band, the On Fires, as a bass player in 2010. I send them a message. I get no reply.

The trail wasn't anything warmer than tepid. Now it's stone cold. There's only one thing for it. It's not a sufficiently serious case to involve Interpol so, inspired by the success that the old bandmates had with tracking down Steve Spooner, my last hope rests with the *Birmingham Evening Mail*. I take out a classified ad.

WANTED

MICK GALIC

I'm trying to track down Mick Galic (possibly spelled Gallick), who was the bass player for Dexys Midnight Runners between 1981 and 1982, and who might still live in the West Midlands. Any information as to his whereabouts will be gratefully received.

Thank you.

I pay my seven pounds. The ad gets published. I get no reply.

Reminisce #5

The Cut, London

Despite the rain, despite the puddles being sent skywards by the wheels of countless taxi cabs, Waterloo is busier than ever tonight. Excited theatre-goers are galloping towards the first night of a new production of Pygmalion *at the Old Vic, round the corner from the station concourse.*

A generation ago, excited theatre-goers were galloping towards the first night of a short residency here by Dexys, the three-night last hurrah of the Projected Passion Revue. It's a happy coincidence, a fortunate echo, that the ghosthunter is out snooping tonight as the most famous play by one of those titans of Irish literature whose name Dexys chant during 'Burn It Down' – 'George Bernard Shaw!' – opens.

Later this evening, the much-decorated actor Bertie Cavell – as Professor Henry Higgins – will issue advice to the impressionable Eliza Doolittle: 'I can't turn your soul on. Leave me your feelings; and you can take away the voice and the face. They are not you.'

Another echo. These could be the words of Kevin Rowland.

11

Paul Speare

Tenor sax, 1980–82

'I got away with not having a ponytail.
You didn't have to have one if you wore a headband.'

If you're making a pilgrimage to Canterbury, whether in search of divine guidance or just to interview an ex-member of Dexys Midnight Runners, be advised not to do so on a Friday afternoon in the school summer holidays.

A spiritual experience it will not be. As it isn't today. Tipsy hen parties are turning the air in this train carriage blue, while a bunch of excitable kids, all seeming to answer to the names Conor or Caleb, are charging up and down the aisles. Margate is the final station stop for these revellers. Canterbury West can't come soon enough.

After I split away from my noisy neighbours, the avuncular smile of long, tall Paul Speare, stood on the other side of the ticket barrier, offers the warmest of welcomes. His chariot awaits outside, an electric car that silently, gracefully, carries us through the cathedral city's streets. Just a few minutes later, I'm sat in the kitchen of the mews house Paul shares with his wife Paula. He pops the kettle on and places a plate of restorative chocolate digestives in front of me, manna after all that on-train kerfuffle.

Tonight, one of the brides-to-be on that train might be wailing along to 'Come on Eileen' in some Margate karaoke bar. Paul played tenor sax on the record, but had left the band before it made its slow ascent of the singles chart. 'I get PPL for playing on it, but as I don't listen to commercial music or commercial radio, I hardly ever hear it. If I'm out with Paula and it comes on in a petrol station or somewhere, we don't even acknowledge it. Even with my own stuff, I never listen to it once it's out. You hear things so many times, you rehearse them, you record them, you hear it hundreds of times. So once something's done, I just move on.'

Paul might not have graced the *Top of the Pops* studio to mime along to 'Come on Eileen', but that was exactly where he made his Dexys bow eighteen months earlier, helping on that reprise of 'Geno' for the Christmas edition, alongside other newbies Seb Shelton, Micky Billingham, Steve Wynne, and his fellow sax player Brian Brummitt. 'I went to my mum and dad's for Christmas 1980 and *Top of the Pops* came on. I said, "I'm on this." They knew nothing about music or the music business. It was totally outside their experience. And they were quite old compared to most parents.

'"Well, that's very nice."

'"Actually, Mum, I might be doing this all the time now. I'm thinking of joining them."

'She was horrified. At that point, I had a nice, respectable teaching job and she liked to tell people that's what I did.

'No one in the family had any experience in the arts at all. My music teacher, Dorothy, was very encouraging. I'm still in touch with her now. If it hadn't been for free lessons at school and being able to use instruments there, and grants to go to college, I would never have been a trained musician. My parents were not wealthy at all. They were just working people from Dagenham, in a council house. I don't know what I'd have done otherwise. I always had a way with words, so I might have gone into journalism. My mother would have liked me to have become an English teacher, which I think would have been the road to doom for me. I get bored so easily.'

That Christmas, Paul wasn't yet a fully fledged member of the band. 'I was being considered. And I was considering, as well. I was very much in two minds about joining. It was by no means a foregone conclusion.'

Having found himself in Birmingham doing a postgraduate teaching year after gaining his diploma at music college, this Essex boy often played on sessions with a few West Midlands jazz-funk and fusion outfits. These were mainly at Outlaw Studios, an establishment that Dexys were known to frequent from time to time. It was the studio owner Phil Savage who played matchmaker.

'Phil rang me up: "Have you heard of Dexys Midnight Runners? They're looking for a tenor sax player." I didn't follow pop music or the charts. I was into jazz and jazz-funk. But I knew they'd had a hit. So Paul "Basher" Burton, their manager, rang me up. And I always find it difficult to say no to things.

'The audition was a total culture shock. It was bloody weird, to be quite honest. The atmosphere was weird. Some of the people seemed weird. Kevin seemed weird. For where I'd come from – through the classical college system, then teacher training, then teaching – to find myself in a room with Dexys was totally different. People were just looking at each other and not saying anything. There were all these long silences while they waited to hear what Kevin thought.

'I was mainly teaching flute at that point and would have to give a certain amount of notice if I was going leave – officially, anyway. But when this came up, the boss was very understanding: "If I were your age, I would do exactly the same thing. I'll make sure you get a good reference."

'But it still took me a little while to come round to the idea. I had a perfectly nice little job, I had my own council flat and I was all right. I didn't feel I needed anything more at the time. But

I couldn't turn down the Christmas edition of *Top of the Pops*. I got tempted in the end and joined properly in January.'

One of the culture shocks that distanced Dexys from the straight-laced musical world Paul had known until then was the new look, the new uniform, that this second coming of the band were issued with – boxer boots and hoodies. 'It went with the job,' he shrugs, 'so I had to wear it. I could see what Kevin was getting at. It made us stand out from other bands, but I didn't feel comfortable in that stuff. It wasn't the sort of thing I would have chosen to wear myself in a million years. It was quite a macho look and I've never been interested in appearing macho at all. And it was made clear to us from the start that we would have to wear some watered-down version of this even when we were rehearsing. I got away with not having a ponytail. You didn't have to have one if you wore a head-band, so I went for the headband option instead.'

They'd accepted the new gear and they'd successfully mimed to 'Geno' at BBC Television Centre. Now it was time for the new line-up to prove their mettle in the studio. '"Plan B" was the first record we did together. I still love that single. I think it's much better than the *Too-Rye-Ay* version. It's got much better groove, the production's grungier and the trombone solo is great. I hated that mouth organ solo on *Too-Rye-Ay*. It's in the wrong bloody key. It doesn't work.'

Paul snaps a chocolate digestive in half.

The failure of 'Plan B' to chart, the exodus from EMI and the heavily pared-down first leg of the Projected Passion Revue tour might well have had Paul wondering whether his decision to escape the sanctity of that steady flute-teaching job had been well-judged. The band's fortunes were low, in both senses. He is far from the first Dexys alumnus to confide in me the depth of their personal poverty during their tenure in the band.

'There were times when I had no food in the house. I was bailed out on one occasion by the wonderful Steve Shaw [aka fiddle player

Steve Brennan, one third of the Emerald Express], who was still a student at Birmingham School of Music. We were good pals and he was on the phone to me. He said, "I'll come round. I'll bring you some chips." He came round with fish and chips for me. And a packet of fags. I've never forgotten that.

'The worst thing was being at home. When you were working, you had that camaraderie. You were focused on that. When you got home, it was horrible. With no money, you couldn't go out. You couldn't do anything.'

In other bands, the harsh commercial realities might have forced the trimming of creative ambitions, the clipping of artistic wings. But it didn't appear so with Dexys Mk II. Rather than scaling back the content of the live show, the urge to present something different to everyone else remained, hence the retention of both the comedy duo the Outer Limits and the dance troupe Torque as intrinsic elements of the Projected Passion Revue circus. Not everyone was necessarily pleased.

'It's all very well realising your vision,' explains Paul, 'but you're actually putting other people you know into difficult financial positions. And it wasn't as if we had any say in any of it. We just had to go along with it, whether it was a good idea or not. And we were the ones paying for it. Putting on this massive show is fine, but it was partly why we weren't getting any pay. We did three nights at the Old Vic that November and the only reason we got any money that week at all was because the T-shirts sold quite well. God knows how much a professional dance troupe costs.'

That wasn't the only source of tension around the Old Vic shows. The horn section were simmering over Kevin's insistence that they rapidly learn – and master – certain stringed instruments in order to widen Dexys' musical canvas. Jimmy and Brian were instructed to take up the cello, while Paul was placed on viola duties.

'I had actually already played the viola. It was among the many instruments I dabbled in before I became serious on the flute and the sax. I'd tried the viola because I was into Curved Air, so I at least had some experience of knocking out a tune on it. But watching Jimmy and Brian trying to get around on the cello was pitiful. Oh, the noise. When we played the Old Vic, it was the only time we ever had to play the strings live ourselves. But Jimmy and Brian were miming. We had this guy backstage playing a 60,000-quid cello with a contact mic stuck on with some gaffer tape. The other two were just scraping away, albeit looking good. But the whole thing was daft. It was a great relief when Kevin said he was going to get fiddle players in. Well, it was to me. The other two weren't happy. But I think all three of us felt insecure that we might get the sack because Kevin didn't need us any more, or that it would be an even larger band and thus even more expensive to tour around.'

Once the Emerald Express were recruited at the start of 1982, Brian and Jimmy stuck their fingers in the air and felt which way the wind was blowing. It was a logical conclusion that it wasn't blowing in favour of the horn section. They made their excuses and left the band, albeit temporarily returning to record the horn parts on *Too-Rye-Ay*. Paul remained in the fold – for a short while, at least. In the team photo on the album's inner sleeve, he's the sole horn player still standing, lining up for the camera and towering over his bandmates, his arms spread across the shoulders of Giorgio Kilkenny and Kevin Rowland. It's almost certainly the last picture taken of him in his Dexys colours.

'What made me leave? I can remember the straw that broke the camel's back. It was literally as we were walking out of the studio after the final mixing. Kevin and Basher were going on holiday to Spain. I had no money, so I was going home to my flat and, with no money, I wouldn't be able to do anything for a couple of weeks. But they were going on holiday. Then Kevin said to me, "Paul, can you book the rehearsal room for when we get back?" Because I couldn't say no in those days, I said, "Yeah, all right then." At some point soon after, though, I thought, *I can't do this any more.* That just tipped it. I think I was just exhausted, mentally as much as anything else – all the tension and the lack of money. It was hard.

'It didn't matter whether it was going to be successful or not. I just couldn't do it any more. It wasn't a choice. But the thing that did it was Kevin, very offhand, asking me to book the rehearsal room for when they came back from their holiday, nice and tanned. I really resented that.

'For years afterwards – decades, in fact – if I got involved in a band, I would never tell them about what I'd done in the past. It's tricky. If you're joining a band that's clearly not famous, you don't want to go in saying "Hi, yeah, I played for Dexys". They'll think you're an arrogant twat. But then the opposite happens. Somebody in the band always finds out. "Why didn't you tell us . . .?"'

Even if at times he disguised his heritage and obscured his past, Paul is nonetheless adamant about what his eighteen-odd months as a member of Dexys imbued and empowered him with. 'It was definitely a springboard. I should make it clear that it was a fabulous opportunity. It was a very difficult time, but I'm grateful for it because it led on to all sorts of interesting work, right up to this day. I can still trace the work I did with Paul Weller back to Dexys via lots of other routes. It would never have happened otherwise.'

Prior to joining, Paul's career had been tracing a trusted linear path. Dexys – and Kevin Rowland in particular – taught him a crucial life lesson. 'You don't have to do that thing. You can actually do that other thing that's less obvious. And I've been like that ever since. That's how I am. It was the first time I'd actually broken out of the mould. It was the best thing I ever did. There's no question about it. The best thing I ever did.'

'I do experiment. A lot of pop music to me is too simple. It's like having a rich, spicy diet and then having to eat sausage and mash.' Paul blows his horn at the Herne Bay Jazz Festival. *Jean Marshall*

The kettle goes back on, ready to provide lubrication for Paul's post-Dexys story, the opening chapter of which found him swiftly reuniting with Jimmy and Brian in what became the TKO Horns.

'I was at home with nothing to do. I'd not long just bought my first bicycle and remember riding over to Jimmy's quite regularly. We would just sit and chat. Occasionally Brian would be there as well, although he still had a flat in Newcastle. At some point, we decided we were going to work together. We put a press release in a couple of music papers – *Sounds* and probably *Melody Maker* – to generate work. The first thing that came up was the John Watts album.'

The former Fischer-Z frontman had gone solo and had the budget to commission these newly liberated horn players. It was an environment that Paul, reliant on the goodwill of student band-mates a few months earlier, particularly appreciated.

'We went down to Ridge Farm Studios near Dorking. It was fab-ulous – a huge place with tennis courts and a swimming pool and a sauna. It was like a holiday camp. And we weren't in Dexys any more, so we could get stoned as well. It was like we were free! You'd be really enjoying the evening and then, about eleven o'clock, John would come over and go, "Right, can we record some horns now?" We'd be like, "Oh God . . ." But it was a lovely period of time. And we were getting paid handsomely. It was the way the music industry should be.'

This new horn section for hire was gathering momentum. Next came that tour with the Q-Tips. 'They had a massive VAT bill and needed to do a college tour to pay it off, before drawing a line underneath things. Paul Young was recording *No Parlez* at the same time.' It was while they were on tour with the Q-Tips that a call came in from Elvis Costello – or, at least, a call from the premier production double-act of the day, Clive Langer and Alan Winstan-ley, the duo who had overseen *Too-Rye-Ay* and who were just about to do similar for Costello's *Punch the Clock*.

The TKO Horns, fleshed out to a four-piece by Dave Plews on trumpet and with Geoff Blythe having replaced Brian, were pretty much exclusively in the employ of Costello and the Attractions for twelve months. Between two nights at the Albert Hall at the tail end of 1982 to three nights at the Hammersmith Odeon at the close of 1983, they recorded the album alongside playing dozens and doz-ens of live shows across a couple of continents and numerous TV appearances. 'I tend to put things to the back of my mind. I have to force myself to stop and think about them. This seems centuries ago now.' A pause. 'Well, it was last century . . .'

The hired help certainly put a shift in as part of the Costello cara-van heading westwards. 'They did a two-hour set every night. We did the first half-hour with them and the last half-hour. We were at the top of our game then. We were probably a bit above our station, but it felt like there was possibly a bit of resentment about having these extra people in the band, where it had always been the four of them. We were smoking weed as well, so that probably didn't help much. In Costello's book, he only mentions us a couple of times and not any of us by name. He's worked with string sections and they all get named and he says how wonderful they are. Also, if I remember rightly, he just refers to us as a bunch of Brummies or something. Geoff was sort of a Brummie, but I wasn't, Jimmy wasn't and Dave was a Londoner. So that was a bit offhand really, when he was so effusive about other people's work. We did add a lot to that album and that tour.

'We had two separate Greyhound buses – one for the Attractions and one for us, the horns. We had our own bus driver and the lighting guy was sort of our road manager. He didn't like us much either.'

After this extended time in the service of Costello, work continued to flow in for the TKO Horns, whether for Madness, Nick Lowe or the post-Squeeze duo of Difford & Tilbrook. It was recording a track for the latter, 'Action Speaks Faster', that prompted a slight, but permanent, change in instrument for Paul. The producer, Tony Visconti, required some baritone sax. 'I'd never touched a baritone sax in my life, but I did it and it was fine. I thought, *I've got to get one of these*. And I did. After a little while, I got some money together and bought one. And that's really what I've played ever since.

'I know I've been a bit disparaging about Elvis Costello, but he did get us other work. Now I look back, with a bit more wisdom and age, I wish I had shown more gratitude to some of these people I worked with. If I were to see Costello now, I would say to him, "I've never thanked you for all that work." I mean, nothing's ever perfect but, bloody hell, it was great.' Costello also passed on another small but significant piece of work for Paul as an individual musician, when he was in the producer's chair overseeing the Special AKA recording 'Free Nelson Mandela'.

'Most people hadn't heard of Nelson Mandela before then. I didn't know. Costello told me to come along, so I came down on the train to Air Studios, but there was another flute player there, David Heath. It was a bit awkward, but luckily I had my tin whistle in my inside pocket, so I played that instead. We just doubled the part and it really sounded good.'

The combination of the whistle and the flute ensured the song was shot through with echoes of South African kwela music. Never had a protest song sounded so joyful and celebratory. 'To have played on such an important song was an honour. And I loved working with Jerry Dammers. I'd love to work with him again.'

For the TKO Horns, the magic was losing its lustre. 'There was a bit of residual work, but basically it was fizzling out and I was exhausted from the touring. I needed to recalibrate. And I think we drifted apart. We were probably sick of the sight of each other by then. People's foibles – my own included, I'm sure – start to get on others' nerves.'

Paul's first post-TKO commission wasn't to play at all. It was to appear in a video for a Don Henley single, 'All She Wants to Do is Dance', the follow-up to 'The Boys of Summer'. 'He wanted a sax player with spiky hair. It was an amazing set. I think it was at Shepperton. It was supposed to be a bombed-out nightclub after a terrorist attack or something. They had an actual Jeep suspended above us as if it had come through the roof.' The idea was that, despite the carnage, all the woman in the song wanted to do was dance. And Paul's sax helped her out in that respect. 'There wasn't even a real sax on the recording,' he chuckles. 'It was a synth.'

The next few years were a tumble of teaching, session work and running a studio near Tamworth. Through the studio, in the early '90s, Paul ended up being involved with the chart-topping act KWS from Nottingham. 'They used to do house versions of old soul records and they had a big number-one hit with "Please Don't Go". I was asked to do the horn arrangements for the follow-up, "Rock Your Baby", and we did PAs and videos and *Top of the Pops*.'

Paul has also worked extensively with the Midlands soul band Stone Foundation. Again, it's a relationship forged out of that Tamworth studio. Paul was around thirty when he first met co-founder Neil Sheasby, then in his late teens, and his mates. 'They found out that someone from Dexys had moved into a village at their end of Tamworth and hunted me out when I opened the studio. They were bonkers about Dexys. Their band at the time was called Dance Stance.' Indeed, Sheasby's fascination has never wavered. Stone Foundation's live sets include a cover of 'I Couldn't Help If I Tried' from *Searching for the Young Soul Rebels*. Along with Paul, another Dexys alumnus has been a collaborator – Mick Talbot.

Stone Foundation record their albums at Paul Weller's Surrey studio; Weller in fact produced (and played extensively on) their 2017 album, *Street Rituals*. This put Paul on Weller's radar, a relationship that later found him contributing baritone sax and flute on a couple of Weller's own records, *On Sunset* and *Fat Pop*.

By now, we've decamped to Paul's music room/studio upstairs and he's rifling through his sizeable collection of laminates and backstage passes. There's one from the Albert Hall when he played there with Weller. There's another from Glastonbury as part of the Stone Foundation line-up. And there are plenty from that year-long nomadic adventure with Costello.

In fact, much of the memorabilia Paul has saved is from that seemingly endless tour. There are itineraries that not only reveal the hierarchy of the entire charabanc (who got their own room, who had to double up), but also the false names the musicians adopted when checking into hotels in order to avoid unwanted attention from fans. The Attractions' keyboard player Steve Nieve chose to sign in as Norman Wisdom, while Costello appeared to switch between Marshal Tito and Grandmaster Grumbling Appendix.

Most fascinating to the music historian is arguably the typewritten letter that the Attractions' legendary manager Jake Riviera had issued to the entire party ahead of that two-month crusade across the US:

A MISSIVE FROM THE MANAGEMENT

Although this tour has been planned to be as enjoyable as is feasible, I would like you all to bear in mind that there are 36 shows in 57 days, so a modicum of pacing would be appreciated.

It is indeed a long way to San Francisco and America is a big country. By the end of this tour, you will have seen most of it. A professional manner will enable you to enjoy it more, and more importantly, the audience will enjoy it more.

God does not allow one several throws at the coconut. Go out there and knock 'em dead!

Best wishes,

JAKE RIVIERA

There's also a cutting from a couple of months after the TKO Horns left the Costello fold. It's from the *NME*, announcing the results of its annual poll, declaring which bands, musicians and singers were deemed to be the cream of 1983. In the 'Miscellaneous Musicians' category, there's good news for Paul, Jimmy, Geoff and Dave. They've taken top spot, holding off the likes of Yazoo's Vince Clarke, Saxa from the Beat, perma-tanned Spandau Ballet saxman Steve Norman, and jazz trumpet legend Chet Baker, who also appeared on *Punch the Clock*. Less than eighteen months after forming, the TKO Horns are kings of the hill, top of the heap.

Paul is now flicking through a photo album that covers the Dexys years. Its pages have corralled promo shots, amateur snaps, newspaper cuttings, that kind of thing – trapping and protecting them under cellophane. There's a cutting from *Smash Hits*, showing the band doing a photo session in running gear at an athletics stadium in Smethwick. There's a terrifically moody shot I've never seen before, taken in the Apollonia and showing the results of a recent command for everyone to dye their hair black and attempt to grow a moustache. And there's a tremendous live shot that captures Kevin in mid-air and Paul's sax partner Brian giving it every last ounce of passion and effort. 'I took this picture to Brian's funeral and showed it to people. It's a great, great picture of him.'

Turn the page and there's a press ad for the 'Liars A to E' single, featuring characteristically lofty words from, presumably, Kevin Rowland:

'In comparison to all that goes on, music is worth nothing, especially when all on sale is shallow, conceited, foul-tasting, non-lasting bubblegum. Music doesn't have to be this way. It just is. Of course, it could never be really important or bring about any change, but it needn't be so proudly disposable. Then again, what can one expect from golden-hearted cockneys, Brummies, Scousers, jocks etc.?' That golden-hearted cockney is surely Dagenham boy Paul.

I gaze around the room. There are sound-dampeners on the walls, sharing space with a couple of gold discs. One commemorates Paul's contributions to *Too-Rye-Ay*, presented to him on the occasion that it notched up 100,000 sales. The other is for *Punch the Clock*. Next to them is a platinum disc marking the seven-figure UK sales for 'Come on Eileen'. 'They're not made from gold or platinum,' Paul smiles. 'I wish. They're just vinyl that's been sprayed. They're a bit faded now. They've spent a long time on walls in various houses.'

Saxes and flutes stand vertical on their stands, buffed and primed and eager to be blown. This is where Paul largely makes his music these days, squirrelling himself away up here when he's not riding his bike, or the tandem he shares with Paula, up and over the nearby Kent Downs.

His most recent project has been a four-track EP, *In Search of Avet*. It's a very varied offering, skirting jazz, jazz-funk, fusion, Afro-rock, electronica, spatial psychedelia and more. Featuring his own compositions, Paul plays flute, baritone sax and bass clarinet on it. One track includes a string quartet. Another is a tribute to electronic music pioneer Daphne Oram, a co-founder of the BBC Radiophonic Workshop who later built her own studio in a Kent oasthouse.

'I do experiment a lot. I'm not trying to be commercial or anything. I'm not interested in that. It is what it is. It's about trying stuff out, stretching myself. A lot of pop music to me is too simple. It's like having a rich, spicy diet all your life and then having to eat sausage and mash. It's just not interesting enough for me.'

Future plans include possibly committing his memoirs to paper ('I don't know if it will be for actual publication or perhaps for my daughter'), along with getting a big band off the ground. 'I love playing baritone in a big band.' Ideas are clearly not short on the ground.

'I had writers' block for a number of years. I couldn't get anything off the blocks, but since we moved here, I turned the tap on and now it won't turn off. It's been hard work, some of it. You know, herding cats and all that. But I'm bloody sixty-seven now. I didn't ever think I'd be doing session work in my sixties. What's happened over the last couple of years has been great – just doing exactly what I want. I've got the time and I haven't got to make a living out of it. No commercial considerations. Just choosing who I want to work with. It's been great.'

We head back downstairs and Paul picks up his car keys, ready to return me to Canterbury West.

'Not to sound morbid, but if I were struck down tomorrow, I'd feel as if I've achieved what I set out to do. But I think there's still more to come. There's no set point where you have to draw the line. I keep reading obituaries of people who are my age and younger. I'm really conscious that I won't be here forever.'

A beaming smile to accompany his parting message.

'Just get on with it. You don't want your final thought to be *If only . . .*'

12

Helen O'Hara

Violin, 1982–86

*'"Come on Eileen" was a summer record. The song just caught everybody.
When I heard it out of car windows, it just felt great.'*

It's a heat-hazed, sun-kissed Saturday in Worthing on the Sussex coast. A small light aircraft passes over the pier while, three hundred yards out to sea, a jet ski traces a perfect figure-of-eight in the water. On the prom, a man on stilts is waving flags in the air, much to the curiosity of toddlers in the long queue for the ice cream stall.

It's an ice cream kind of day. Along the prom, a seafood stall is doing very little trade. Their takings might be down, but they do bask in an excellent name: Shrimply the Best.

Not everyone is soaking up the sun. Across the road, on the other side of Marine Drive, a few dozen sensible souls have opted for the shade of a basement. Here, at the Cellar Arts Club on this Saturday afternoon, Dexys' principal violinist, Helen O'Hara, will be guiding the congregation through the gospel of her life and times.

Worthing is the latest stopping-off point in the promotion of her memoirs, the Penderyn Music Book Prize-longlisted *What's She Like*. The book is a clear-eyed and faithful account. While there has been no small amount of myth-making about Dexys throughout the band's lifespan – most of it authored by its more vocal members – Helen's retelling of her five years in its service doesn't amplify or exaggerate. She is a reliable witness. If she were giving evidence in a criminal trial, her testimony would be the one that the jury would believe the most.

But this afternoon's event takes a different shape to the usual author talks, as shown by the carrier bag of precious records Helen has brought down with her from her Greenwich home. These are the records that mean the most to her, the ones which go beyond being mere physical objects, the ones which helped shape her into who she is today. The occasion is the latest instalment of The Defining Ten, a tremendous series of events where a notable musician selects the ten records that most shaped them into being the person they are today. Previous guests have included Pete Wiggs from Saint Etienne, the Orb's Alex Paterson, the free jazzer Evan Parker and Steve Mason from the Beta Band. Think of it as a more in-depth version of *Desert Island Discs*; rather than a mere forty-five minutes, we'll have at least a couple of hours. Plus, we'll hear the songs in their entirety.

The afternoon's format takes a parallel path to the book, a strictly chronological journey to reveal those way-markers on Helen's musical hike. First, though, Luther the host explains the effect of Dexys' music on him as both a young boy and a young man. He was five years old when *Too-Rye-Ay* came out, becoming familiar with the album when his dad bought a vinyl copy and taped it so he could play it in the car. 'Obviously I was always worried that the police would knock on his door: "Mr Jones, you've been recording your *Too-Rye-Ay* album, haven't you?"' Luther then had his own home-recorded copy, which he played on the same mono cassette player usually used for his ZX Spectrum computer games. 'For some reason, "Until I Believe in My Soul" really resonated with me.' By 1997, Luther was working in a record shop when Creation Records reissued *Don't Stand Me Down*. 'My boss at the time, Basil, felt absolutely vindicated that this album was finally getting critically reappraised. We were drawn in by his worship of it. I think it's my favourite Dexys album.'

Luther's gushing monologue lasts a full seven minutes before he finally turns to his guest. 'That's probably the longest intro you've ever had,' he says, apologetically. 'You're probably wondering what time your train's leaving . . .'

There's no rush, though. The lazy afternoon stretches out in front of us as we're taken on a deep dive into Helen's musical evolution. Luther's friend Jim is operating the decks today. At regular intervals, Helen will reach into that carrier bag and hand Jim her next choice, whether an LP, a seven-inch or, in the case of her classical music selections, a CD. And it's a classical music selection to start proceedings – Chopin's Nocturne, Opus 9, No. 2 in E-flat major – which prompts recollections from her childhood.

'I'm one of seven children,' she explains. 'Number six. And I had this privilege of having all these older brothers and sisters who played musical instruments. Two of my sisters played piano and I remember hearing them play this. It's probably my earliest memory of music. It's really beautiful. I certainly learned it when I was older.'

Helen swapped to violin during her primary school years and showed instant prowess, reaching and passing her Grade 5 within a year of taking up the instrument. 'I just loved it. I practised a lot. I've never found it really easy to play. I still find it hard now. Sometimes I wish I'd never started . . .'

As she talks, the room is rapt, acolytes and fans to a person. No floating voters here. These are Helen's people, and the records that she played on are the soundtrack to their youth. One man in the second row has come dressed for the occasion. He's in a denim jacket rather than dungarees, but wears a Dexys-issue red kerchief tied around his neck.

The second record is the Rolling Stones' '(I Can't Get No) Satisfaction', a song that prompts a recollection of the time that the thirteen-year-old Helen tried, and failed, to get into either of two Stones shows at the Colston Hall in her native Bristol. 'I was devastated.'

The story has a happy ending, though. In 1982, the Stones returned to the West Country to play a bigger gig at Ashton Gate, home of Bristol City FC. This time, an old friend was working at the concert as a driver, ferrying people around, and he got her in. 'I was at the side of the stage and the Stones walked past me. And Keith smiled at me. "Oh, hello Keith." It was just so sweet. And you know how your heroes are always twenty feet tall? I was taller than them. They weren't that big.'

The next record out of the bag is David Bowie's 'Starman', which elicits another tale of seeing another hero in Bristol ('Certain people are very special. And he was.'). Then we're treated to the first record of the day that Helen played on – the only single put out by her pre-music college band Uncle Po. Helen actually played piano on 'Use My Friends', a chunk of era-specific new wave from 1978 that occupies a similar ballpark to Martha and the Muffins' 'Echo Beach', albeit with male vocals. 'We probably went as far as we could,' Helen reasons. 'We just couldn't make that extra step to be signed.'

With Uncle Po 'hitting a brick wall' and her options appearing 'slightly dead-end-ish', Helen – via her sister Liz – experienced 'a lightbulb moment': she'd enrol at music college. It seemed likely that she would need to wait another year to apply but, in the event, it just so happened that the Birmingham College of Music still had a couple of places remaining. Of course, had Helen gone anywhere but the second city, ultimately linking up with one of the most successful West Midlands bands of the time, her professional life wouldn't have gone in the direction it did. From such compara- tively small decisions are bigger destinies forged.

Helen was very studious when she arrived in Birmingham. 'I just really gave it everything,' she tells the audience. 'I got into college at eight in the morning and used to leave at nine at night. And I'd go in at weekends. I just worked and worked and worked.' Her dedication bore fruit. She rose to become the violin leader in the college's orchestra, once playing under the baton of Simon Rattle.

The piece of music Helen has selected to represent her college years is the last movement of Bach's Violin Concerto in E major. 'I deliberately didn't listen to pop bands when I was there and in my final year I was applying for professional orchestral positions.' One of those applications was returned with the offer of an audition, the successful execution of which delivered the offer of a permanent position. It was with the Bilbao Symphony Orchestra, a precious first role after graduation. That was the plan, anyway.

First, a post-Dexys Kevin Archer came calling, diverting Helen's gaze away from her strictly classical world. And then, following his old bandmate's suggestion, Kevin Rowland sent his 'heavies' – the gentle giants Jim Paterson and Paul Speare – to go knocking on the door of Helen's practice room at college. 'They seemed to take up all the space, which wasn't much anyway,' she would later write. They proposed that Helen come and play on some demos with Dexys. 'It seemed more like an order than a request, and like in a gangster film when "no" isn't the right answer, I obviously said yes.'

After playing on a couple of sessions, Helen was asked to recruit two more violinists from the college. Steve Shaw was one, the co-leader of the orchestra's second violin section. Roger Huckle was the other, Helen's deputy in the first section. Once the trio gained Kevin's approval – and after being drilled into shape by Seb Shelton, who emphasised the need to play with 'feel' more than with exacting, precise technical virtuosity – the singer bestowed a name upon the string section: the Emerald Express. Then, in time-honoured fashion, Kevin also rebadged each player individually, this time to impose a certain degree of Irishness upon them. Helen's surname of Bevington was ditched for O'Hara, Steve was now billed as Steve Brennan and Roger became Roger MacDuff. 'I loved my new name,' she later noted. 'Steve seemed happy too, but Roger didn't say anything.'

Despite being in her final year of college, and despite the offer of that job in northern Spain, Helen became seduced by this strange bunch of characters and their obsessive search for perfection. The bar was set high and nothing that failed to reach it was acceptable. As someone so dedicated to her studies, such an approach presumably chimed with Helen. And the music they made matched the level of commitment.

'Kevin Archer's band had been amazing,' she tells us of the Blue Ox Babes, 'but this was something else. I'd signed the contract with the Bilbao Symphony Orchestra, but I knew there was no going back.' Into the final months of her final year, this previously ultra-disciplined student could be found bunking off college for the *Too-Rye-Ay* recording sessions. 'I told the director of studies at the college that I'd just been having the most amazing time. He could see the enthusiasm, so he was OK in the end. Steve got an absolute bollocking.'

Defining Ten host Luther Bhogal-Jones shows off his well-worn copy of *Don't Stand Me Down*, freshly signed by Helen O'Hara.

There is only one song that Helen can select at this point in the proceedings. She hands Jim a seven-inch copy of 'Come on Eileen', explaining to us that she gave all her copies of the single away back in the day, thinking she could easily ask for replacements from the record company. But she never did. The copy she's brought along this afternoon is a comparatively recent purchase from her local Oxfam shop, where she'd gone to buy some birthday cards. 'I don't have a record player, so I never normally look through the records, but for some reason I did that day. And this was there. Ninety-nine pence!'

The needle hits the groove with a crackle and Helen's solo fiddle curls its way out of the speakers, like a whisper of smoke. A warm glow fans across the room. And spontaneous applause breaks out at the end.

'It's so joyous, isn't it?' she rhetorically asks. 'For me, "Come on Eileen" was a summer record. The song just caught everybody. When I heard it out of car windows, it just felt great. It was a hot summer and the song kind of fitted with everything.'

Despite the single's rampant success, and despite the band's ubiquity, Helen's material world hadn't improved much – a recurring motif in the Dexys story. She was still sharing a student flat and, when she returned to Bristol for a brief visit, faced an embarrassing situation with her former bandmates. 'I wasn't signed to Dexys or to the record company, so I didn't have very much money. I was on *Top of the Pops* but I couldn't afford to buy a round for the guys from Uncle Po. And I didn't have the confidence to tell them why.'

The next selection is Al Green's 'Belle', a formative record in the embryonic stages of *Don't Stand Me Down*. By now in a relationship with Kevin Rowland, and with the band's nucleus shrunk to them plus Billy Adams, the search was underway for a new collection of musicians to achieve the desired sound of the record. The position of drummer posed a particular challenge. They were after a drummer who could replicate the feel of the groove on Al Green's records. Etta James's drummer, Crusher Green, was on board for a time; David Bowie's drummer from the Ziggy Stardust era, Woody Woodmanscy, was also part of the sessions for a while. 'Woody was great and obviously a great guy,' Helen explains diplomatically, 'but he didn't have the right feel. Most people find where they fit. I'm not the right violinist for other bands, you know.'

In the end, Helen made a call to Memphis, to Willie Mitchell, Al Green's long-time producer. She wanted the number of his drummer. 'I said, "Have you heard of Dexys Midnight Runners?" He said, "Of course I've heard of Dexys Midnight Runners!"'

The drummer, Tim Dancey, was perfect and he recorded all the tracks for the album in a couple of days. 'Tim played differently to all the British drummers that I've heard. It was the way he tuned his drums. It was the way he hit the hi-hat. It was just beautiful.'

The folk down here in the basement now get the chance to run the rule over Tim's playing. It's time for the magnum opus from *Don't Stand Me Down*, the song that Kevin wrote about his love for Helen: 'This Is What She's Like'. There is a slight catch, though. It might be a lazy afternoon, but Luther still has half an eye on the time. The band who are playing a gig here tonight have arrived and are patiently waiting on the stairs to load in. 'I would have loved us to play all twelve minutes of it,' he explains, attracting a low groan from the back row, 'but I think unfortunately we're only going to be able to play just a highlight.'

Jim puts the needle down about two-thirds of the way through the song, at the point at which the band are soaring in full flight. It is such a majestic record. Helen's head, nearly forty years on, can't stay still. The fingers on her left hand are moving too, forming shapes on the neck of an imaginary violin. The soles of her red Converse boots tap out a silent beat.

As the final notes fade, Luther reads out a couple of quotes about the song. One is from the music writer Gary Mulholland, who describes it as 'a work of bloody-minded ambition by a man completely out of time', noting that its influences include the Beach Boys, Van Morrison, 'deep-soul weepies' and the informal, chewing-the-fat conversations of Peter Cook and Dudley Moore.

The other is from the man out of time himself. 'My biggest regret is that "This Is What She's Like" wasn't a ten-minute single,' declares Kevin Rowland. 'I think it might have done for Dexys what "Bohemian Rhapsody" did for Queen.' Back in 1985, by refusing to release a single from *Don't Stand Me Down* – or, at least, agreeing to a chopped-in-half release of 'This Is What She's Like' too late in the day – the band lost any remaining support from their record company. Mixed, potentially misunderstood reviews of the album ensured the charts weren't set ablaze and it would be a decade or so until it was reclaimed as a lost classic. The band dissolved in 1986, although their split wasn't publicly announced until the following year.

'The album was so out of step with what was happening at the time that it didn't stand a chance,' laments Helen. 'And by the time everything came to an end, we were all absolutely exhausted. Well, we still made "Because of You" for [the TV sitcom] *Brush Strokes*, which was actually great because there was a deadline. It had to be done quickly.'

With Kevin having designs on becoming a solo artist, it was time for Helen to re-evaluate her career too. She worked on an album of instrumental music, *Romanza*, while also undertaking session work, most notably for Tanita Tikaram, with whom she also toured. After five intense and dedicated years with Dexys, the notion of being a freelance musician who could set her own agenda and workflow felt decidedly alien. 'My head was still in the weird Dexys world where you didn't work with anyone else.'

The penultimate record out of Helen's bag is Tanita's 'Good Tra-dition', her debut single which made the top ten in 1988. Helen's violin is all over the song, in particular her swinging, bluesy solo. The pair share a working relationship to this day. 'It always felt very natural to play with her. I find a similar sort of thing with Tim Burgess. I'm so lucky to play with him too.'

The quantity and range of Helen's work commitments in recent years is particularly gratifying as they represent a renaissance, a come-back. She spent twenty-three years away from life as a professional musician while she raised her two sons. As they reached adulthood, Helen returned to the wider world, studying for an Open University degree and undertaking work as an extra for television and film; sharp-eyed viewers can catch her in the likes of *Call the Midwife* and *Paddington 2*.

The violin was also dusted off, initially to play in pub sessions, but then for a return to the professional arena. In 2015, Kevin invited Helen to play on the next Dexys album, *Let the Record Show: Dexys Do Irish and Country Soul*, a collection of covers of traditional songs, such as 'Carrickfergus' and 'Curragh of Kildare', alongside choice cuts from the songbooks of folk like Joni Mitchell, Johnny Cash and the Bee Gees. She was also invited to be part of the post-production inner circle.

Some live dates and radio shows with Dexys followed. Although a tour reviving *Too-Rye-Ay* had to be cancelled after Kevin seriously injured his leg in a motorbike crash in Thailand, the closing ceremony at the 2022 Commonwealth Games in Birmingham found Dexys reprising 'Come on Eileen', Helen joined on stage by Jimmy Paterson and his trombone, having been lured down from the splendid isolation of his Highlands home. Kevin, Helen and Jimmy were back together, just a handful of miles from where it all started.

HELEN O'HARA

Helen's final choice in her Defining Ten leads Luther to muse whether its title is a deliberate reference to the resumption, the reawakening, of her career. It's the Beatles' 'I'm Only Sleeping'.

And then we're done.

No one's in a hurry to leave, though, and while tonight's band bring their gear in, Helen's only too pleased to meet and greet anyone and everyone who wants to chat. The man in the red neckerchief is first in line.

Some have brought items for Helen to sign, mostly their lovingly worn copies of *Too-Rye-Ay*. The person who's brought the most items for some Sharpie-based embellishment is Luther himself, an impressive pile of records and posters to mark another successful Defining Ten event. All that seems to be missing is that illegally recorded cassette from his childhood.

Helen and I walk through the still-warm Worthing streets back to the station, she with that carrier bag of precious records back in her hand. We talk about literary events, about the warm fuzz of nostalgia and about the fast-accelerating passing of time. And we talk about our kids and their music making. My youngest passed his Grade 5 piano a couple of days ago. Her youngest, Billy, is a professional drummer. Indeed, he's been an on/off member of the latter-period Dexys, including playing with the band at that Commonwealth Games performance. It turns out that acquiescing to the request of those two horn-playing 'heavies' in that practice room at Birmingham School of Music four decades ago not only diverted Helen's own professional path, but also helped shape that of one of her offspring.

Back then, Helen O'Hara gave the answer that the Dexys henchmen wanted to hear. It turned out to be the right answer for herself too.

163

Reminisce #6

Brook Drive, Southwark

Things round here have changed.

Forty years ago, the Elephant & Castle was one of south London's more down-at-heel quarters, a dark corner of fume-choked traffic junctions and in-decline building stock. The developers have moved in since, fanning out from Southwark and Borough, and turning the skyline into something resembling a mini São Paulo. Futuristic high-rises reach for the skies. Boulevard dining has come to the area too.

Things are different down on Brook Drive as well. Back then, there were long terraces of three- and four-storey Victorian dwellings on both sides of the street. One side has gone, replaced by newer, more prosaic architecture. The other retains its Victorian houses, many now converted into flats. Vi's Stores, at the junction with Hayles Street, closed for business quite some time ago. The cigarette-advertising signage – for Silk Cut and Embassy No. 1 – was long since chucked into a skip.

These days, number 151 is an advertising-free, five-bed private house, the old shop front now painted powder-blue. These days, too, there aren't seven raggle-taggle musicians stood out front, play-acting for the cameras as they belatedly shoot the video for a single that's already in the top ten. There are seven wheelie bins standing sentry outside instead.

A photograph is taken to commemorate the changes.

'Excuse me . . .'

A young woman, who's been marching up and down the road approaching people, steps up.

'Are you Matt? I'm waiting for Matt. Matt the estate agent.'

'No, sorry.'

'Are you sure?'

'Yup. Not me.'

'Then why are you taking a picture of that house, if you're not an estate agent?'

'To commemorate a great moment in pop music history.'

She shrugs.

'The "Come on Eileen" video. It was filmed here. Dexys, you know?'

'Dixie Chicks?'

'Dexys. Dexys Midnight Runners.'

Another shrug.

'Never heard of them.'

Things round here have changed.

13

Steve Shaw (aka Steve Brennan)

Violin, 1982–83

*'There was a clear sense of change about.
Kevin was incubating his ideas for the next chapter.'*

There are few more goose-bumping, more tear-jerking sounds in British football than when the terraces at Easter Road in Leith, home of Hibernian FC, break into song. Not any old song, but one in particular: 'Sunshine on Leith', arguably the most beloved tune from the pen of those Hibs fanatics, the Proclaimers.

Whether sung to celebrate a famous victory or to commemorate the passing of a much-respected club chairman, the song is always delivered with strong measures of gusto and soul, cutting straight to the heart. Indeed, in 2018, BBC Radio 6 Music voted it the greatest football anthem ever, even outscoring 'You'll Never Walk Alone'. There's rarely a dry eye in the house when it comes over the PA.

It's a love song in the traditional sense, but also a love song to one of Edinburgh's more maligned quarters – and, now, to its football club. At Easter Road, by the time the violin solo comes in, the terraces have either broken into applause or are picking out the melody – 'Da da da da da . . .' – drowning it out. This is harsh on the violin player, as that solo is every inch as stirring as the Reid twins' lyrics. It was played by Steve Shaw, better known to Dexys disciples as Steve Brennan.

It was as Steve Shaw, the Birmingham College of Music student, that he was recruited into the Dexys fold ('with thanks to Helen,' he says, four decades on. 'I don't think I ever thanked her'). But it was as Steve Brennan that he helped unleash the full fury of the Emerald Express's strings, that he scored big hits, that he filmed pop videos, that he travelled the world. And once his time in the band was up, unlike Helen O'Hara he reverted back to his birth name. Steve Shaw played that solo on 'Sunshine on Leith', not Steve Brennan.

'The period leading up to me leaving Dexys was a very unhappy time,' he reveals. 'We'd done a lot of great UK and European dates, then things changed massively for me during the US tour. Kevin and Helen were travelling across the American cities separately from the group, mainly as they had lots of interviews and promotional work to do, plus they were in a romantic relationship at the time too.

'I'd never experienced paranoia before Dexys, but because I was so in love with – *obsessed* with – being in the group, I became insecure about my role as a second fiddle. Kevin was planning to marry Helen and I missed the working rapport I had with her. I felt less important to Kevin. I don't think these were just my feelings. There was a clear sense of change about. He was incubating his new ideas for the next chapter.

'I must have been difficult to be around. I was unhappy and had become quite miserable. Detached, even. I was paranoid about my future role in the group. I would pester Helen, Seb and Billy. Helen and Billy were always willing to try to reassure me, but I couldn't be convinced by anything they would say. I never spoke to Kevin about it, which is odd. I must have feared he would confirm my suspicions and increasing anxiety.

'It seemed remarkable to me at the time that *Don't Stand Me Down* was released that there's that dialogue near the beginning of "This Is What She's Like", where Billy asks Kevin, "What were you all talking about when I came in?" Hearing that on record for the first time made me wonder if I'd planted a seed, if my own feelings of paranoia had become acknowledged.'

Unsure of his role in the band, watching that next chapter take shape without him was surely worse than simply receiving a P45. Unsurprisingly, Steve gradually felt frozen out.

'I wasn't involved in *Don't Stand Me Down*. Kevin, Billy and Helen were writing and working things through as soon as we got back to the UK after those US dates. I was doing some playing for an indie group from Coventry called the Letters, who'd been given some studio time by EMI Publishing. I would often bump into Kevin and Helen outside the Ivy Bush pub, as we all lived quite close to each other on Hagley Road. They would be wearing their Brooks Brothers Ivy League clothes and I felt envious I wasn't part of that period too.

'As well as living close to them, Kevin had bought his brother a flat in the block next to mine, and Kevin Archer lived just up the road. John Taylor from Duran Duran lived on Hagley Road too, and Dennis Seaton from Musical Youth lived almost opposite him. It must have been like the original Stella Street.' Having moved to Birmingham from his native Liverpool for music college, Steve has lived in the city ever since. He no longer lives on 'Stella Street', though, preferring instead the suburb of Moseley, south of the city centre.

'I met up with Kevin many years later at the Hotel du Vin in town, probably around 2000, during his 12-step recovery. He told me he thought I'd lost interest in the group, which must have been how I had appeared. The meeting didn't go well. I wasn't in the best place when I met him. I was angry and upset at the way things had turned out – too displaced to actually talk about it to him and unable to be honest with him. I never did speak to him about how things changed for me and how I'd felt.

'I think Kevin had tried to ring me several times before we finally met up, and he'd contacted other people I knew too, but I didn't fully understand or recognise the process he was going through at that time. It's remarkable that Kevin sorted out his addiction problems and got back to doing what he's meant to do. It's a brilliant outcome. I have the highest respect for his recovery and determination.'

Kevin Archer's proximity to Steve's flat meant that, despite their respective times in Dexys not crossing over, they'd spent plenty of time in each other's company. So, with the band drifting away from him, Steve instead found musical inspiration within the second coming of the Blue Ox Babes and he was to prove a pivotal figure in the band's resurrection. If Dexys had left Steve questioning his musical worth, hitching up with Kevin Archer – along with Yasmin Saleh and Steve Wynne – helped to restore his faith in himself and his abilities.

'We worked together writing songs, although Archie wrote the bulk of them. It was a great time and he was a joy to be around. He was so inspiring, always encouraging me to write. Though I couldn't sing a note, he would always – and almost immediately – grasp the musical ideas I had, which made the process easy and exciting.'

'I was so in love with – *obsessed* with – being in the group.'
Steve Shaw contemplates the past at home in Moseley.

STEVE SHAW (AKA STEVE BRENNAN)

If Steve felt excluded from post-*Too-Rye-Ay* Dexys, the Blue Ox Babes placed him at the heart of the creative process. He co-wrote six of the songs on the *Apples & Oranges* album with Kevin Archer, including their debut single – and best-known number – 'There's No Deceiving You'.

Highly spirited as part of the Dexys string ensemble, being the sole violin player in the Blue Ox Babes allowed Steve's playing to stand on its own, to take centre stage as and when the song allowed. The versatility was on show. On 'Bedlam', his playing pricks the skin as much as it does on 'Sunshine on Leith'. On 'Thought as Much', there's a whiff of the Scottish Highlands about his styling, while 'Gregory Right' finds Steve evoking the Cajun fiddlers of southern Louisiana.

As creatively freeing as the experience was, the passage and lifespan of the Blue Ox Babes was nonetheless an undulating one. 'Unsettling and disruptive,' says Steve. 'As the song "The Ballad of the Blue Ox Babes" says, "We had our trials and tribulations". The album wasn't well-received. I don't think anyone realised or acknowledged how original and creative Archie had always been in Dexys, so we got described as a poor Dexys soundalike, which devastated him. And the rest of us too. "Walking the Line" was released as a single, but it didn't get on a decent radio playlist. And despite us being the UK tour support for the Proclaimers, the album was never released. We were all severely disheartened.'

During that tour with the Proclaimers, Steve had a dual role. In addition to playing the whole set with the Blue Ox Babes, he would later return to the stage to play on 'Sunshine on Leith' alongside the Reid brothers. When the latter were booked on a tour of both the US and Australasia, Steve went with them. Yasmin was heading Down Under too, but on a permanent basis with her then boyfriend. The Blue Ox Babes were over.

By this point, Steve had already recorded his part on 'Sunshine on Leith'. He knew the twins from some years before after Kevin

Rowland had invited this pair of Dexys fans down to Birmingham to record a demo. 'They were great people as well as great musicians – full of warmth and sincerity,' says Steve. 'Charlie, Craig and their manager Kenny were always very good to me.'

Steve had been called down to Chipping Norton to lay down his violin part. He was no stranger to the studios, having recorded *Oranges & Apples* there. Pete Wingfield again was the producer.

'They had had some difficulty finding the right instruments for the melodic break in the song. I think they had tried bagpipes and harmonica, so Pete suggested they try violin and they invited me down. Pete had the part written out – two melodic lines in B-flat. I played it straight into the desk in the control room, with Charlie and Craig listening. And that was it, in the bag.'

Before, during and after his spells with the Blue Ox Babes and being part of the Proclaimers' live band, other session work came Steve's way, whether that was playing alongside André Previn's daughter Alicia for General Public (a gig secured through his old Dexys pal Micky Billingham) or supplying spiralling violin on the Deacon Blue top-ten hit 'Twist and Shout'.

But a long and lengthy career playing freelance fiddle to whoever wanted extra colour on their records or in their live shows wasn't forthcoming for Steve. 'In around 2000, I acquired a shoulder injury due to long hours of playing with poor posture. It stopped me from playing. I had to turn down a lot of work with the Proclaimers due to not being able to play at all. I think one doctor diagnosed my condition as ankylosing spondylitis – which I thought sounded like some rock drummer . . .

'I became severely depressed and anxious as a consequence. I couldn't comprehend what was happening to me. It was a devastating time and my depression grew deeper and darker. I exchanged exciting tour dates with the Proclaimers for bags of antidepressants, anti-anxiety meds and sleeping pills. I'd lost all sense of myself and my purpose in life. It was a desperate and challenging time for me. This depressive illness stopped me doing almost everything. It mithered my soul and the medications sedated me. Anxiety robbed me of most everyday experiences. I was only present in the constant painful turmoil going on within me.

'My sister had always been severely depressed when I was growing up, but I never tried to understand it or tried to be helpful to her. I could never understand why she didn't have any connectedness to life, why she would rather sleep and avoid the outside world.

'It was a consequence of my own depression that led me to work in mental health. I work for an NHS mental health trust and have had that privileged role for about twenty years now. I'll always remain frustrated and disappointed that many people who experience mental health problems rarely recover. At best, they have to accept what's happened to them and adapt to living their life managing the enduring symptoms they may have. There may be no full clinical recovery for many, but a personal acceptance of the condition, and being kind and supportive to the new you, can help a more personal, meaningful recovery.'

The injury has removed Steve's ability to resume playing his instrument. Instead, he remains a keen listener.

'Today I listen meltingly and enviously to players like David Oistrakh, Isaac Stern, Nigel Kennedy and Tasmin Little, dreaming I am playing again. Playing music halts time in its tracks. Minutes cease to exist as we hold people's attention through letting music speak, establishing a connection through melody and harmony. What else is there?'

The Hibs faithful, standing to attention at Easter Road, communally bathing in the warmth of 'Sunshine on Leith', would surely agree.

14

Roger Huckle

Violin, 1982

'I remember coming back home from that orchestral tour and turning the telly on. There were Dexys, either at number one or pretty close to it. "Oh, shit . . ."'

At five minutes to seven on a warm spring evening in a concert hall in central Bristol, around two dozen classical musicians saunter on stage. They find their allotted places and warm up their instruments. The violinists practise their bowing, while the notes of the clarinet spiral up towards the ceiling. The xylophone player gently caresses his instrument with his beaters, but his comrade in the percussionists' row at the back – the timpani player – doesn't dare try out his instrument for fear of startling the last members of the audience taking their seats.

Tonight, these musicians – known collectively as the Bristol Ensemble – will be playing an orchestral arrangement of Mike Oldfield's *Tubular Bells*, it being the 50th anniversary of the album's release next week. This isn't uncharted territory for the Ensemble. A couple of months ago, they did the same for another album marking its half-century – Pink Floyd's *The Dark Side of the Moon*.

The lights go down and the Ensemble's leader and conductor strides purposefully onto the stage. He wears a dark suit over a ketchup-red T-shirt. All the musicians' eyes fix on him as he picks up his baton and issues his first instructions.

His name is Roger Huckle. He was once known as Roger MacDuff.

That Roger is a very busy man is shown by the fact that, after tonight, it takes a full six months before there's room in his diary for him to reminisce with me about his Dexys days. And even then – and despite him living little more than twenty miles from me – it's on a Zoom call from Bergen. 'I kind of live over here as well,' he explains. 'My wife is Norwegian.'

Before he originally moved to Norway's second city in the mid-'80s, Roger studied for four years in England's second city, during which time came his six-month Dexys adventure. Like Helen O'Hara, he grew up in Bristol's northern suburbs, although he was a couple of years behind her when he enrolled at Birmingham School of Music. As her deputy among the first violins in the college's orchestra, Roger was an obvious candidate to fill one of the band's violin vacancies. Helen's book tells us that the twenty-year-old Roger 'could have passed as an art student', making him the best fit among their cohort to join a pop band. He and Steve were arguably the least straight-laced students on the course, and the most likely to be able to handle the unusual ways of the world of rock and pop.

'We were in each other's pockets all the time. Steve and I both came from comprehensive school backgrounds in pretty rough areas. I went to Henbury Comprehensive in Bristol. To survive in a comprehensive school playing the violin meant you had to be a bit streetwise. You couldn't be a nerdy violinist.

'But, at the same time, your late teens are a formative social period. I was out partying a lot, mixing with art students, dressing in different ways. The world I inhabited in Bristol was very eclectic. It wasn't the serious classical music world. I do remember arriving at

Birmingham School of Music, walking into the canteen and going, "Ah, OK". There were definitely a lot of geeky, very straight classical musicians in there. Then we arrived. We were really good players. We just weren't from that intense classical background. I'm not being rude to the classical world, but it is quite a rarefied thing and it is very, very straight. That's changed a little since then. People have been forced into occupying all sorts of different arenas to make a living. In those days, it was "You either do this or you do that". You didn't mix things.'

The invitation to audition for Dexys was an attractive one. 'Helen approached me and Steve, and we said, "Yeah, why not? Let's give it a go and see what it's like." It was very exciting, because we were in the intense, small world of classical music training where everyone's obsessed with fine details. Then this other thing came knocking on the door. I had actually been doing lots of folk music in that period because I was house-sharing with some guys who were into that at university, so I wasn't just doing classical music – some folk music and a bit of improvisation/crossover jazz stuff.

'When I walked into that rehearsal room, I didn't feel uncomfortable. It was an interesting set-up. They were a motley crew, but they were kind of fun and really friendly. I liked the guys and I liked the vibe, the whole feel of it. We weren't met by a kind of scepticism. They were exploring stuff as well. They were trying to find something. The weirdest thing was that the brass section was still hanging around, kicking their heels at the side of the room. "What's going on here, then?" And then we know what happened.

'When we first started rehearsing with them, we were playing with a slight refinement and that was obviously not what they were really after. They wanted this raw, dynamic string sound, so we had to completely change our mindset. All the refinements that you're required to do with classical music training just went out the window. And that was perfect for what they wanted. It was still musically driven.' It was about the passion, not the delicate, technical finesse being taught at the Birmingham School of Music. 'I don't remember anyone actually breaking strings, but we must have been pretty close.'

Dexys' move towards folk music fitted Roger well. He was no square peg trying to squeeze into a round hole. His edges had already been shaped and sanded and smoothed by playing with his folkie housemates. 'All that hard playing that Dexys wanted – they wanted to get the hardness of a brass sound onto violins – fitted well with the rawness and slight roughness of playing folk music.'

Despite their studies – and bear in mind Helen was in her final year – the Dexys schedule was unrelenting. Creative, too. 'We did a lot of rehearsals. There was a lot of discussion and a lot of exploration and a lot of changing. "This works. That works. What shall we do here? What shall we change?" We got to know everybody pretty well.

'It was really interesting to immerse yourself into their world. At that time, they were still wearing their boxing boots and tracksuits. I remember Steve and I going off to buy that kit. "This is the uniform. We need to do this." So we turned up in college with that gear on . . .'

Kevin had swiftly dubbed the trio the Emerald Express, as well as dishing out aliases for each of them. 'I wasn't so cool about my name. "MacDuff? Hmmmm, OK . . ." But it's entertainment. It's showbusiness, isn't it? At the time, I didn't think too much about it at all, but I probably should have done. If I'd have objected and suggested an alternative, I'm sure that would have been fine. But it was all a bit of fun. We were just getting swept along. And we were pretty naive about self-image at that age. I didn't have a profile. I was just a fiddle player at Birmingham School of Music.'

Roger never actually played live with Dexys; his time with them was limited to rehearsal and recording. The first experience of the latter was at Air Studios for 'The Celtic Soul Brothers'. 'I'd done a lot of small-scale recording by then, but it was the first time I'd been in a studio as prestigious as that. Even so, I still think I was not that aware of where this could go. The idea that we could end up looking at having a number one seemed very far removed. It wasn't getting all intense. From what I remember, I was still enjoying having a laugh. I wasn't overwhelmed. I was just along for the ride.

'It was exciting at Air. That was the first sense I had that it was getting serious as a project. I seem to remember there were lots of cases from other musicians scattered around. "Oh, look. There's Paul McCartney's case." It was like walking into a hall of fame of pop music. I've since done all sorts of recording there – film music and stuff.'

The project might have been gaining momentum, but Roger had to decide whether to stay on board or jump off this accelerating train. 'Helen was in her final year, so she was having to make some big decisions about which direction she wanted to go and I think Dexys really ticked a box for her in particular. It was a bit like that for me in the end, when it came to the crunch. I had to weigh up Dexys against another two years of study. The college wouldn't accept me disappearing: "You either stay at college and do what you're meant to be doing or that's it."

'I think it was close to the release of *Too-Rye-Ay* when I felt I had to dip out. Dexys needed everybody to be available for a long period and that was getting close to the end of my second year, when I was due to be going on an orchestra tour to France. I talked to my tutor: "I'm not really sure what to do here." I was told, "Well, if you're walking out on this tour, you're walking out on your course." It was a very clear ultimatum. I couldn't do both Dexys and my training. It was either/or. I had to think what was really in my heart to do. And that was to stick with the next two years of training.

'I let Helen and Steve know. I think they understood. They were a bit sad that I wasn't going to do it any more, but they could see the rationale behind it. The Dexys experience has stayed with me all these years, but I wasn't as really, really into it in the same way that Helen and Steve were.

'It was very gutting. It wasn't an easy decision to make. I had to think about it a lot. Sometimes you have to dig deep and look into yourself. A large part of me wanted to do the pop stuff, but the bigger part was saying, "No, come on. You need to get yourself trained up properly first."

'Everyone knows the pop world is very transient. One minute you can be at the top, the next no one's talking about you any longer. So I always knew it would be a pretty short-term career move and that's what was playing on my mind – the longevity of getting a proper degree and getting skilled up, set against the hype and the excitement of six months or eighteen months or however long it would be. And then you'd be left high and dry. You are kind of dispensable. And it was clear that people were dispensable. That's stayed with me throughout my whole career. People are dispensable in classical music too. I started my own chamber orchestra to avoid being at the beck and call of other people and their decision making. You can be flavour of the month and suddenly you're not – and there can be no apparent reason for it. Suddenly your diary's empty. "What the hell happened there?"

'In the end, I think it was probably the right decision, although I remember coming back home from that orchestral tour and

Roger Huckle – the artist formerly known as Roger
MacDuff – on his home turf of Bristol. *Matt Lincoln*

turning the telly on. There were Dexys, either at number one or
pretty close to it. "Oh, shit . . .'"

Roger continued with his studies at the college and would later
meet a Norwegian woman by the name of Liv, who was spending
her gap year in Birmingham. Once he graduated, a position in the
Bergen Philharmonic came up. Roger applied, passed the audition
and moved to Liv's home patch. Reader, he married her.

The couple moved back to Roger's hometown at the turn of the
'90s when, after 'messing around for a couple of years', he began to
foster notions of starting Bristol's first professional orchestra. 'I realised I had to do something that had my own stamp on it. I needed
to start my own thing that I could be in charge of and where I could
just work with people I wanted to work with.'

What would later be rechristened the Bristol Ensemble was originally known as the Emerald Ensemble, a nod of the head, a tip of the hat, to the three-strong string section he'd been part of more than ten years earlier.

'I remembered a discussion with Kevin Rowland about names and marketing and stuff like that. He was explaining why the name was really important, that it creates a picture. The name "Dexys Midnight Runners" had some sort of aura about it, some sort of picture in your mind: "Dexys Midnight Runners? What the hell's that?" So we were looking to name the group. We were considering gemstones and then "emerald" came into it. "Oh yeah. That matches up!"'

'Bristol didn't have a professional orchestra. It was very much dominated by the amateur music-making scene – a mixture of semi-professionals and some good amateur players. I wanted to create a professional scene but it took far longer than I expected. At that point, there weren't that many professional players in Bristol, so I had to use my freelance connections and pull people in from further afield. It took a few years to get going, but was really popular as soon as we first started. We were selling out concerts of Bach or Vivaldi's *Four Seasons*.'

Was the aim that this orchestra, fronted by the former comprehensive school kid, wouldn't exclusively play in well-heeled auditoria to well-heeled audiences? 'Very much so. That was very much part of my thinking – to engage lots of different people. That's certainly something that's stayed with the Ensemble right up to today. We do lots of education work in disadvantaged areas of Bristol. We see about 1,600 kids each week.

'And we tried to make our concerts accessible for people and not snobby. We talked to the audience, we dressed differently. We were trying to rethink it. In fact, I was possibly too far ahead of the curve. We were doing these things to popularise classical music way before it became the thing to do. We were trying to open the doors, to open classical music to wider audiences.

'I want us to get out into places across the city like Knowle West and Whitchurch and Easton, so we're not just playing out of the more obvious venues like St Georges. Get out into the community, get our fingers dirty. Thirteen of us went into the Merchants Academy in Withywood [a low-income area on the southern outskirts of Bristol] and did a whole forty-five-minute concert, playing a mixture of music – classical and pop. We got them up to conduct and they absolutely loved it. They were totally caught by it. It was magical.'

The Ensemble's diary – and thus Roger's too – is bursting at the seams. Over the next few weeks comes a series of performances across Bristol and the wider West Country, recitals of the works of Bach, Vivaldi, Mendelssohn, Rachmaninov, Brahms, Handel and, with multiple reprises of *The Dark Side of the Moon*, Waters/Gilmour/Mason/Wright. Then there are performances featuring music from the BBC wildlife documentary series *The Blue Planet*, and even a tango concert in a local village church. Most tantalisingly, though, they'll be providing live orchestral accompaniment to showings of the short Aardman film *Shaun the Sheep: The Flight Before Christmas*.

As Bristol's first and only chamber orchestra, the Ensemble have largely remained anchored to the city, often found to be collaborating with the more creative Bristolians, whether that's Aardman, Roni Size or the BBC Natural History Unit. Plus, for many years Roger has been a lecturer at Bristol University. Think global, act local.

'I just see it all as music. If I like it, I like it.' Roger is the boss, so he has the final say. You could say, in a way, he's the Kevin Rowland of the Bristol Ensemble – the director, the auteur.

Playing such an untrammelled, open-ended variety of material can only help the Ensemble grow even further than it already has in its thirty-year history. 'Doing so has expanded our musical expression, away from the rigidity of classical music, away from all the pickety-picky stuff that totally kills it for me. Doing folk music, and then doing Dexys, absolutely freed up my mind. If I hadn't done all that stuff, and if I'd only inhabited the rarefied world of classical music, it would have been suffocating.'

Most recently, Roger has been writing music in collaboration with another British musician living in Bergen called Marcus Davidson. Roger describes the project – called Standing Waves – as 'East–West electronica with improvised violin over the top of it'.

Bergen offers a chance for Roger to come up for air, to have a breather. Cloudless blue skies like today's allow him to clear his thoughts. 'It's a bit of a whirlwind when I'm back in Bristol, when I'm back in the UK; then I get to Bergen and chill out. Recovery time!

'I've got a fantastic group of lovely, lovely people. The social thing is just as important as the music making. We have a great time. I've got a really good associate leader now, Simon Kodurand. He's also our artistic director and he takes on quite a lot of our leading when I've decided I've just had enough and need a break. I administer most of our concerts and play in quite a few, but I just need to find space to get out because it's too much otherwise.'

And this space allows Roger to dream up the next unlikely musical voyage for the Ensemble. With one eye on their adaptations of the works of Pink Floyd and Mike Oldfield, could a revisitation of one of his past lives soon appear on the runway?

'I have been thinking of an orchestral take on Dexys,' he confirms, with a hearty laugh. 'But I haven't quite got there yet.

'I'd probably need to drop Kevin a line first . . .'

Dexys Midnight Runners, September 1982. (*l-r*) Spike Edney, John 'Rhino' Edwards (*crouching*), Andy Hamilton, Nick Gatfield, Steve Shaw (aka Steve Brennan), Seb Shelton, Kevin Rowland, Helen O'Hara, Kev 'Billy' Adams, Micky Billingham and Simon Walker (*crouching*). *Brian Cooke/Redferns/Getty Images*

15

Simon Walker

Violin, 1982–83

'In the short distance between the stage door and the door of the bus, I lost my beret, I lost my neckerchief, and they tried to take my T-shirt off.'

Brighton has some notable architectural gems. There are the domes and minarets of the Prince Regent's Royal Pavilion. There are the Italianate stylings of the Grand Hotel. And there's the handsome frontage and curved roof of the Palace Pier.

New England House isn't in the same bracket. It would never adorn a seaside postcard. Situated round the back of Brighton station, it's eight storeys of 1960s architecture, all glass and steel and concrete and stairwells and loading bays and graffitied metal shutters. Constructed in 1963, it prided itself as being 'the world's first purpose-built, high-rise industrial business centre'. Sixty years on, it's still serving its original purpose. While enterprising property developers might have fancied carving it up into hundreds of tiny pods for those in search of urban living, it instead remains a hub of enterprise and entrepreneurship, home to all manner of light industry, from graphic design studios to French bakeries. And, on the sixth floor, a modest recording studio that's occupied New England House for a large chunk of the building's lifespan.

This is the Loophole, the working environment of one Simon Walker, a man who, for a good few globetrotting months between the autumn of 1982 and the spring of 1983, answered to a different name. He too would answer, publicly at least, to the name Roger MacDuff.

Unlike his fiddle-playing predecessor, Simon hadn't been lifted from his studies at the Birmingham School of Music into the world of rock and pop. He was already very much in that milieu, as he'll soon be telling us. Prior to that, though, he was headed, like Helen, Steve and Roger, down a classical music route. It had seemed like that was his destiny, that it was in his bloodline.

'My father was in the Royal Artillery Orchestra and Band,' he explains, setting a mug of tea down in front of me once I've found a perch here in the Loophole. 'He was a fantastic classical harpist. And a pianist. And a clarinettist. When he finished his national service, he got a job with the Royal Shakespeare Company in Stratford and ended up composing for the theatre. All my friends thought he was a *magician*, not a musician, so I let them think that.

'I was volunteered to play the violin. In 1969, aged ten, I vividly remember the headmaster pulling me out of class and telling me I'd be having violin lessons. I was very timid and didn't kick up a fuss. So I took up the violin and, a year later, I was playing concertos. I had a natural facility for it, but I was a reluctant player. My dad would tell me to do half an hour's practice and I'd stare at the clock until that half-hour had gone, and then I quickly put the violin back in its case.'

However reluctant he was, Simon's talent was undeniable. He auditioned for all the top music schools in the country and was accepted by each and every one of them. 'It wasn't a case of "Are you going to music school?" It was "Which one are you going to?" I went to Cheethams in Manchester on a scholarship and don't regret it. I was idle. I did no work there. If I had my time again, I would go back there and be idle again. I was actually given the accolade "King Dosser".' One of his friends there was Mike Lindup, later a lynchpin of Level 42.

Simon then auditioned for music colleges, repeating the same high strike rate on audition. With a range of offers to choose from, he plumped for the Royal College of Music. However, unlike Helen and Roger, he didn't see the four-year course to its natural end, leaving after a couple of years when he got offered a job at Olympic Studios in south-west London. Recording studios had emitted an allure for him since his early teen years.

'When I was thirteen, I turned pages for my father at a recording at Pebble Mill in Birmingham. I walked into the control room there, which is two or three times bigger than my whole studio here, and just fell in love immediately. The job at Olympic was a lowly position, the way most people start out – a tea maker.

'I knew my dad would be devastated, because it was a given that I was going to follow in his footsteps. Ultimately, though, he respected the fact that I was my own person and had made up my mind what to do.'

But the job at Olympic fell through and, having left college for a role that never materialised, Simon then formed a number of bands with his friend and flatmate Nick Page, the future co-founder of Transglobal Underground. Most notable of these was the reggae-flecked Bumble and the Beez. 'We did really well. We got signed by EMI and played all the big halls in the UK, supporting John Martyn, Hazel O'Connor, the Selecter, Third World . . . But we'd also play the likes of the Half Moon and the 100 Club. We were gigging three times a week, minimum. It was a time of great confidence for me. You couldn't get me off the stage.' Members of Bumble and the Beez, including Simon, would ultimately form the Reggae Philharmonic Orchestra.

Then, in the summer of '82, after Roger Huckle had served notice of his departure, word reached Simon that Dexys needed a new third violin player for their upcoming UK tour. 'So I went up to Birmingham to Diamond rehearsal studios. It was a bit daunting as they were already a ten-piece band and I didn't know anyone from Adam. But I'd done my homework and I'd learnt the songs. And I got the gig. During Bumble and the Beez, I had to take the sideline of playing keyboards because the violin was not considered commercial in pop music. Then, suddenly, Dexys came along. I was despairing, but then I got this phone call. Two weeks of solid rehearsal later, we were out on the road.'

For a young man who'd grown up in Stratford-upon-Avon ('a town where theatre was everything'), and who'd even been a child actor at the RSC for a couple of years, the theatrical element of Dexys' shows made perfect sense.

'There were various rules, including no smiling on stage. The trick was to give someone a wink and a smile without Kevin noticing. But I soon realised the importance of presenting an actual show, rather than standing there in a T-shirt and jeans, just playing. There was a degree of choreography. Steve and I were on a riser to the right of the drums and, at the beginning of "Plan B", the sax players would back out of the way and we would run and jump on the monitors. One time, Steve's lead got caught on something and so, halfway towards the front of the stage, his violin just flew away.

'As part of the show, Kevin was very keen for us to break our bow hairs. He wanting to see them dangling down from the bow. Actually, the Dexys experience ruined my playing for many years. I forgot how to play subtly.

'We started the tour in Glasgow and that was when I realised the extent of the fandom going on. When we finished the gig, in the short distance between the stage door and the door of the bus, I lost my beret, I lost my neckerchief, and they tried to take my T-shirt off.'

The whole adventure was unfolding before him, the direction of travel often seemingly improvised quite late in the day. 'At the beginning of the UK tour, we didn't know we'd be going to the States, and then Europe, and then the States again. No idea. It was almost like we bumped into the next tour. Or maybe, towards the end of a tour, Basher the manager might say, "I take it you're free for three-and-a-half weeks from the such-and-such of whenever." And then it rolled on again.'

In the New Year of 1983, on the first leg of the two-stage US tour. Simon struck up a close friendship with Bob Noble, the keyboard player drafted in to replace the now-departed Micky Billingham. 'I was twenty-three and Bob was thirty-five, but we just got on really well, spending our time playing chess or dirty Scrabble.' They would be lifelong pals.

When the band arrived in New York City, they had a surprise – and not necessarily welcome – visitor. 'Yoko Ono came to see us before the show because John Lennon had been a big fan of the first album. Sometimes people want peace before a gig and Kevin was visibly peeved that she'd invaded his space. But I had a little chat with her. Little Sean was only about six or seven. They stood at the side of the stage, about two metres away from me.'

After the second US visit, the final leg of the *Too-Rye-Ay* tour, those at the pumping heart of Dexys – Kevin, Helen, Billy and, for a while at least, Seb – began to flesh out the band's next chapter. The other players slipped away in various directions. Before too long, Simon got a call. 'I had to drive up to Birmingham, with a cellist who was also based in London, to do some demos for *Don't Stand Me Down*. I remember thinking, *Ah, kiss of death*. They'd hired a Fairlight – a very expensive sampling machine.'

Further flirtations were to come. 'Many, many years later, I got a random call from Kevin. I'd moved several times since Dexys so I really don't know how he tracked me down.' Kevin wanted Simon to find another fiddle player and for the pair of them to appear with the band on a forthcoming appearance on Jonathan Ross's new Channel 4 show, *Saturday Zoo*.

'My criticism of the two tracks we did was that they had promise but they were like demos. They were works in progress, not finished tracks. That's how they sounded to me, especially from where the band had come, the accomplished albums they'd made to that point.

'I did one more thing for Kevin, also in the '90s, I think. He was working in Camden – just him and an engineer – and he wanted me to put some violin down. I think he sent me a cassette and I worked out some ideas. And that was the last time I saw Kevin. Even though he lived here in Brighton for years, I never bumped into him.'

The Dexys connection also led to another touring engagement, namely stepping in for Helen in Tanita Tikaram's band when Helen was off having her first child. 'I got the job by default,' he smiles. It also reunited him with Tanita's keyboard player, his old pal Bob Noble. 'More chess, more dirty Scrabble . . .'

'The show must go on.' Simon Walker contemplates the final days of his Loophole Studio in its current Brighton location.

Throughout the '80s, Simon had continued his musical adventures with his pal Nick Page, forming a number of short-lived outfits. The most successful of these was the Rain Gods, after they were courted by Culture Club/Curiosity Killed the Cat manager Tony Gordon. 'He said, "I want to manage you. I want to get you a huge record deal." A few months later, we had a major deal with RCA. I think it was four hundred thousand pounds, of which we were given a hundred and fifty thousand upfront.

'We made an album at Livingston Studios and it was the most expensive recording project I've ever been involved in. I had to score some strings and we hired a twenty-six-piece string section and recorded them at Abbey Road.' The album had a limited release; it wasn't put out on CD. 'I thought, *Well, that completely shows me how much confidence they've lost in us.*'

After all these various musical projects with Nick, Simon's story becomes clearer, cleaner and more straightforward as we reach the tail end of the '80s. In 1988, he opened the Loophole, initially in Leyton, where the studio was in operation for five years. During this time, Simon and his partner Sally had had twins and were desperate to leave the area – 'It was rough. An industrial through-route, a no-man's land.' The family swapped the East End for the south coast, and the studio's been here, on New England House's sixth floor, ever since. 'This,' he says, extending an outstretched arm around the Loophole's modest dimensions, 'used to be a toilet in the '60s and '70s. There would have been cubicles just over there.'

This has been Simon's place of work for thirty years. But not for much longer. He drops the bombshell that he'll soon be leaving the building. The lovely wooden desks will be ripped out and reused, and much of the equipment rehomed. 'Soon' is actually very soon. 'Soon' is almost now. Today is Saturday. On Tuesday, the Loophole, at least here in New England House, will close its doors for the last time.

'Do you know who the first person to ever book the Loophole in Leyton was?'

I shrug.

'It was a guy called Karl Wessel, who goes by the name Moving in the Right Direction. He was signed to Soul Jazz Records for a while. It's kind of reggae fused with jazz. He was seventeen when I first met him. He was the first person to reply to the little box ad in the paper and was the first person to record there. And he's coming in tomorrow. It'll be the last music session here at Loophole. It's poetry, isn't it? He's bookending it.'

Much of Simon's work in more recent times has been voiceover and spoken-word sessions; among many others, Brian Blessed has put the Loophole's recording levels through their paces. These days, much of this work finds Simon simply editing recordings people have already made at home. 'Some of them still come in, but not enough to justify the £650 monthly rent. Every month that goes on, my savings are going down. I just thought I needed to nip it in the bud now. I'm keeping the Loophole name, but I'm just going to be working from home, reducing the overheads.'

It turns out the studio's closure might hit close to home, namely his three children. 'The kids will get a shock,' he explains. 'They come here every Christmas and we do a record for their mum. We split up years ago, but we get on fine. Me and the kids did "Ghost Town" last year. We've done about seventeen tracks so far. It's a great sort of diary. The first one we did for Sally was little Finn, aged eight or nine, singing "Walking in the Air" in his unbroken voice. He's twenty-six now and the twins are thirty-one. I can't believe that. They're older than I was when I opened the studio. They'll miss this place. I'll have to try to do a more humble version from home this Christmas. We have to do it, though. The show must go on.'

I don't need to ask if Simon will miss this place, his bolthole here on the sixth floor. He obviously will. But the raw economics have overpowered any sentimentality.

'I am tempted to get a job that's a no-brainer,' he sighs. 'I really am not proud. I'll quite happily gather trolleys in the Asda car park for the last few years. Maybe I'll be a traffic warden and become one of the most hated figures in Brighton . . .'

16

Andy Hamilton

Tenor sax, 1982–83

'It was almost as if shooting yourself in the foot was seen as a victory.'

'My dad used to go to the Westminster record library. This was a long time before we had the money to buy our own albums. He borrowed a record that had a picture of a guy playing the saxophone on it. It was an album called *Schizophrenia* by Wayne Shorter. My dad didn't know who he was and neither did I, but Wayne Shorter turned out to be one of my all-time heroes. I met him a couple of times. And this album was life-changing for me. It was 1968 and it just fuelled my tank. I thought, *My God, this is me. This is what I want to do.*'

It's a damp and miserable day in the flatlands of Suffolk, but Andy Hamilton is warm and dry in his house in a village just outside Bury St Edmunds. He's busy recalling the moment that the destiny of his fifteen-year-old self was crystallised, the moment at which a portal opened up to a musical life far less ordinary. It's a cliché, but it's possibly quicker and easier to name the A-grade pop acts that Andy *hasn't* played sax for and alongside over the past forty-plus years. We'll get to the roll-call later; suffice to say it includes an intense spell as Paul Speare's replacement as Dexys' tenor player. For now, though, Andy is offering chapter and verse on his early musical evolution.

'I was always fascinated by the look of the sax. There used to be a youth club near where I lived in Portsmouth as a teenager, which is where I saw Sounds Incorporated, who were a sort of pop band from the '60s. I was fascinated by their horn players. And my sister's boyfriend had a couple of jazz records. Listening to people like Stan Getz and Johnny Hodges, I thought, *I want to do this*. So I bought a saxophone for nine pounds in a junk shop. I can't even remember if it actually played or not. I think I just liked owning it. It looked kind of cool. I remember Wayne Shorter said the same thing. That was why he chose the saxophone. I joined my first band probably more on the basis of *owning* a saxophone, rather than actually being able to play it. I didn't realise it was going to prove such a fearsome adversary, though. It's hard work, you know. That's the nature of the instrument.'

That first band was the Portsmouth outfit Smiling Hard. It was the summer of '71 when the rest of the band came calling. 'I don't know why their sax player left, but they just turned up at the door one day. "We hear you play the saxophone. Do you want to join a band?" I'd been through school and had got a couple of A-levels. I was wondering what the hell I was going to do and the idea of joining a band sounded very appealing. I guess there weren't many sax players in Portsmouth in the early '70s. I was probably a good bet as at least I owned one.

'We went to Hamburg, where we played at the Top Ten Club on the Reeperbahn. We did a month at a time there, playing eight half-hour sets a night. Eight sets every night meant that you had to stretch out your repertoire, so there were sax solos in every tune. That's where I learned to solo – because I had to, otherwise the songs would be over in three and a half minutes. It was great experience. And great fun.'

'Smiling Hard were very ambitious and we were good. All the players were good. But the trouble was that we weren't specific enough about what we were doing. There were some elements of the band who wanted to do this, some elements who wanted to do that. We were basically a funky soul band with hints of jazz and a little bit of rock thrown in.'

It was within the Smiling Hard ranks where Andy first encountered Spike Edney, with whom he would strike a close bond for many years – and with whom he would later join Dexys. 'Spike played piano and keyboards, and a bit of trombone. I could play sax and a little bit of guitar and keyboards. And Kev Gilson the singer could play sax and guitar.'

This versatility came in useful later in the decade when they became the first-choice backing band for visiting US artists, such as the Tymes, Ben E King and Edwin Starr, able to alter the line-up depending on what instrumentation each song required. Starr was particularly impressed by his young charges; he took them with him on an American tour, as well as bringing them into the studio over there en masse.

'When we came back from the US, Spike and I moved up to London, sharing a flat in Pimlico. The next day, we were walking along St Martin's Lane as a couple of jobless musicians when we bumped into Peter Stringfellow, who we knew from playing in Cinderella Rockerfellas in Leeds and Manchester. We'd played in his discotheques. He said, "What are you doing?" I replied, "What are *you* doing?"

'"I'm opening a nightclub tonight. Look, you play the sax and you play the piano. Have you got white jackets? Sit in the entrance and play some smooth music as the customers come in. We'll see how it goes. Tomorrow!"

'It was an amazing stroke of good fortune. We must have been the only two musicians who landed up in London and then ended up getting full-time jobs the following day. The gig allowed us to rent a flat and get some solidity. We played there every night for about a year.'

The good fortune continued to flow. A friend of Andy and Spike's from the south coast had also moved to London from Southampton and had secured himself a job as a tape operator at Tony Visconti's Good Earth Studios. As one of the few sax players he knew, Andy got involved at Good Earth and it was there that, in 1981, he hooked up with a promising new band from Birmingham, both recording and touring with them. They were going places. Their name was Duran Duran.

The next twelve months were something of a blur. Andy played the sax solo on 'Rio', although he didn't get to jet off to Antigua to film the video; Nick Rhodes and John Taylor shared dubious sax-miming duties on that instead. Andy did get to go to Montserrat and Australia to record with them, though. A taste of the high life, at least.

Between Duran albums, though, Andy fell back into the role of the unemployed musician hawking for work. And that's when his and Spike's Dexys sojourn begins.

With the horn section of Jimmy, Brian and Paul having retreated into the sunset, and with 'Come on Eileen' having topped the charts in the UK – and later to do so in the States – there was much touring and promotional work to be done. Even though by then the fiddles were arguably the instruments chiefly defining the Dexys sound, the horns – Andy and fellow new recruit Nick Gatfield on saxes, with Spike taking Jimmy Paterson's role on trombone – were out front alongside Kevin Rowland, giving it as much as their predecessors. These were no half-hearted session musicians going through the motions, largely hidden at the back of the stage. No one in the audiences on The Bridge tour of the autumn of 1982 would have thought they were anything other than full, permanent members of the band rather than being the hired help. Their performances and playing rivalled the passion of the band's two previous horn sections.

'I was in it 100 per cent,' confirms Andy. 'I gave it my best, my absolute best. We were flying the flag. We were definitely up for making it as good as it could possibly be. As musicians, that's what you do in every situation. You give it your all. And everybody in that band worked really, really hard to give it everything they could. It was so intense. Everything was at full volume. It was exhausting.'

Another newcomer whose commitment couldn't be questioned was John 'Rhino' Edwards, Giorgio Kilkenny's replacement on bass. At every show, he played like his life depended on it, a man possessed. 'The first time I met him, we walked into Diamond Studios in Birmingham and here was this tall, skinny guy with spiky hair. Then we start playing and he starts writhing on the floor. What is this? Some kind of cosplay? It turned out he'd grabbed the mic, which was live, and he was being electrocuted. Once we managed to save his life, that was my introduction to Rhino . . .

'For Kevin, it was part of a spiritual journey. I don't know quite where he was going spiritually, but there were moments when it truly worked. I've got a tape of a gig in Houston where it was positively inspiring. When it was good, it was great. But when it was bad, it could be bloody appalling. And no amount of commitment could get over the fact that sometimes it was just that.

'Kevin was insistent on everything being played at full tilt with maximum passion. I understood that. I got it completely. But in order to make sure everyone played as loud and as intensely as they could, we'd have virtually no monitoring down the front. So Nick and I would be playing our saxes full tilt, and when you do that, you can't hear it and you blow it out of tune. I think I made an enemy of them by saying, "Look, let's get to the point where we can hear ourselves clearly first with decent monitoring, and then let's play intensely." Trying to play intensely without being able to hear what you were doing is absurd. Billy would think the gig was great if he came off stage with only one string left on his guitar because he'd broken the rest from playing so hard. That was his idea of commitment. I thought that was ridiculous.

'Musically, there were some fabulous songs on *Too-Rye-Ay*. I'm very fond of that record. I used to love it when we played "Let's

Make This Precious". And "Come on Eileen" is an ingenious song. It's just that Kevin did some stupid things, including that thing he did in Paris with Bowie.'

In early June 1983, Dexys found themselves supporting David Bowie at the Auteuil Hippodrome, a racecourse west of the city centre. This was Bowie in his rediscovered pomp, having just scored a number-one hit with 'Let's Dance', before repeating the trick with the album of the same name. This was the Serious Moonlight tour when he was playing to phenomenally large audiences. The crowd in Paris was estimated to be a six-figure one. But it wasn't a crowd that, in its restlessness while waiting for Bowie, was pleasing Kevin. He launched into a diatribe, aiming sharp invectives at them and ending with his observation that Bryan Ferry was infinitely more talented than that night's headliner.

Standing along the line from Kevin, Andy was understandably surprised and confused by the outburst. 'I thought, *what an odd thing to say*. And, of course, I turn around and David is sitting on a flight case just behind me. Ten seconds later, the power was cut and we were escorted off the premises. I slipped into the crowd and watched David's show, which of course was fabulous.

'Then I went back to the hotel and walked into the bar. Some of the band were going "We fucking showed them!" I just said, "You twats!" We'd done loads of gigs in France and the crowd loved Dexys. They loved them. There was a huge following to be had there and he just pissed it down the drain. What a stupid thing to do, insulting the audience for coming to see Bowie. How ridiculous was that? It was almost as if shooting yourself in the foot was seen as a victory.

'I said, "I think you're a bunch of wankers if you think that was a good thing to do something so stupid." I didn't think it wasn't my place to say that. I could say whatever I wanted. And that was the last time I saw them.'

After the intensity of those nine-odd months on the road with Dexys, Andy returned to London, the demobbed soldier readjusting to civvy street. It was a routine he was already familiar with. 'You go back home and you go down the supermarket. Life goes back to normal. It was very strange after Duran Duran tours. You'd finish one of these enormous glittering tours, with God knows what going on, and the next day you'd be taking the cat down the vet's. Duran Duran came home but had to continue being pop stars. They had to live that life. I had the best of both worlds. I've played with lots of different people and I've been able to live a relatively normal life at the same time.'

'It was so intense. Everything was at full volume. It was exhausting.'
Andy Hamilton recalls his breathless time as Dexys' tenor saxman.

Another world tour with Duran took up much of 1984 before Andy found himself supplying sax for Wham!. This again came via that old friend working at Good Earth. 'I played on three or four of their songs. I got on well with George Michael and toured with him a few years later on a solo tour. There is a huge element of luck, being in the right place at the right time. But God knows what opportunities I missed . . .'

There is one particular missed opportunity, one that would have greatly benefitted his bank account, if nothing else. 'I came back from the US with Duran and we had to go to this film set in Birmingham to do some close-ups they hadn't been able to film on tour. Then I got this phone call from Good Earth. George had this nice song. Did I want to come and have a go at playing sax on it? I couldn't. I was stuck in Birmingham.'

That song was 'Careless Whisper'. George Michael famously went through eight sax players before he found one who could nail exactly what he wanted. That player was Steve Gregory. 'He had the good sense to varispeed the track down a tone because it was too high for the tenor,' explains Andy. 'Would I have had the wisdom to do that? Would I have had the wherewithal to think about taking it down a whole tone? I don't know. But, anyway, it worked great for Steve. He still gets royalties from it to this day.'

The next staging-post in Andy's top-line career occurred on 13 July 1985 at a football stadium in north-west London. 'The night before Live Aid, I was in Bermuda with Rhino, playing in this nightclub with his band, the Rhino Express. Spike was out there too, playing keyboards. Afterwards, Spike and I flew back. Spike was playing keyboards with Queen at Wembley, while I was with the Boomtown Rats. I was at the airport in Bermuda and there was an announcement: "Mr Hamilton, please come to the information desk." I thought, *Geldof is going to kill me. If I don't get on this plane, I'm going to be dead.* The person at the airline said, "Somebody is looking after you" and he gave me seat A1 in first class. Geldof obviously made sure I was definitely going to be there.'

'We landed at Heathrow on the morning of the gig. *How am I going to get into Wembley? I've got no pass. All I've got is my saxophone and a bag.* There was no traffic on the North Circular because everybody was already in the stadium. I was in a taxi, sweating. I arrived and then I heard a voice. It was Big Jim Callaghan who used to work with the Stones and Bob Dylan, and who I knew from Duran. "Andy Hamilton? Come this way."

'The Rats were getting changed in their caravan, just about to go on stage. I didn't realise I'd arrived within fifteen minutes of going on. Geldof said, "You're leaving it a bit fucking late, aren't you?" "Listen, I've just flown across the bloody Atlantic . . ." Then we went on stage and I was scared shitless.'

Spike enjoyed a more leisurely preparation that day, thanks to Queen going on six hours after Geldof's gang. In the years since, Queen has been his main employer, but he's also found time to create and steer the SAS Band (aka Spike's All Star Band), the ultimate party band for hire. It's an outfit that certainly lives up to its billing: over the years, these all-star guests have included Chaka Khan, Jack Bruce, Jamelia, Lionel Richie, Mark King, Mel C, Roger Daltrey and Jeff Beck. I approach Spike for a chat, but there's a conflict of interests. 'I've been writing my own book,' he tells me, 'and I'm in the final throes of a fairly extensive piece on my time in the Dexys camp.'

Andy's contacts book is as plump, and equally as impressive, as that of Spike. Alongside Duran Duran, Wham!, George Michael and the Boomtown Rats, those who've commissioned him for session work and/or tours include Paul McCartney, Elton John, Tina Turner, Pet Shop Boys and Bon Jovi. He's also been the musical director for the rejuvenated ABC.

'I don't regard myself as being at the top of the tree. I think I do a good job and I've been lucky. Also, one of the things about being a muso is being able to get on with people. I'm a relatively easygoing person and I'm easy to talk to. So if you're not a pain in the arse or a cocky bastard, you can get on with most people – even if some of the people you might be working with are cocky bastards . . . After all, a sax player is dispensable. I'm only one rung above a percussionist when it comes to the essential elements of a touring band.'

That said, Andy has taken his foot off the gas – or, at least, the travelling – since he and the family moved out of London up to Suffolk, via Surrey. 'We just wanted to have a bit of land, a bit of space. There's a lovely feeling of freedom here.

'But since being up here, a few of the small things I used to do have disappeared. I used to play with a couple of local soul bands before I moved, but in rural Suffolk there's hardly any of that here. The openings for me to do the kind of work I did in the '80s and '90s are limited now. When we got established here, I knew the writing was on the wall, that I wasn't going to be able to do that forever. I'd already done that for thirty, forty years. I did do quite a lot with Dire Straits Legacy before and just after Covid, but apart from that, I've hardly done any live playing, which is a shame. But I have to be match-fit, just in case the phone does ring and I get offered something really nice. I record myself all the time, so I'm always practising. And when you teach, you have to be good.' Andy's most recent lesson was just a couple of hours ago.

'Up here, I write music all the time. I've written lots for TV and stuff like that, which I love. I started writing with Dave Clayton, who was the piano player in Simply Red for twenty or so years. We wrote some real wild electronic dance music together. We wrote three pieces and played them to some people, but hardly anyone got back to us. But the owner of a big production music library in London got in touch. "Andy, you know those three tracks? I really like them."

'So we signed a little non-exclusive deal and I ended up doing four or five albums for this company. That was how I paid the bills. I've built up this repertoire of writing stuff for them. Some of it doesn't get used, but other pieces end up being used all the time, such as this one track that's always on *The Big Bang Theory*, *Gray's Anatomy* and Nigella Lawson's cookery programmes. Oh, and *Homes Under the Hammer*. I've written so much stuff. I've got about 175 pieces that have been published. Four times a year you get royalties from them and it's lovely.'

Outside the window, the Suffolk drizzle is still heavy as the afternoon deepens.

'So my hunger to do what I've done for the last thirty years is not so great now. I've been there and done that, from playing eight sets a night in Hamburg in 1971 to playing with George Michael on the 25 Live tour. I'm happy. And I can wake up in the morning comfortable. During the '70s, I lived in the back of a van for eight years. I've done sleeping on floors, I've done sleeping in vans, I've done travelling up and down the A1, earning no money.'

Not having to slum it on tour any longer is one thing, but a downside of life off the road is no longer sampling those moments of high living, as Andy concludes. 'With Duran, we never ever – well, rarely, at least – checked into an airport. We always had private planes. Looking back, it does all sound rather glamorous, doesn't it? And I would certainly never describe myself as having done what I consider to be hard work.

'Playing music in front of people who love your music isn't hard work.'

Reminisce #7

RCA Building, Manhattan

The elevator up to the eighth floor of the RCA Building – the sky-scraping centrepiece of the Rockefeller Center, later colloquially known as 30 Rock – has heard a good few Brummie accents of late. It's May 1983 and several of the Second City's musical turns have recently ridden upwards to Studio 8H, home of Saturday Night Live. In this particular series of the show, bands from Birmingham have appeared in three of the last five episodes. Last month, Musical Youth were here. The week before that, Duran Duran performed two numbers. Today, Dexys push the button to the eighth floor. We're in the epicentre of the Second British Invasion of the US charts.

Tonight's episode is guest-presented by Ed Koch, the mayor of New York City. Wearing a navy blazer with gold buttons and a primrose-yellow tie, he attempts to transfer his skills on the campaign trail to a television studio. The results are mixed. The band are still in their dressing room when the mayor opens the show, so they don't get to hear him describe President Reagan as 'a wacko', nor hear him send himself up in an awkward fashion ("'Ronald Reagan" sounds like a president. "Ed Koch" sounds like a ball-player from Cincinatti.').

By the time Koch introduces 'the real-good Kevin Rowland and the [sic] Dexys Midnight Runners', Koch's delivery is no less stilted. He hands over to the professionals, a slimmed-down version of the touring band, who run through a live version of 'Come on Eileen'. Although the single is no longer roosting at the top of the Billboard Hot 100, it only vacated the number-one spot yesterday and so tonight's performance will attempt to slow its descent down the charts. Later on, they also play a spirited version of 'The Celtic Soul Brothers'.

Enthusiastically received by the SNL audience, this is one of the last outings for the band in their raggle-taggle phase. The well-heeled displays of Brooks Brothers, whose 6th Avenue branch stands in the shadow of the RCA Building, are already calling.

17

John 'Rhino' Edwards

Bass, 1982–83, 1984

'I absolutely adored being in Dexys. I loved it. I'd have done it for no money.'

He's played thousands of gigs, tuned up at thousands of sound-checks, sat in on tens of thousands of rehearsals. But John Edwards isn't averse to learning something new, even now that he's crossed the threshold into his seventies. The man known as Rhino has just discovered a knob on his amp that he's not noticed before. And he hasn't got a clue what it does.

Not one for unsolved mysteries, John plugs in his bass and enlists the chief tool of tonight's sound engineer – his finely tuned ears – to see if turning the knob up and down makes any discernible differ-ence to the sound. If it does, it's minimal – and, even then, it's only detected by a professional with acute hearing.

'How have I not spotted that before?' John rhetorically asks his fellow bandmates. No one answers. I ask whether it's a new amp.

'Nah. I've had it for eight years . . .'

It's a late Saturday afternoon in the back room at the Railway Inn in Winchester. John is the first member of his trio, Rhino's Revenge, to set up for tonight's gig. Leon the drummer – who, rather notably, has been Status Quo's drummer for a decade now – walks back and forth between his car and the stage, carrying drums of varying size.

Craig the guitarist, also of the outfit Romeo's Daughter, takes the tool of his trade out from its case. At the back of the room, Adam, who sells the band's records and T-shirts, is wrestling with a trestle table.

While he waits for his two bandmates to set up, John tests his mic by reciting the day's football results. Or, rather, one result in particular – that of the west London derby between his beloved Brentford and a certain team from just off the King's Road.

'Chelsea 0, Brentford 2.'

A pause while he savours the sweet taste of these words.

'That's Chelsea 0, Brentford 2.'

Another slight pause before the facade of the impartial results announcer slips.

'Get in!' he yells, launching into the bassline from the Stranglers' 'Peaches'.

With seven decades under his belt – and looking, in hoodie, jeans and trainers, ridiculously younger than his years – John shows no sign of slowing down. He's been Status Quo's bass player since the mid-'80s when he replaced founder member Alan Lancaster. But decades of playing some of the largest venues across Europe haven't dried up his enthusiasm, nor blunted his blade. The urge to play live, whether in a well-upholstered enormodome or, as tonight, in the back room of a pub, has never evaporated. He'll barely break even this evening, but that's not the point. Love, not money.

Half an hour later, with the soundcheck done, we head upstairs to the dressing room, where I want to grill John not so much about the Status Quo years, but more about the period in his professional life directly before that, namely his tenure as Giorgio Kilkenny's replacement in Dexys.

But, first, we need to trace the time prior to then, to understand how he got to the point of receiving a nod from Kevin Rowland. But before even that, a disclaimer is issued from across the table. 'One of my school reports said, "John possesses a mass of irrelevant information, which he chooses to impart to the whole class at random." I'm afraid I do flit around a bit, that's all I'm saying.'

It turns out that his first instrument, which he took up at primary school, would have been the perfect fit for *Too-Rye-Ay*-era Dexys. 'I was taught violin at school. After two lessons, my violin teacher, Mrs Shipton, walked all the way to my mum and dad's house, as we were quite hard-up and didn't have a phone. "I really need to teach your son. He's really, really good." So she gave them a rate and they scrimped and saved. And I was good. I got a weekend scholarship to the London College of Music. The idea was that you do three years there, keep in touch and then go there properly from school.'

That was the plan, at least.

'Then I heard the Beatles. I heard "Love Me Do" and that was it. I wanted to be the fifth Beatle. By the time I was fourteen, I'd lost all interest in the violin.'

Another revelation would arrive when John was sixteen. He's very precise about the date: 7 November 1969. 'I went to see Free at Richmond Athletic Ground. I saw Andy Fraser and said, "That's it. I want to play the bass. That's what I want to do." It was a complete epiphany. I knew McCartney was a good bass player, but I saw this guy and I just fixated on him. He's still my favourite bass player to this day.

'It was where he played the notes, where he left the gaps. I'd never heard anyone play like that. I thought, *Yeah, I can do that. What you do is my thing. That's what I want to do.* A couple of weeks later, my dad saw an advert in the paper for this band called Maniac Mouse, so I borrowed a bass and went down. We played "Born To Be Wild" and "Hey Joe", and I got the gig. They were a lot older than me. I was in my teens and they were in their mid-thirties. They treated me really badly, though. I used to get a hard time. I was playing in Plymouth in the late '90s or early 2000s, and this guy came up to me. He was the drummer in Maniac Mouse. "We never told you," he said, "but after about three weeks, we realised that, even though you'd only just started playing the bass, you were already better than we were going to be. If any of us were ever going to get anywhere, it was going to be you. And you did it.'"

After Maniac Mouse came a string of bands that benefitted from John's playing. 'It was just gig, gig, gig, gig, gig, gig, gig. I backed Elvis impersonators. I played in loads of working men's clubs . . .' These years as a semi-pro were balanced financially with a job at Exquisite Knitwear, first in the warehouse and then a promotion into the office. Until his phone rang one day in 1976, that is.

John didn't know the voice on the other end of the line, but it belonged to someone who'd been admiring his bass playing from being in the crowd at a gig at the Fulham Greyhound. He was sounding John out about a job playing bass for the French superstar singer, Nino Ferrer. 'After a lot of rigmarole, which involved me telling my work I'd been taken to hospital, I signed up. I went out to live in France for six months. We recorded the worst album known to man. I can't tell you how bad it is. It was appalling.'

John's time in France bore riper fruit through what he labels 'unconscious networking'. The following year, he got another call, this time from a French producer asking if he wanted to try out for a band called Space. They were an electronic outfit who, wearing astronaut helmets while they played, showed themselves to be the Daft Punk of their time. They had a massive hit too; 'Magic Fly' topped the charts across Europe, requiring John – with a bass synth around his neck – to perform with them across the continent. 'That was good fun. I was living in my bedsit in Teddington, getting up at 8 a.m., going to the airport and flying first class to Paris or Rome or wherever. Then I'd be back in my bedsit that evening. It was the most bizarre thing. John Flying, they called me.'

The jobs continued to roll in. Next up was a spell in Judie Tzuke's band, which is where he was anointed with the nickname 'Rhino', on account of his clumsiness. Again, his recruitment into the role yields something of a story. He had bumped into Judie's co-writer at a party, where his level of refreshment had slightly emboldened him.

'He said, "I come to watch you play in Hounslow every Sunday. We've just got the money from Rocket Records to do an album. Do you want to audition for it?"

'"No, not really. I don't want to do auditions."

'"OK, if you can remember my phone number, the gig's yours. 940 5196."

'I phoned him up the next day: "All right? Are we on?"'

Impressively, nearly half a century on, John can still remember that number. 'I'm quite retentive,' he confesses. 'And not necessarily in a good way.'

Then fate, destiny, kismet or providence – whatever you want to call it – intervened. John was on his way to a meeting at Rocket Records' offices when he realised he'd left a cassette in his flat, so he dashed back to retrieve it. When he arrived home, the phone was ringing. Should he answer it? He was already running late for that meeting. But he did. Opportunity knocks, but it also rings.

'"Hello John, it's Steve Torch."'

Steve Torch was a bass player who would later co-write the Cher monster hit, 'Believe'. He was also an associate of Kevin Rowland.

'He said, "Kevin's just asked me to join Dexys. I've told him I'm not good enough, but that I know someone who is. And that someone is you."

'They were at Good Earth Studios, so I went down there without my instrument.

'"Where's your bass?"

'I thought they just wanted to say hello. They had this image of them being really spiritual and heavy, so I had to find out if we got on. They got me a bass and I added a couple of licks in the song we played. Kevin stopped everything. "What did you do that for? Just play what's on there."

'I got a phone call from them the following morning, asking if I could do this TV show at the BBC. I needed to be there in an hour and a half, but as I was living in Chiswick at that time, I was near Shepherd's Bush. It was for *The Young Ones*. We were playing "Jackie Wilson Said" in the toilet of the house. That was my first appearance with Dexys. I watched the rehearsals of the show with Micky Billingham. "What the hell is this?" It was mental.'

Slipping into the Dexys dungarees for the cameras was no problem. 'I've worn spacesuits, I dyed my hair black for Kim Wilde, I've backed Sandie Shaw while wearing Roman armour, I've worn ski suits in studios where the temperature was thirty-eight degrees . . . I don't care. A uniform is a uniform. It's the music that counts.'

John joined just as 'Come on Eileen' was beginning its descent down the charts, but was an integral part of the promotion for 'Jackie Wilson Said', and on The Bridge tour on both sides of the Atlantic. He wasn't the only newcomer: the new horn section of Nick Gatfield, Spike Edney and Andy Hamilton had just been constructed, and Simon Walker had been appointed to the vacancy in the Emerald Express. 'There was a nucleus of six in the band – Kevin, Seb, Billy, Micky, Helen and Steve. The rest of us were what they used to call the Glittering Luxuries.

'I liked everyone in the band. Kevin had quite a charisma, and it could be quite a negative charisma. He could walk into a room and cast a shadow. Everyone would stop talking. But I never had a single cross word with him. Seb was great. He was basically the sergeant. Micky Billingham was a fantastic player. Listen to the keyboard playing on *Too-Rye-Ay*. It's brilliant – very tasteful. He really was a quality act.'

On one of John's first episodes with the band came the near-death moment that greeted Andy Hamilton on his first day: that electric shock during rehearsals. 'It got up to my shoulder before I managed to throw the guitar off. If it had reached my heart, it would have killed me. It was a proper, proper shock. Then I touched the plug and got another belt. Then this geezer came in. "It's only a bit of electricity." I nearly killed him.'

Serious electrocutions aside, John was in his element in the new band. 'I absolutely adored being in Dexys. I was in the band for the right reasons. It was just a gig for some of the other guys, but I was really, really keen. I loved it. I want Kevin to know that, whatever he thought of me, I was really into it. I'd have done it for no money if there hadn't been any around.'

His love shone through, despite the strictures of the Dexys system. 'Oh, we were regimented. We weren't allowed to look at the audience. We had to stare past them at the exit signs instead.'

John's commitment, his devotion, could be seen every time he was on screen or stage, whether on Saturday-morning kids' TV with a tea-chest bass, or on countless full-blooded performances on The Bridge tour. During the latter, he was nothing short of mesmerising, driving the band along and providing sturdy backing vocals. Other than Kevin himself, it's hard to find anyone else on stage who was more committed, more in the moment than John. And this was despite him being a freelancer, a supposed glittering luxury.

'I almost had a punch-up on stage with this geezer. Well, not a punch-up, but I pushed him really hard. He got up and was giving it all that, so I thought, *Come on then* . . . I was prepared for a serious bundle because I was really into the whole ethos of it.

'I was living the dream. We did *American Bandstand* and *Saturday Night Live*. But there were some long journeys in a sit-up-and-beg bus. I remember one time it was really hot on there. Steve Brennan walked up to the front to ask the driver to turn the heating down.

A voice suddenly comes out. "Turn it back up! That's why it's Kevin Rowland and Dexys Midnight Runners . . .'"

When the second American tour finished, the extended promotional campaign behind *Too-Rye-Ay* was finally over, a full ten months after the album came out. Then came that fateful, prematurely ending evening in Paris supporting David Bowie, after which the band went back to domesticity on civvy street. John returned to being a bass player for hire.

Despite the tour being over, Kevin appeared to still want the band to rehearse. By then, though, John's diary was filling up. His first priority was a month spent zigzagging across Germany with the Climax Blues Band.

'Kevin said, "So, you can't do it?"

'"No."

'"OK, fine."

'And that was that. I was out. But I wasn't sacked.'

It's now time for John's band to take on some pre-gig sustenance. The six of us – me, John, Leon, Craig, Adam and tonight's guest harmonica player, Neil – head out onto the wet, greasy streets of Winchester. Over steaming bowls of chicken hot pot and vegetable yasai, John continues the story. It turns out there's a coda to his Dexys time.

'I got a call from Helen one day.

'"Hello John."

'"You all right, Helen?"

'"We're at Westside Studios."

'"Oh, that's nice."

'"Can you come down? But can you wait in your car? And if you see Randy Hope-Taylor, can you make sure he doesn't see you?"'

So John drove over to Holland Park, where he did as he was asked and sat tight in his car. Then he saw Randy, another bass-playing session musician who would go on to play with the likes of Incognito and Jamiroquai, leave the studio.

'I guessed that some of his work wasn't going to make the cut. So I re-did "This Is What She's Like" and "One of Those Things". There was only Kevin, Helen and Billy from the old band there. Seb had left by then. We were playing "This Is What She's Like" without a click-track, but they were clicking the outro and if it wasn't 124 bpm, we had to do it all over again. I had to do one particular lick on that song about thirty times. But I enjoyed working on *Don't Stand Me Down*. I really got into it. And I note that it made it into the *Observer*'s list of greatest British albums over *Too-Rye-Ay*.'

John wasn't part of the subsequent tour, but he did go to see one of the three nights the band played at the Dominion Theatre on Tottenham Court Road. 'And that was my last connection with Dexys, until I went to see them just a couple of weeks ago, which I really enjoyed. It's a shame that Kevin's got to get his hits out, but that's how it is. I think he got quite realistic about it in the end. I have the utmost respect for him. Huge respect.'

After the *Don't Stand Me Down* sessions came a return to the ranks of the Climax Blues Band, along with work for Peter Green and Kim Wilde. The opening to join Status Quo arrived soon after. 'I was still with Kim when I did my first TV show with Quo. They were both on it. I played with Kim at four o'clock and Quo at six.'

Having swapped the denim dungarees for the trademark double denim, John's life with Quo had begun when he was invited to play on a Rick Parfitt solo album, after which he was co-opted to play on the band's next LP, *In the Army Now*, following Alan Lancaster's move to Australia. 'Then they said, "Do you want to do some gigs?" I didn't really. I was busy. I was touring with Judie Tzuke, plus I'd just got married.

'I said, "How much is it?"' John pauses for a beat, long enough for me to start imagining what the day rate would be for the bass player in Status Quo. It's probably the same amount of time that he spent considering whether to take the job. '"OK, I'll do it!"

'About three weeks into the tour, we were in the Holiday Inn in Belgrade. I was walking along the hotel corridor with Francis Rossi. I said, "I really need to know if I'm in or out." He said, "Oh, you've been in since day one . . ."'

John is now a couple of years shy of having been Quo's bass player for forty years. It turns out that the peripatetic life of a free-lance musician, hopping from job to job, from studio to studio, from tour bus to tour bus, wasn't what he was searching for.

'I've had the most unbelievable career,' he smiles. 'Unbelievable. I've worked for a lot of bands. You develop an innate sense of when to shut your gob. But I always wanted to be *in* a band. That's one of the reasons I loved being in Dexys so much. I always wanted to be in something that's insular. I'm not very good at being matey with other musicians, so Quo is the perfect band for me. I'm among very loyal people. I'd take a bullet for them. No problem.

'Another great thing about Quo is that I'm a good tourist. I like seeing stuff. We'd go to these really obscure places, like Rügen Island off the coast of Germany, and do a gig there. I've been to a lawnmower museum. I've been to a hammer museum. I've been to some amazing art galleries. I always take a big walk on the day of a gig, wherever we are. I try to open my mind regularly. Everywhere, there's something to do and see. Everywhere.'

And between times, in the gaps separating one Quo tour from another, John can then prioritise his own band, switching between songwriting, recording and gigging. 'I have fun with this. It's my ball, whereas Quo is Francis's ball.' He scoops up a final spoonful of chicken hotpot and pushes his bowl towards the centre of the table. 'And a gig's a gig. I don't care where it is.'

Tonight's gig is half a mile away, so it's back out on those wet Saturday-night streets to return to the Railway Inn. An hour later, John, Leon and Craig take to the modest stage, ready to deliver what the hundred-odd punters in the pub have come for – a set of arrow-straight, steel-toecapped bluesy hard rock.

For the next hour and a half, John is given up to the groove, as he invariably was in all those shows with Dexys. Lost in music. No turning back. His head is constantly nodding and moving from side to side. He's locked in, a study in total concentration. It could be a scene from 1982 – only he hasn't got that gravity-defying tam o' shanter perched on his bonce.

Not remotely looking close to someone in their eighth decade, John 'Rhino' Edwards calls the shots at the soundcheck at Winchester's Railway Inn.

Other things are different. John's no longer staring at a faraway fire exit sign. He's looking into the whites of the crowd's eyes. And he's wearing a big beaming smile too. There are few rules in the ranks of Rhino's Revenge.

And there's plenty of banter with the crowd, too, with John's quick, ready wit often called into action. 'That was very Winchester,' he mock-grumbles when greeted by an underwhelming audience singalong.

When the last cheers subside at the end of the night, the punters head home. A night of rocking with Rhino's Revenge will see them through until the next Quo tour next spring. The band soon follow suit. Instruments and amps and musicians disappear into their respective cars, which themselves disappear into the dark, rainy Saturday night, back to London, back for tomorrow's show at the storied Half Moon in Putney.

'And it's a lunchtime gig,' cheers John, punching the air and showing the night's first concession to his age. 'Home in time for *Antiques Roadshow* . . .'

18

Bob Noble

Keyboards, 1982–83, 1984

*'All credit to Kevin. He put his own money where his mouth is and proceeded
to pay for the rest of the album. I hate to think how much it came to.
Probably more than a million quid.'*

In Lake Worth, it appears that only mad iguanas and Englishmen
go out in the midday sun.

The clock has just struck twelve here in the West Palm Beach
suburbs and the temperature is in the nineties. As he has done for
the last twenty-eight years, Bob Noble sits in his favourite chair on
his back porch. There's a fine view of the freshwater lake beyond
the bottom of his backyard, but Bob's only got eyes for the iguanas clambering up one of his palm trees. This is how it rolls in
Florida. It's not only several thousand miles from Bob's hometown
of Leicester, but it's also a lifetime away, a lifetime of being a keyboard player for hire, a keyboard player to the stars.

From January 1983 until the autumn of the following year,
Bob was an on/off member of the Dexys circus. After Micky
Billingham rejected out of hand the idea of touring the US, despite
having no other clear career options, the invitation was extended
to Bob on the recommendation of his old pal Rhino Edwards.
Both had been members of Judie Tzuke's band; indeed, Bob was

still a vital cog in her set-up, but the Dexys tour fell neatly during a fallow period.

Half a decade older than Kevin Rowland, Bob was in his mid-thirties when he received his Dexys call-up papers, by which time he had already made a couple of circumnavigations of the musical block. When he was a teenager, his band travelled to Germany and played the US airforce bases for five years before he joined forces with a singer/guitarist called Paul Muggleton to form a band called Omaha Sheriff.

'I co-wrote the songs with Paul and we got a deal with Tony Visconti's label Good Earth. We released an album, which came out on RCA here in the States.' The problem was that this was 1977 and circumstances beyond their control would dictate the record's trajectory. 'Elvis Presley died and RCA turned their whole plant over to pressing Elvis records. Our album sank like a stone. We did do another album, but it never got released. With Omaha Sheriff defunct, Judie was looking for both a keyboard player and a backing singer, so we joined her band. I played on four albums of hers and toured with her, including being on the bill for that Elton John gig in Central Park in 1980.' Paul went one further; he and Judie got married.

What did he make of the raggle-taggle Dexys brigade on the day he first reported for duty?

'All the people in Dexys were lovely people. I can't say a bad word against them. I'm still friends with some of them to this day, especially Simon Walker and, of course, John. Helen was wonderful and Billy was really nice. I mean, everyone was. Now Kevin, he was a little bit of a different proposition. But he was Kevin Rowland and he always treated me fairly.'

Bob did both US tours, and a European tour in between, during which 'Come on Eileen' reached the summit of the Billboard Hot 100 chart. 'That was why we went back to the States but, strangely, I don't think the gigs that we did on that second American tour were as big as the ones we did initially. They were maybe 2,000-seaters. Something like that. I would have expected bigger crowds than we got.

'It was a strange thing to get to number one in the States. The Dexys sound was different to that of anybody else at the time – maybe more English-sounding. And England is not as straightforward as the States. But, strangely enough, when people have approached me in the past when I've been playing here in Florida, they ask who I've played with. I reel off a list of names, but the one they're most interested in is Dexys.'

On that second trip across the Atlantic, there was the small matter of that *Saturday Night Live* performance. I ask Bob about it, but quickly realise I've made a faux pas. 'I didn't do it. They had a limit to the number of people you could have in the band, which I think was eight. We were an eleven-piece. So I got the heave-ho.' Bob stayed on the sidelines as Nick Gatfield switched his sax for keyboards. Andy Hamilton also sat it out. As the third violinist, Simon Walker didn't make the cut either. 'The performance is probably on YouTube, but I've never looked it up.'

Cruelly denied his moment in the sun on television screens across all fifty states, Bob was nonetheless at one with life on the road. 'It was very hard work but I enjoyed the touring. When I was younger, I actually had a career as a singer. I lived my life backwards, like Orson Welles. I was a great singer when I was eight, but really crap later on. My voice had gone downhill. But when I joined Dexys, there was a lot of backing singing involved. There was a tendency to do a three-minute song and then go over the end for another five minutes. Us backing singers would sing whatever we were singing over and over, while Kevin would be ad-libbing in a soulful way. When I started the tour, I think my top note was E and it went up three semitones during the tour. It was a hard-work gig, but it actually stretched your vocals.'

Once the second American tour was done and dusted, the core of the group went off to plan the next chapter. The hired help went off to find work.

'I didn't feel cast adrift. I toured with Judie when I wasn't touring with Dexys, and I was also working in the studio, doing sessions with several different people. And that was good. That was how I was earning my living. I definitely didn't feel cast adrift.'

At this juncture, Bob reaches into his pocket to retrieve a piece of paper, just as his predecessor Micky Billingham did. 'I actually made a list of people that I played with,' he says, unfolding it. 'I tend to forget.'

There are some impressive names on the list. There was the Japanese tour he did with Bob Geldof, replacing his double-booked former bandmate Spike Edney on keyboards. There was also time served with Feargal Sharkey during the most successful moments of his solo career; with Elkie Brooks, with Belouis Some, with Tanita Tikaram . . . and with Whitney Houston. 'I did a session with her at one point, a backing track for what I think was her fourth single. We used to do backing tracks for people who were doing TV programmes. I think she was doing *Wogan*.

'I did a Brazilian tour with A-ha. That was great – 60,000 people every night for five nights. They were huge in Brazil. There were fans everywhere. There'd be three hundred people outside the hotel at any given time. One day, we were leaving a studio in Rio – me and the three of them: Morten, Pål and Mags. We're walking out and one of these fans turns to me and yells, "'Ere! Are you Pål's dad?" Very humbling.'

A-ha weren't the only representatives of Scandinavian pop royalty whose careers were touched by Bob. He and Paul Muggleton were prolific songwriters and had been signed to a publishing deal by EMI. One of their songs, 'Just One Heart', had been covered by a very high-profile artist – Abba's Agnetha Fältskog, on one of her solo albums. The modest ping of a cash register could be heard.

By this point, though, Bob was back in the Dexys fold. The initial recording sessions for the third album, *Don't Stand Me Down*, had been held at great expense in Mountain Studio in Montreux, but the level of output didn't match the level of outlay. The band returned with just one finished song, 'Listen to This', in their luggage. With pianist Vincent Crane struggling with his mental health, Bob's services were called on again.

'I took the bait,' he chuckles. 'It was strange at the time because I went for an audition with Spandau Ballet, who were going off on a world tour. I phoned them up afterwards to ask if I'd got the gig, but the manager wasn't there and nobody called me back. Then Kevin called me up. "Can you do this album? You'd be on a retainer." So I said yes. Of course, once I said that, I get a call from Spandau's manager, saying I'd got the gig for a six-month tour of the world. But I'd already committed to Dexys.

'Then I got offered a slot on Kim Wilde's tour, but I had to turn that down as well. And then our old tour manager, who was working with Tina Turner, asked if I wanted to audition for her tour. All these things came in at the same time.

'Anyway, we started rehearsing the songs for *Don't Stand Me Down* at Marcus Studios in Fulham and it was very interesting. There was this one twelve-minute number, "This Is What She's Like", which started off at one speed, then slowed down, then gradually slowed down even more, and then sped up to a slightly faster speed than the initial tempo. When we were rehearsing it, Kevin decided that the first part would be at – and I'm using a rough example here – 120 beats per minute, then it would slow down to 80bpm before coming back to 124bpm. Helen would be recording the song on a cassette, then Kevin would play it back and one part might be two beats per minute too slow.

'We went over and over and over it. We must have spent at least a couple of months rehearsing the album. But I was being paid every week, so I was happy enough. Kevin was very insistent on us playing very passionately. This meant he and Billy would play their guitars at full throttle, often breaking strings. I'd previously noticed this on tour – that the roadie was constantly changing strings. Kevin wanted to record everybody at the same time, so we would all come to the studio. He was paying retainers to ten musicians the whole time. Ten musicians were playing and everybody had to get everything right all the time because there weren't supposed to be overdubs. Well, because of guitar strings being broken or people fouling up, it took a long time.

'So we were playing "This Is What She's Like" over and over. Billy had broken a few strings and I think he only had two left, so Woody Woodmansey, the drummer at that point, stopped playing because obviously it wasn't sounding very good. But Kevin says, "That's the one! That's the one!" So even though it had broken down, Woody started playing again and we finished the track. Woody had to tidy it up with overdubs. So, in the death, instead of us playing it all together, everybody finished up doing overdubs.

'Then Woody got replaced. Kevin kept saying to him, "I want you to sound like Al Green's drummer." Woody's really good, but he's not Al Green's drummer. So, ultimately, Kevin actually had to get Al Green's drummer in.' That drummer, Tim Dancy, came with an advantage. A couple of advantages, actually. 'One, he was really good. Two, there was a finite time that he had to do the album before he had to go back to the States to keep playing with Al Green.' Minds were focused. Efforts were productive.

'By this time, we'd moved on to other studios. Vince came back so I started playing organ. We would play throughout the day. All credit to Kevin and Helen and Billy. They would take the day's tapes and listen to them overnight – all night sometimes, however long it took. They put the work in.'

All of this meticulous marshalling of the process came with the meter ticking. 'I can't remember the exact figure – and this is probably hearsay – but I think Phonogram had spent £450,000 on it already and wanted to pull the plug. So, again, all credit to Kevin. He put his own money where his mouth is and proceeded to pay for the rest of the album. I hate to think how much it came to. Probably more than a million quid, a huge amount of money at the time. But we did finish the album.

'I didn't hear from him for two or three months. Then I got a call. "Bob, you've got to come in. The organ was out of tune. You need to redo all your parts." So, having spent months rehearsing and meticulously going through all the tracks in the studio, I went in and, in just one afternoon, did it all.

'I think the album only sold 20,000 copies, something like that. It was a real shame. But Kevin didn't want to put out a single. I think he thought that because people loved Dexys, they wouldn't mind. But the record industry at that time revolved around having hit singles. Unless you were Led Zeppelin, that's what the game was.

'After that, I did an album and a world tour with Joan Armatrading. I also did a tour with Murray Head. One day, his guitarist Phil Palmer called me, asking if I wanted to play with Paul McCartney. Paul wanted to have a blow with some different people. Phil was going to play guitar with him and had recommended me for the keyboards. As luck would have it, Nick Gatfield was working at EMI by then and he recommended me too. Terry Williams from Dire Straits was going to be on drums and obviously Paul on bass. It was 18 June 1987. I remember the date precisely because my wife was pregnant and that was the due date. In fact, she gave birth on 14 June but had to stay in hospital as there would have been nobody for her to go home to. I was with McCartney.'

Bob Noble at home in West Palm Beach, Florida. 'People ask me who I've played with. I reel off a list of names, but the one they're most interested in is Dexys.'

Bob then hooked up with Tanita Tikaram, which meant a reunion with his old fiddle-playing Dexys buddies Helen and Simon; he also played on Helen's debut solo album, *Romanza*. 'After Tanita, I got a gig with Cliff Richard and was with him for seven years, up until 1997. To be honest, I wasn't particularly a fan and the music wasn't my forte. But we broke records. We did eighteen Wembleys and fifteen NECs – the record for playing consecutive nights at each of them. Twelve thousand people a night.

'It was while I was touring with Cliff that we decided to move to the States. I was travelling all over the world, so it didn't matter where we lived. We moved to Seattle, where my wife is from. I met Jan in 1980. We met halfway up the Eiffel Tower. I was on tour with Judie, and

Jan was spending the money that she got from her divorce. We met waiting for the lift to go to the top. And we're still married.

'To be honest, moving to the States wasn't a wise career move. When I arrived in Seattle, I visited all the studios. Then, though, the place was in the middle of grunge. Everything was Nirvana, Soundgarden, you name it. I couldn't get arrested. There just wasn't the session work for keyboard players. We spent three years there. One day we were visiting friends in Florida and I just said, "Why are we in Seattle, where I don't know if I can get any work, when we could be sitting in the sunshine? I could set up a studio here." And that's what I did.

'Somehow, I ended up playing in Irish bands too. We got a great band together called Fire in the Kitchen, with a couple of members of the Irish Rovers and a violinist from China who could play Irish music. She came to live with us for nine months and became part of our family. We had a residency in Fort Lauderdale for seven years, before it whittled away to being just me and a guy called Bobby O'Donovan playing the pubs.

'In the meantime, I'd set up the studio and started producing a Gaelic singer called Jennifer Licko. I've done four or five albums for her, and toured with her in North and South Carolina. She's currently doing a revue called the Highland Echoes Show – basically it's a Scottish version of *Riverdance*. Nobody's been coming here to record it, though. Jennifer lives in Brazil, as does the drummer, and the fiddle player, Pat Mangan, lives in New York. They send me tracks, I send tracks out, and somehow it gets done. Then it gets mixed and mastered by my friend Mike Paxman in the UK.' It's a global endeavour: Brazil, Florida, New York . . . and Walton-on-Thames.

Bob doesn't have to travel far to his studio. From the backyard, it's just through the fly screen door and down the hallway. All those years ago, he commandeered a bedroom for the purpose, in which a large mixing desk takes centre stage, along with his piano. An adjacent room houses the sound booth. Just as in the homes of other Dexys alumni, there are gold and silver discs on the wall. But these are from Bob's work with Judie Tzuke. His only recordings with Dexys were for *Don't Stand Me Down*, which certainly didn't win any accolades for bountiful sales. There is also a plaque commemorating that record-breaking run of shows with Cliff Richard.

Bob apologies for the mess in the studio. 'We're moving back to Seattle next year and have started packing everything up in boxes. It's a nightmare as we never throw anything away. It's going to cost a fortune to move us over there, so we've got a few months ahead of us of selling things or giving them away.' Whether the mixing desk makes the journey with them has yet to be decided. 'We've been looking at how much it costs to move it and it's a bit frightening. I'd like to keep it. I wouldn't get much money for it. Of course, that size of desk isn't necessary these days. You can do everything with a small desk. But . . .

'Also, Seattle is one of the most expensive places in the States, so we would probably get a house less than half the size of this one for possibly more money. Our son and his wife live there, and Jan's family. As you get geriatric, you want family around you to wheel you into the emergency room. I'm seventy-five now. I'm ready for the old people's home.'

Bob closes the door of the studio, closing the door on the mess. Back on the back porch, the iguanas are still scurrying up and down the palm trees, much to his continued amusement. After nearly three decades in Florida, he'll miss the mixing desk if it gets left behind. But he might just miss his reptilian friends even more.

Reminisce #8

Hagley Road, Birmingham

The end of the working day. The hour when the city turns blue. Twilight.

A mile west of Birmingham city centre, a crescent of five-storey brick apartment blocks sits anonymously out of sight, largely hidden behind trees as tall as the buildings themselves. This is Kenilworth Court, a gated – if not guarded – community.

The black metal gates ease open every couple of minutes, a soft parade of Audis and BMWs bringing executives home. Forty-odd years ago, a white Volkswagen Golf convertible would slide in and out of these gates, driven by one of the country's most recognisable pop stars. Artisans used to live here among the executives, you see. Musical craftsfolk. Kenilworth Court was once the home of Kevin Rowland and Helen O'Hara. The Kennels, they called it.

This is where the couple, plus Billy Adams, drew up the blueprint for what would become Don't Stand Me Down. *They worked out of their flat, with Billy arriving every morning, ready for business. Close your eyes and you can hear the growl of his motorbike arriving at the gates.*

The only music being made here these days is the ambulance's siren song, a frequent refrain along Hagley Road. Repeat to fade.

At lunchtime, every lunchtime, the Golf would leave the premises, heading west on Hagley Road, down towards Bearwood a couple of miles away. There the three of them would carry on their discussions, fine-tuning their ideas at a neighbourhood tea-room called the Little Nibble. It was an extension of the first Dexys gang chewing the fat at the Apollonia – a reprised, reduced version of the teams that meet in caffs.

The Little Nibble served its last pot of tea many moons ago. But its memory lives on in song, immortalised by a namecheck in Kevin and Billy's spoken-word intro to 'This Is What She's Like'. Nowadays, sandwiched between a laser hair-removal specialist and a chiropractor clinic, 522 Bearwood Road is a fast-food chicken outlet – Metro's. It boasts about its wares with the slogan

231

'It's the Real Taste'. The schoolkids mingling outside, counting their change to see if they can afford some after-school peri-peri fries or a portion of onion rings, have no idea about what used to go on behind these doors. And, let's be honest, nor would they care.

19

Kev 'Billy' Adams

Guitar and banjo, 1981–86

'At the time, it did feel like we'd ultimately failed as a band.'

There are no iguanas in Kev Adams' back garden. Bridgnorth isn't known for them.

But all manner of wildlife is currently invading from every direction. The bird feeders are swinging wildly, thanks to the acrobatics of a pair of magpies, while a squirrel bounds across the lawn, followed by a waddling female Mallard duck, newly arrived from the lake across the open fields beyond.

None of these creatures seem perturbed by Kev's partner Sara painting the back fence. A-level student son Jake will soon be home from college. BBC Radio Shropshire plays softly on the kitchen radio.

While the kitchen and dining room are show-home spotless, it's a different matter in another reception room off the hallway. Behind the door is a delicious jumble of instruments – from mandolins to modular synths – and general ephemera: a collection of Kev's notebooks and diaries from his time in the group; tour programmes; computer keyboards; leads and cables; several books on the Fall; and even the match-day programme from a recent Wolves home game against Brentford.

At the far end, a table-tennis table stands upright, folded in half and gathering dust. On the wall is a framed four-foot-high poster featuring Dexys in 1985, shot on the streets of New York City. Kevin Rowland, obviously, takes centre stage, looking – in his fedora and wearing a mac over his Brooks Brothers suit – every inch the young Sinatra. Helen and Kev are to his left, equally well-attired. Nick Gatfield is on Kevin's right, the furthest away, gazing in the opposite direction. He appears not to have got the memo: he's wearing jeans. 'He's got nice shoes on though,' notes Kev, coming to the sax player's defence.

This particular image was part of the limited promotional campaign around the release of *Don't Stand Me Down*. Despite the amount already spent on multiple recording studios and multiple session musicians, the expenses kept racking up. Nick Gatfield flew to New York just for this photoshoot. He arrived on Concorde.

Gazing at this photo takes Kev back to 1985. He, Kevin and Helen were already in Manhattan to apply the finishing touches to the album. For Kev, this involved him endlessly recording his spoken-word contributions to certain songs, the in-song conversational passages between him and Kevin.

'The ad-libs in rehearsal were often quite funny, but as time went on, there were less ad libs and more set lines. It became "acting". The very last overdubs in New York at Electric Ladyland were an absolute nightmare. It was just me on the mic, with Kevin and Helen in the control room and Kevin clicking on the talkback every two minutes going, "No, not like that". We rolled again and again and again . . . I'd usually back any decision until it was bang-on, but it had just got too much by that point. I couldn't wait to leave New York and get away from it.

'Acting was out of my comfort zone. I felt a fraud and didn't believe in myself. If it were part of a natural performance, as "This Is What She's Like" became, then that was fine. But I never enjoyed "One of Those Things". It just seemed a bit glib with me going "Oh yeah" in the right place every time.'

It had been a long, sometimes tortuous process to reach the stage of the final overdubs, beginning many, many months before with those initial songwriting sessions at The Kennels, Kevin and Helen's flat in Kenilworth Court on Hagley Road. 'I remember it being a great flat,' says Kev, 'high ceilings and nicely furnished. And I do remember, right at the start, Kevin playing the Beach Boys and the main take-away being that this was a fantastic opportunity to use any line-up needed for the songs. No more "We are a brass-led band" or "We have a strings-led sound". It was a completely blank slate.'

After recruiting what turned out to be the first *Don't Stand Me Down* line-up, and rehearsing intensely at Outlaw Studios in Birmingham, the first stop was Mountain Studios in Montreux, with the sainted Tom Dowd as producer, the veteran of many legendary soul and jazz recordings. A month in Switzerland only yielded that one song, 'Listen to This'.

'I think we were actually quite pleased to have at least one song from it. The main frustration was that everything had sounded and felt so good back in Brum at Outlaw, but it just didn't come together in Montreux. We weren't quite burnt out from it yet, though, so probably raring to get going with the next line-up. I don't think any of us suffered from despondency. We were very driven and we knew those songs could work with the right line-up. I can't speak for the session players, though. We must have been a nightmare.

'We put pressure on ourselves to get it right and the money could take care of itself. Fine in theory! Obviously re-setting each time, including another round of auditions, became a little frustrating by the third time. On each occasion, though, we thought we'd cracked it before we arrived at the studio.

'The live recording was mainly to capture the feel for the bass and drums. That period was *all* about the feel. The tempo had to be bang on, so part of the reason was that it was so hard to find a drummer with the right feel and great time-keeping. Finally, Tim

Dancy came in from Memphis and there it was, right there. Tim arrived and we recorded the rest of the songs in a few days.'

When those last overdubs were in the can and the final mixing was complete, the three-person nucleus were both pleased and relieved with the results. 'We were very proud of the finished record. There was never any doubt about that. It was a complete album and we didn't think there was an obvious single on there, so when Kevin suggested releasing it only as an album, I supported that 100 per cent. With hindsight – and with the record company giving up on us – obviously that wasn't a good decision. But, who knows, it may have worked, had we had the full backing of Phonogram.

'It's been said more than once since, and I probably agree now, but "Listen to This" would have made a great single. It didn't feel like that at the time, though. I don't think it represented us, or the album. It's one of my all-time favourite Dexys tracks now – easily in my top three.

'As we approached the release date, Kevin and I went to visit the chairman of Phonogram. He had an enormous office with a huge, roaring log fire and a lovely big dog on the rug in front of it. He was very amiable and seemed supportive, but ultimately it made no difference.' He pauses for a beat or two. 'It's weird how my main memory is of that dog and that roaring fire.

'It was the bane of a multi-album deal. You sign up with a super-enthusiastic A&R person who fights your corner in the weekly promo meetings. If they know their arse from their elbow, soon enough they get headhunted and are off to greener pastures, leaving a band without anyone in their corner at the record company. All is fine while the band is making money for the company, but once that dries up, no one cares a jot about the band's development and future possibilities. You're either cash cow or history. It makes you realise that there are many, many decent albums out there that got shelved without even getting released, for want of an insider with a little imagination and clout.'

Kev runs a palm over his silvering goatee.

'At the time, though, it did feel like we'd ultimately failed as a band. The album disappeared without a trace for most people. It's been mythologised over the years, as these things are. It's mostly a revisionist success story, but that's just fine. It has meant a lot to people and that's a success in itself. But the reality at the time was that it was a struggle to get this band of very good musicians to play the songs the way we wanted them to be.'

He turns to face that framed poster, here in his room, here behind a door that's usually closed. 'It's the only place I could put it. If it were out on display and I saw it every time I popped upstairs, it would be too much.'

We head into the dining room and take our seats. At the point of *Don't Stand Me Down*'s release and rapid invisibility, Kev had served in three iterations of Dexys across nearly five years. When he joined in January 1981, the well-heeled recording studios of Montreux and Manhattan would have felt very remote. They would have felt even more remote a few years earlier, in the Bridgnorth household in which he grew up. Here, the Dansette record player had long since been terminally damaged by one of his younger brothers snapping the arm off it. So when Kev wanted to play the first album he owned – one by local heroes Slade – he had to go round to friends' houses to hear it.

'I remember hearing "Gudbuy T'Jane" in a music lesson at school and my ears pricked up: "What's that?!" That was the first band where I noticed the guitar looked cool. I loved the sound of it. And as ridiculous as it might seem, I thought Dave Hill looked quite good, with the glitter and the platform boots and everything.'

Another epiphany was hearing the Isley Brothers' *3 + 3*, an album-of-the-week selection on Radio Luxembourg. Ernie Isley's guitar grabbed the young teen's ear, turning him onto soul and funk. He began to amass a sizeable collection of northern soul singles. When he was fourteen, an acoustic guitar arrived at Christmas and led him towards heavy rock, in particular Status Quo and Black Sabbath. 'I was a typical obsessed teenager. It was music and motorbikes. I had a BSA Bantam when I was fourteen for dicking about with in the fields. I later drove my parents mental as I wanted a moped, but instead they bought me an electric guitar and amp for my sixteenth birthday.'

With his mates, he was playing rock 'n' roll, 'like Chuck Berry, but quite fast and through fuzzboxes that I'd made. When punk happened, we just had to play a little faster.' Punk had another effect on the eldest son of the Adams family. 'At sixteen or seventeen, I thought I didn't need those records of mine any more, so I sold all my classic old northern soul singles and my rock albums, just so I could go out and have a couple of beers in town.' The note of regret is still sharp.

After two years at college in Wolverhampton, at eighteen Kev moved to Bearwood in Birmingham to live with his grandparents while he studied at the city's polytechnic. He answered an ad in the paper placed by a new-wave pop band in search of a guitarist. 'Pop wasn't ideal, but it was in Bearwood. So I went to the bass player's house. He was getting his hair cut. The guy cutting it was a musician himself, but also a jobbing hairdresser. He was really chatty. It was Kevin Rowland.'

Kev was invited to audition for this new-wave outfit that weekend, at a rehearsal room they shared with Dexys in Birmingham city centre. Having passed the test (his main competition was a guy with a Fender Stratocaster who 'took about twenty-five minutes to tune up and then struggled with what they wanted him to do'), he then went out with his new bandmates that evening to see a certain band at the Barrel Organ. 'Dexys came on and they completely blew me away. I'd never seen anything like them before. It was the way they were spread out across the front and attacked the microphones. They wore soul on their sleeves but were rooted in punk.'

Kev then also started getting his hair cut by Kevin Rowland. 'One day, he said, "That band you're in. They're not really going anywhere, are they?" I said, "They're my mates, you know." Then he said something quite Machiavellian.

'"Well, you can be loyal to your mates or you can be successful."

'He asked me what sort of band I'd like to be in.

'"I love Dexys. I love what you're doing."

'"I'll remember that."

'I took it with a pinch of salt. Then, a few weeks later, he came around and asked if I'd go for a walk to have a chat. So we did. He said, "I've fallen out with Kevin Archer. Would you be interested in playing guitar in the band? The only thing is, we'd need you to sing." I said I wasn't sure about singing. Kevin Archer is a great guitarist and singer in his own right. I didn't hear from him for a couple of weeks. Then I went to see them play and Kev Archer was still there. They'd obviously patched things up. He was a big part of the band.

'Then they started disappearing off my radar. Throughout '79, they were slowly playing less and less. And I never gave it another thought. I was studying for my HND and also still coming back to Bridgnorth, where I still had a significant group of friends. We had a car between us and we started travelling around going to gigs. We'd go all over the shop, seeing Buzzcocks or the Ramones or Siouxsie and the Banshees or whoever. I told them about Dexys. The first thing they saw of them was Dexys doing "Dance Stance" on *Top of the Pops*. It would have been fantastic to someone who didn't know what they were, but I was appalled they'd turned "Burn it Down" into "Dance Stance" and watered it down. I thought, *What a shame. They could have been great*. Then the next thing was "Geno". And I didn't like that. And I never bought the album because I'd heard it and I knew they were loads better than that live.'

Kev takes a sip from a *Twin Peaks* mug with the legend "Damn Fine Coffee" on the side. Today it contains tea.

Come Christmas 1980, Kev had returned home from Birmingham to his mum and dad's in Bridgnorth. Waiting for him was a message to call Kevin Rowland. 'I hadn't seen them since late '79, so this was more than a year later. I phoned him back. He told me about the band splitting up, how it had been quite acrimonious, and how Kevin Archer had also decided that he'd like to go and try his own thing. So would I like to come over for another chat?

'We met at the Hasty Tasty café in the Bullring. I was straight with him. I told him that I'd always loved Dexys, but that I wasn't knocked out by *Searching for the Young Soul Rebels*, that the recording hadn't captured their raw power and their live magic. But I'd still love to join them.'

Kev had become the final member of the second coming of Dexys, joining the new rhythm section of Seb Shelton and Steve Wynne, sax players Paul Speare and Brian Brummitt, and keys player Micky Billingham. Just as Kevin Archer had become 'Al' to avoid confusion, another Kevin in the line-up required another change of name.

'If you really believe in what you're doing, you keep going and you make it work.' Kev Adams on holiday in Pembrokeshire.

'I was quite happy being Kevin. It felt like a big decision because I was going to carry it around with me for a while. But I couldn't come up with anything. Then Kevin said, "I've written a few ideas down." It was just stream-of-consciousness stuff. He'd just written names as they occurred to him. The list literally started with Tom, Dick, Harry . . . I can't remember whether it was him, or someone else in the band, who came up with "Billy". A few people said that would suit me. So I agreed, as long as no one called me William. And from that day after, Micky Billingham would always go "William!" And, unfortunately, "Billy the Boy" became a thing too.'

Having only just left his teens, the newly christened Billy was the baby of the bunch. The likes of Kevin and Seb were in their late twenties by then. 'To a baby-faced twenty-year-old, that was as old as the hills. I was slightly in awe of these guys with their experience. I remember going into the first rehearsal and knocking the guitar amp over on its wheeled flight case. Seb goes, "It's nice to know we're working with professionals." Seb was the guy whose job it was to drill the new boys. He got me a metronome, which wasn't too subtle.

'Seb also told me I wasn't playing the guitar correctly – that, in order to look as if I meant it, I had to play from the shoulder. That sounded ridiculous but it's what I then did. I learned a style where I absolutely destroyed guitars. Strings would be flying off all over the place. And that all came from Seb telling me to play with my shoulder. Also, the two Kevins had developed this love of super-heavy guitar strings, with lots of tension, being wound so tight. That's part of the reason they would break too. They were practically bass strings. The guys in the music shop on Broad Street used to laugh. "We only keep these for you."

'My fingernails used to break and my fingers would be bleeding at the end of the day. My nan told me I needed to grow the fingernails on my right hand. Apparently, the best way to grow them faster is to eat whole packets of jelly. It might have been an old wives' tale, but I did it because I was in so much pain. I also put my sore left hand in a bowl of white spirit to soothe it.'

All eyes were on the new boy, whose youth and comparative lack of experience meant he had much to prove. 'When I joined in January '81, I wasn't the least bit influential. I was more fighting for my place. I'd walk in the room and I used to overhear Brian Brummitt in his Geordie accent, deliberately talking loudly, saying, "Of course, you're only as strong as your weakest member." It wasn't just Brian. Because I was really baby-faced, I think they thought I was about sixteen.'

Billy joined just in time for the journey down to west London to record 'Plan B'. 'The first studio I ever walked in in my life was Abbey Road. You can imagine that was an experience. We got there a little early. We checked in, took the gear into the live room and said hello to the engineer and the tape op. Brass players are famous for liking a drink and one of them said, "Have you heard? There's a bar here." So we went through to the bar and got a pint in. All of a sudden, there's Kevin stood there, absolutely seething.

'"What are you playing at?"

'"We've got a bit of time to kill."

'"You wouldn't drink if you were in an office job, would you?"

'Seb had quickly reinforced to me on day one that I had joined Kevin's band. He explained the hierarchy, with me pretty much on probation as the last to join. And Kevin was right about the drinking thing. Sometimes the way he went about things wasn't the most tactful, but his intentions were good.'

Not only did Kevin outlaw pre-rehearsal/pre-recording session drinking and instigate a no-drugs rule within the band, but he also attempted to instil a culture of physical fitness and discipline. Several of the band took up running, an image reinforced by that photo session at Hadley athletics stadium in Smethwick that Paul Speare showed me. Kev digs around in a cardboard folder, trying to locate a photo or two of his own from that very shoot.

'We were telling that story – that we all go out jogging in the morning, that we jog to rehearsals. But the only two occasions that all eight members of the band ran together was for this photoshoot and for a segment on the *Oxford Road Show* on TV. It was all for show. I remember Kevin telling me, "If the truth is too boring, you've got to make something up."' Just like his story about finding Helen. 'It wasn't "Oh, Kevin Archer passed me her number and Jimmy and Paul Speare popped down to find her". It was "I met this girl at a bus stop and she was carrying a violin case . . ."'

Presumably not by design, today Kev could be auditioning for Dexys circa 1981. He's got his hair pulled back in a ponytail. He's wearing a light-coloured T-shirt underneath a zipped-up hoodie, and tracksuit bottoms. All that's missing are the boxer boots. But he is indoors, I suppose.

His ponytail is far more developed than it was in 1981. 'There's only one photo with me in my headband before my hair was long enough to have a ponytail. Amazingly, some people's hair would never grow. They were obviously having secret trims.'

The personal discipline ran in parallel with the collective discipline. And the new eight-piece, with Kevin and Jimmy the only survivors from *Searching for the Young Soul Rebels*, were in deep preparation for their first tour, the Projected Passion Revue. They retreated en masse to Newcastle, hometown of manager 'Basher' Burton. Alongside his hairdressing salons, he also owned a cinema in Gosforth, inside which Dexys were swiftly installed to rehearse their new stage show.

'We went up there for about three months and that's what we did all day, every day. We'd rehearse stage movements during certain songs, where exactly you'd put your feet so it wasn't just people running about, tangling guitar leads and mic leads. We even got wooden pretend monitors made as there were certain songs where we'd charge to the front and leap onto the monitors. These weren't going to be gigs. They were going to be *shows*.'

However, despite the intense and lengthy rehearsal schedule, the curtailing of the first wave of the Projected Passion Revue left just those three dates to fulfil. 'There was quite a short attention span for bands at the time. If you hadn't had a record in the shops for six to twelve months, you would be relatively forgotten. So the tour was shorter than it was supposed to be. I think only the Dominion show in London was sold out.'

It turned out that attempting to include the audience in the phi-losophy of personal discipline, by closing the bars in the theatres on the tour, wasn't the most commercial of moves. 'It was a daft idea,' declares Kev. 'It didn't bring more people out. No one said, "Oh fantastic, they're closing the bars. I'll *definitely* go now."'

'Musically, and as a show, that original Projected Passion Revue tour was a success. We were getting better all the time. By the end of the year, we were so tight. There was a spiritual element too, where you were trying to get outside of yourself. The "projected passion" thing came from playing with your head up, looking right to the back of the room or right to the top of the balcony, and you project to every single person in that room. It might sound slightly pretentious to the wrong person, but this is what Dexys were.'

The three shows at the Old Vic at the end of 1981 were among the greatest performances any incarnation of Dexys has ever pro-duced, but – with the horn players playing (or miming) their new stringed instruments on a couple of songs – the foundations of future discontent were being laid, especially when the Emerald Express were recruited early on in the New Year.

'I would hear things that Kevin wouldn't hear because they wouldn't say them in front of him, but they were happy to say them in front of me. I think they were trying to recruit me into the brass-is-best team, but I was actually on the let's-do-something-different side. That's the way I am anyway. I was agitating for change. In retrospect, we'd never be as good as the first band. They made those songs their own and we could only be an imitation. We had new songs like "The Celtic Soul Brothers" and things were evolving – just not fast enough for me. I always want to do something new. I never finish anything myself ever.'

Just as Micky Billingham had swapped the organ for piano and accordion on *Too-Rye-Ay*, so too did Kev trade his guitar for banjo on a handful of tracks, most notably 'Come on Eileen'. Kevin Rowland's first suggestion had been the mandolin, so Kev popped to his local music shop round the corner on Bearwood Road to buy both instrument and a book on mandolin chords. 'It was an absolute nightmare to play. I found it physically difficult to hold down the strings. I gave it a good go for at least a week but wasn't getting anywhere with it, so Kevin suggested banjo instead. I thought it was a comedy instrument. I wasn't interested in bluegrass or country music or trad jazz, but I'd give anything a go. Again, I got a banjo and a book of chords. Eventually I found a tuning that fitted with most of the songs that we'd already written. Years later, I was round a mate's house and he had a mandolin. I picked it up and it was so easy to play. Back then, I'd simply bought a cheap mandolin which hadn't been set up properly. I'd been thinking that all mandolins were a bastard to play . . .'

At this point, I rudely interrupt Kev mid-flow. I can hear something from the kitchen. He suffers from poor hearing – the result of playing too many loud guitars and riding too many noisy motorbikes, plus a fondness for techno in the early '90s. So quiet is the radio that he can't hear what I'm hearing, so I signal to him to follow me into the kitchen. The afternoon presenter on BBC Radio Shropshire is playing 'Come on Eileen'. I've identified Kev's twanging banjo from an adjacent room.

It's great timing as, with the horn section having departed and the Emerald Express taking that lead guitar role, we've arrived in the summer of 1982 – the time of *Too-Rye-Ay*, the time of 'Come on Eileen'. Of the latter, Kev reveals the crucial factor that earned the struggling single crucial radio play. 'It could have quite easily flopped were it not for a radio plugger called Brad. He was owed a couple of favours at Radio 1 as we'd played a big live show in Newcastle for them in June. A few of the producers refused to play the single, so Brad went in to see the people behind some of the evening shows. He called in favours and got some plays. People bought it and it snowballed. But it was so close to not happening. And then the band would have split up, without a shadow of a doubt.'

That Radio 1 show in Newcastle, with the already-departed Brian and Jimmy returning to the fold for one night only, was the last that the line-up on *Too-Rye-Ay* would play together. From then on, for both extensive promo work and that autumn's tour, Dexys was now an amalgam of an ever-shrinking nucleus of permanent members and a shifting cast of session musicians. And that's how it would be from then until today. 'Not to do them a disservice – as we played with some excellent players and they were great to travel with – but it was a totally different dynamic. They were on much better money for starters . . .'

After the second US tour the following spring, that restless urge to move on, which Kev shared with Kevin, closed the door on the *Too-Rye-Ay* era. 'People fell away. Seb was probably the last to go but that was fine. He was newly married and obviously wanted to spend more time with his wife. Perhaps he wasn't so much into the new material, although he remained as positive as always.' Dexys, once an eight-strong democracy, was now a three-person nucleus.

Then came the extended and extensive work to fashion the new songs into what ultimately became *Don't Stand Me Down*, those innumerable recording sessions that were, says Kev, 'somewhere between intense and batshit'. For him, the year 1985 was 'all about the unfulfilled potential of a band that could have been huge and it felt like we failed. Helen and I had gone to Nashville to audition musicians for the Coming to Town tour. We got a largely American band together to go on the road and promote the album, but the dates were relatively poorly attended. There was also little TV. We were supposed to do a feature on *The Tube*, but there was industrial action and it got cut short to ten minutes.'

That year, Kevin and Helen moved out of Kenilworth Court and down to London. After contributing 'Because of You' as the theme tune to *Brush Strokes*, work began on the next Dexys album. Still living in Shropshire, Kev's week consisted of 'dicking around with my motorbikes and then, every Wednesday, riding down to London to see Kevin and Helen. They'd use me as a sounding board. "This is what we've been working on. What do you think?" That was my contribution. Then I'd ride home.

'I wasn't sure what to do with myself. You know how you can just blunder on day to day but drift apart. I wasn't enjoying it but only afterwards, when it was all over, did I realise this. I enjoyed messing around with motorcycles more than playing with Dexys, but couldn't for the life of me work out a way to make a living out of that . . .

'It was a massive relief when Kevin said he wanted the new songs to be for a solo album. He didn't know how I'd take it, having worked together since 1981, five years earlier. It was like the world was lifted off my shoulders. I wouldn't have wanted to walk away from Dexys because it was my life, but this was the kick up the arse I needed in order to go and do something different.'

After a spell living in London himself when his girlfriend got a job in Harrods ('while she went to work, my morning routine consisted of having breakfast, watching *Neighbours* and fiddling with my synths and samplers'), Kev retreated home to Shropshire. Back in 1983, looking for somewhere to store his growing collection of motorbikes, he'd bought a derelict house a dozen miles outside Bridgnorth with the proceeds from the previous year's royalties. 'I bought it for £26,000. I just wrote a cheque.' One day, while having an oil tank installed, such was his mania for all things motorbikes, he asked the guy driving the JCB if he could construct a few jumps on the two-thirds of an acre of land that came with the house. The driver created a full motocross track in the back garden.

Having spent £30,000 doing the house up, Kev found he didn't have the money to continue making music professionally, especially when he discovered the dire financial straits in which he'd been placed by the band's accountants. The house had to be sold off; Kev was only saved by the strength of the housing market at that point. 'I did have some hard times in the early '90s,' he confides. 'Mum and Dad would come round with a box of groceries.'

Kev's old Dexys bandmate Nick Gatfield, who was in his job at EMI by then, gave him some money to make a demo, so a studio in Coventry was booked and three songs recorded. Kev opens his laptop and presses play on one of these songs, 'You Drive Me Mad'. It's a fine pop song, with a big synth-driven melody, and male/female vocals interweaving with each other. Kev's vocals are very strong, with echoes of Pete Wylie, Marc Almond and Dr Robert from the Blow Monkeys.

'I remember seeing someone at EMI Publishing. "I'm very sorry, but this sort of thing doesn't appeal to me. Let me play you a tape of the sort of thing we're supporting at the moment." It was just big, crashy '80s drum synth bullshit. I said, "I don't want to hear any more. I'll have my tape back now." It's easy to think, *What if, what if*... but if you really believe in what you're doing, you keep going and you make it work. I just didn't have enough songs. And it always comes back to the songs, doesn't it?'

Kev then set up a video business, making martial arts demonstration films and, more often, wedding videos. 'I had to edit about seven hours of footage down to an hour and a half or so, but I was good at it. Everyone was always really pleased, even if I had to use the Carpenters' "We've Only Just Begun" more often than I would have liked. But I didn't want to do it for a living. There wasn't the job satisfaction that I got from music.'

Around this time, though, Kev got a call from his old friend Kevin, who wanted him to work on new material with him and Jimmy. He spent the summer with them working on some demos, and there was also a live appearance, on that episode of Jonathan Ross's *Saturday Zoo*, playing a couple of new songs while wearing a pair of Kevin's leather trousers and a frilly shirt. But the spark never truly ignited. With both Kevin and Jimmy working through addiction issues at the time, Kev was 'in the middle and none of my ideas were of interest to anyone'. Feeling like a glorified computer and drum machine operator, he promptly made his excuses and left.

Constantly fiddling about with computers 'while living on a diet of French-bread pizza and Budweiser', Kev decided to turn this hobby into something proper. He enrolled at university in Wolverhampton, timing his return to academia with the arrival of the internet. 'That looked like fun and that's what grabbed me. Before I finished my degree, I was earning money from building websites. And that's what's kept me going all of these years, up to about two or three years ago. Now I'm much happier making music instead.'

Kev last recorded properly in 2002. 'Choosing not to record is part of the process – making music without the performance of recording. It's an end in itself and only has to please an audience of one right now. I'm not sure it's even music as such. It's noise, it's sound, and it evolves from machines that I build and operate.

'It's bliss to these ears,' he concludes. 'But I'm not sure the world is ready for my three-hour-long, slowly evolving soundscapes just yet . . .'

20

Nick Gatfield

Alto sax, 1982–85

'Amy Winehouse was probably the purest artist I've ever worked with. She had zero consideration for sales, for commerciality. She couldn't care less.'

South-west London is beat.

Seven days into September and we're suffering the hottest day of the year, the mercury cruising well beyond thirty degrees. On Barnes Common, everyone is sticking to the edges, to the trees, to the shade. The local teenage goths have been hiding there all the time, but now they're joined by pram-pushing parents, pale pensioners and sunburnt students. Aside from the dizzy spaniels splashing in the stream or skidding among the first fallen leaves of autumn, we're all beat.

Thank goodness then for the ceiling fans and air conditioning of the members' club upstairs at Olympic Studios.

Now back to its original use as a cinema (tonight they're showing *Reinventing Elvis*, the documentary about his '68 comeback, which I fancy hanging around for), Olympic is the most notable rock history location in Barnes, aside from the sycamore tree into which Gloria Jones' purple Mini crashed in 1977, the accident that killed her partner, Marc Bolan.

The feet passing over the studios' threshold during their heyday belonged to the absolute top table of late-20th-century music makers. The Beatles, the Stones, Hendrix, Led Zep, Ella, BB, the Who, Roxy Music, Queen, Madonna, Prince, Björk . . . U2 were the last band booked in here. They emerged, blinking into the sunlight, with their twelfth studio album, *No Line on the Horizon*, in 2009.

Such a pedigree means Olympic is an entirely appropriate place to meet the man who not only played both sax parts on one of the finest songs ever recorded (which is obviously the twelve-minute glory of 'This Is What She's Like' from *Don't Stand Me Down*), but who also, after his days in Dexys, signed and nurtured many of the great successes of British music over the past thirty years. A recording studio – even a decommissioned one – is a natural habitat for Nick Gatfield.

Nick's having work done today at his house on the other side of the common, the noise from which rules it out as the venue for our interview. But Olympic makes an excellent substitute. The members' club is quiet but not oppressively hushed, and the background music (currently some Bowie, someone else who graced Olympic's vocal booths) is perfectly pitched volume-wise – nothing to get in the way of Nick's twin stories of Dexys antics and record exec triumphs. He pours himself a glass of iced water and begins his tale.

'I was destined for a life in classical music. I went to Surrey University in 1979 to study for a music degree, specialising in performance. My instrument at the time was the clarinet. I had been the best boy in my school at music, but suddenly I was in an environment full of good musicians. I realised I was right in the middle of this group. I wasn't rubbish but I wasn't spectacular. And I found the reality of making a career out of music as an orchestral or session player very depressing. But Surrey was the only university at the time that had a recording studio attached to it and they had a degree course called Tonmeister, which I think they still run. It was unique in Europe. It was a music degree, but the Tonmeister element taught recording techniques. It was a producer's workshop before they had courses like that. It was a four-year course and in year three you went on a year's practical. You might blag your way into Abbey Road or one of the other key studios for that year. "Hi, I'm doing the Tonmeister." "Well, that's lovely. The broom's over here and the coffee machine's over there." You cleaned up and you made the drinks. That's what you did.

'I dropped out of Surrey. At the time, I had a semi-pro band called Polo Club and we wanted to be pro. It was an unwieldy thing, which probably prepared me for Dexys. It was an eleven-piece band, very much in the mould of Blue Rondo à la Turk. And we started to get a lot of traction and attention from record companies.

'To supplement my very meagre income, I was selling shirts door to door, cold calling. So I'd do the Soho area, with a cassette of my band in my hand. All the record companies were pretty much based in Soho in those days, or in the West End at least, and I'd mysteriously leave a cassette behind every time I tried to flog a shirt in one of them – assuming I'd got through the door.

'I remember sitting in a café one evening. It was late and it was miserable and it was cold. The job was commission-only and I'd sold nothing. I saw there was a single light on in a nearby building. It was the offices of the Derek Block Agency, quite a significant agency in the early '80s. "Right, I'm going in there." A guy called Rob Hallett, who's still a very successful agent, worked at Derek Block. Rob, who I have a lot of time for now, at the time was this flash guy and here was a kid trying to flog him a shirt.

'"Yeah, I'll have one of those, and one of those, and one of those. I've seen you around. You're in a band, aren't you? How's it going?"

'"Well, I'm selling you a shirt out of a bag, so not great, not brilliant."

'"Do you want to do a session?"

'"Yeah, yeah."

'"Get yourself down to Maida Vale."

Maida Vale was the BBC's studio complex where radio dramas and classical recitals were recorded. It was also where the sessions for Radio 1's evening and late-night programmes were committed to tape. Nick was being sent to play on one that would be airing on David 'Kid' Jensen's show. He didn't know who he'd be playing with. The name of the band requiring his services turned out to be some outfit called Dexys Midnight Runners.

'I'll be honest – I was shitting myself. I wasn't much of a sax player. I was a clarinettist. That's what I was. I played sax in my band, but nothing on this kind of scale, nothing where I had to be on my A game. So I was incredibly nervous. And Kevin is quite an intimidating character when you first meet him. But the session went OK and he was actually perfectly pleasant. I didn't really say more than two words to him. I was told what to play and it was fairly straightforward. And then I was off.

'Then I got called back to do another session. Then after that, I got another call, this time asking me to join. All of the horn section had left by then, so there was a vacancy in that department. I took it gladly, dumping my bag of shirts. By then, I was a student at Goldsmiths College, so I quit that as well. I remember telling my parents, "Don't worry, this band's good, this band's successful. It's not like the other one I dropped out of college for . . ."'

Nick took his place alongside those two other freshly signed-up horn players, Spike Edney and Andy Hamilton. They weren't exactly contemporaries, either in age or experience. Or, it turned out, expectations. 'Spike and Andy were definite session players. I was twenty-one when I joined. I was the kid. Spike was in his thirties and had had a degree of success, and Andy played with Wham! and George Michael. For me, it was more than a gig. I wanted to be in the band. I wasn't going to go and do another gig down the road the following week. It wasn't a conscious "I'm going to make myself indispensable", but I was committed. I think maybe that was recognised. Or maybe my youth was part of it. I certainly brought the average age down.'

The band spent the autumn of 1982 gear-jamming their way up, down and across the UK motorway network on The Bridge tour. Their show was polished but also charged. Session players or not, all eleven members of the concert party gave their all on stage every night, their reward being the rapturous adulation of post-'Eileen' full houses.

'It was quite a weird experience because Dexys' audience was really split at the time. You had the original audience who were quite tribal, quite skinhead, and then you had the new audience who came because they loved "Come on Eileen". And then they met at places like Shaftesbury Theatre. I got my parents tickets to one of the Shaftesbury Theatre shows. Afterwards, they said, "OK, fair play." I think the most significant thing was that I'd been in debt for ages, borrowing money from my mum for years. The first cheque I got from Dexys was for two-and-a-half grand, which at the time was an unbelievable amount. So it was good to be able to look my parents in the eye and say, "All your money on education was probably wasted, but the music lessons might have paid off . . ."'

After the turn of the year, this welcome experience wasn't necessarily replicated on the first US tour. The band had to retrace its steps somewhat.

'I took it for granted at the time. In the UK, obviously we'd had success, so the touring was actually relatively comfortable. But the first time I went to the US, it was pretty grim. The first time I went to LA was with Dexys. I ended up living there for most of the '90s, but at the time I remember thinking, *This place is terrible.* We were staying in some horrible little motor hotel in North Hollywood and it was about a hundred degrees outside. As "Come on Eileen" took hold, the venues got bigger and the hotels got slightly better. And then it was genuine fun. I mean, it was a thrill to sell out the Greek Theater in LA, which has a capacity of around six thousand.

'"Come on Eileen" was number one here in the summer of '82. It took the best part of a year to do the same thing in the States. Nothing exploded simultaneously across the world. It was a market-by-market process. That's where it was really exciting because you could see it grow. And the States at that time was a really tough nut to crack. That's the thing I miss about the business. You release a piece of music and then you actively go out and promote it and people experience it in a different setting. And a recording has a life cycle. It wasn't just like "Bang, there's your drop" and on to the next, which frankly is the way it works now.

'But there were some classic moments where we got to the States and Kevin suddenly decided to refuse to play "Come on Eileen", just to be perverse. Fair play to him. Nobody could categorise the band. From my business experience, generally speaking, when you have an artist who cannot be put anywhere, they fall between the cracks. But somehow – perhaps because "Come on Eileen" is just one of those songs and because of the power of live performance – Dexys took hold.'

On the US tours, Bob Noble had, of course, filled the vacancy left by the departure of Micky Billingham. But when it came to stripped-down TV appearances, most notably that one on *Saturday Night Live*, Bob was relegated to the subs' bench. Nick – possibly because he regarded himself as more than just a session player, a thought presumably shared by Kevin, hence the switch – mimed the keys. Until one night in a TV studio in Manhattan, that was.

'I had no idea of the significance of *Saturday Night Live* when we played it. I mainly bluffed keyboards when we played the song on TV and hadn't really played it live. We turned up at the studio and went, "It's live?!" "Yeah, it's called *Saturday Night LIVE*." It was a terrifying experience. Thankfully the keyboard was particularly low in the mix.'

On their return from the States, with *Too-Rye-Ay*'s serpentine, cross-continental promotional schedule finally complete, work began on the next album. Most of the session musicians moved on to their next paying gig, but Nick stayed in the fold. 'It became a natural thing that – partly because of the demands of TV, partly because of the way we were working together – the band became a smaller unit. And as we went into the *Don't Stand Me Down* era, that got whittled down even further. It was a re-engineering of sound, but of personnel too. The core personnel at that time were definitely Kevin, definitely Helen, definitely Billy. I was kind of the fourth part of the equation. I remember lobbying for John Edwards to be part of that because he's such a good bass player. I think Kevin was very suspicious of anybody who seemed too session-y – or too freaking good.'

As Kev Adams also remembered, the vocals of a certain Californian group were flavouring the initial conversations about the next record. 'There were various writing sessions and listening sessions. Kevin used to listen to a lot of records. The Beach Boys were a big thing at that particular time, especially the harmonies. We demoed the entire record in the studio in Birmingham and I still think it's the best version of it. The demos are raw, but there's a real excitement about them. It was a great A&R lesson for me. There comes a time when you suck the life out of something and beat it to death, but there's an energy about those demos.'

There is artful photography on the walls here in the members' club, beautiful black-and-white shots of past recording sessions held in this building. There's Jimi Hendrix perched on a stool, guitar in hand and wearing, despite it being a monochrome photo, what is clearly the most psychedelic jacket imaginable. There's Keith Richards, equally focused while playing his instrument, headphones fastened to his ears and a cigarette dangling from his lips. And there's Dusty Springfield, her cheek tight to the microphone, wearing both a magnificent turban and the warmest of smiles.

The various *Don't Stand Me Down* sessions, held in various studios, aren't commemorated in photographs. Instead, the pictures only remain in the heads of the protagonists. Nick paints the scene.

'When it was time to record it "properly", we started in Montreux with Tom Dowd producing. I loved it. I was staying in a really stunning hotel in a beautiful room looking over the lake. This was obviously before my record company days. I look at it now and wonder just how much money we spent. It was not an inexpensive studio. Kevin was trying to capture the band live. He'd been listening to *Pet Sounds* – that idea that you have the full band in the room, trying to get real dynamics. I understand the process, but it's tricky. Tom was a lovely pipe-and-slippers type of guy. It was like your granddad making a record with you. But I think Kevin traumatised him, to be perfectly honest. Tom would go, "I don't quite know what's happening here." Then he did a runner in the middle of the night.

'We spent a long time out there, but got very little out of it. I always remember our A&R guy, Roger Ames, sitting on the steps of the studio for about six days because Kevin wouldn't let him into the studio.'

The next producer hired was Jimmy Miller, most famous for producing a string of untouchable Rolling Stones albums over a five-year period, including *Let it Bleed* and *Exile on Main St.* 'Jimmy didn't engineer and he didn't play anything. He would just say things like, "Hey, you guys ever thought about doing this?" It was like what Rick Rubin does now. People accuse Rick Rubin of doing nothing, but actually there's a role for that kind of approach.' (The Stones were clearly some kind of influence on Kevin at this point; he insisted that Nick be credited as Nicky on the album sleeve, a nod to the Stones' piano player, Nicky Hopkins.)

The turnover in producers continued. John Porter held the position for a day, before Alan Winstanley took the reins alongside the nucleus of Kevin, Helen and Billy. And eventually the process got smoother. It gained momentum. It got done.

But it didn't get done until that final trip out to New York where Nick met up with the other three, who were redoing the vocals at Electric Ladyland, and to undertake the photo session from which that poster on Kev Adams' wall was taken. And, yes, Nick did fly supersonic. 'There was a strike going on and the only way I could get out to New York was on Concorde. I was so excited. I remember being in the queue, clutching my ticket. "Ah, yes, Mr Gatfield. You'll be coming back with us? Oh, no you're not." We were coming back on TWA or whatever at the back of the plane.'

As well as appearing on those promotional shots taken on the streets of Manhattan, Nick was also part of the photoshoot for the album sleeve, suited and booted alongside the other three in a formal set-up that was not dissimilar to a Victorian parlour photograph. But before the album was released, before Nick's face was looking out from the nation's record racks, he handed in his notice.

'I thought it would be stupid to leave just as it was released, so I left a little while before it was. I quite enjoyed touring *Too-Rye-Ay*, but one of the reasons why I left was that I couldn't face going on the road to promote *Don't Stand Me Down*. It was nothing to do with the record. The record is great.

'Playing live with Dexys was a fundamentally uncreative process, particularly the way that Kevin organised it. It was very choreographed. There wasn't room for expression. It was very strict. You're doing this, you're standing there, this is happening. After twenty shows, it was almost like a West End theatre band. I just found that uncreative. It started to wear thin after a while.

'Also, brought on by the multiple times of making the record and the tortuous recording process, I'd got to the point where I was kind of played out. I wasn't happy with my tone on the saxophone. I wasn't happy the way it had been recorded. I was doubling up on saxes too and, at that point, I much preferred playing keyboards. And I wanted to do my own thing. Me and a mate had started putting some songs together, doing a bit of writing. Nothing serious, just when we could grab some time together. Then it came the time to make the crunch decision. *Do I really sign up for the next two years? No, I don't want to.* So I called Kevin. I don't think he was drastically surprised.

Post-Dexys, Nick Gatfield – pictured here with Pharrell Williams – went on to sign and work with some of the world's biggest names.

'I had no money – literally. I had twelve quid in my bank account. My girlfriend at the time was a PA to the head of A&R and marketing at EMI Records, a guy called David Munns. I'd met him socially many times. In the past, I probably moaned to him over a beer about *Don't Stand Me Down*.

'"I can't make this record *again*. It's driving me mad."

'"Well, come and be an A&R man instead."

'I didn't want to be an A&R man. That was the ultimate sell-out. Now, though, I had no money. So I called him up. "Yeah, start on Monday."

'I thought I'd do it for three or four months and then quit. That was in 1985 . . .'

Despite his initial reticence about his career move, despite the motivation behind it being purely financial, Nick entered the corporate world with no small amount of confidence and bravado.

'I blagged my way in. I said, "Because I've been in a successful band, because I'm a musician, I want to come in as an in-house producer as well as an A&R guy." Which I did – over-promoted, to be totally honest. It was a tag that enabled me to feel better about quitting the musician's lot. What I didn't do was schlep up and down the M1, going to gigs. All the work I ended up doing was creative. I had no idea at all what a budget was. I'd go into the studio, working with artists from Talk Talk to Sheena Easton. I liked the variety. It was exciting.

'And, to be totally honest, I got too used to having an expense account and a company car. The idea of throwing that away to chip away at a few songs . . . Shocking, I know. But I also got a kick out of working with hugely talented artists. You realise that there are some people who are carved out for that existence – and I wasn't one of them. But I think I had a role in terms of helping these hugely talented people get where they wanted to be.

'David Munns left maybe a year after he'd hired me. His replacement was a guy called Rupert Perry, who actually came in as MD of the company. He looked around and said to me, "You could be head of A&R." "Me? What, really?" I was an unqualified twenty-five-year-old and I had frankly no idea about what I was doing. As it turned out, it wasn't rocket science. It was just about trying to find a group of people who a) had a work ethic, because that wasn't a particular trait of our people at that particular time, and b) had the ability to speak with artists. I was constantly stunned by how so many record companies, particularly their A&R people, couldn't properly articulate their thoughts on music.

'"You know that banging thing . . .?"

'"What, the drums?"

'"Oh yeah, those."

I'm not kidding . . .'

Armed with both his musical nous and the confidence of youth, Nick took up his new position at the top of EMI's A&R tree in 1986. At first, his pickaxe didn't strike gold, but a couple of years into the job, a rich seam of success was discovered. He signed the likes of EMF and Jesus Jones, both of whom would later, in July 1991, sit in the top three on the Billboard Hot 100 for three weeks. Nick also brokered the arrangement with the indie label Food Records, the first deal of which was a band called Seymour – later to change their name to Blur. 'We signed them for three thousand quid,' he smiles.

Nick also nurtured another band yet to rename themselves: On A Friday, later known the world over as Radiohead. 'I remember going to see them for the first time. I was actually taken along by a kid who was in the singles sales team in the days when you used to drive around to record stores in your Ford Escort estate with boxes of singles in the back. His name was Keith Wozencroft and he ended up becoming MD of Parlophone further down the line. He covered the Oxford area and he used to bug me to death about bands. One day, he said, "I've found this band called On A Friday." Their bass player,

Colin Greenwood, was the singles buyer for HMV in Oxford. Keith played me a track – I think it was "Stop Whispering". It was really interesting. So I went to see them in the Jericho Tavern on a Sunday or something. There were literally ten people in the room, plus the band. But they just made an incredible noise. We signed them with no view of where their place in the market was. They were just really, really good, so would hopefully find their spot. And, interestingly enough, they didn't when they first came out. They were hated in plenty of quarters.'

In the early '90s, with some formidable signings under his belt, Nick was offered the position of MD of EMI. He was barely into his thirties. Instead, though, he moved to Los Angeles to start a label for Polygram. His first experience of the US market – beyond being fascinated, ten years earlier, by how 'Come on Eileen' slowly seduced American punters – was a tough baptism.

'I was thrown in at the deep end, starting right from the bottom again. I had to make the connections and it was hard. I set up shop to put out UK music in the States, which was fairly tricky at that particular time. I was kind of second-guessing myself a lot. I didn't know what to expect. It wasn't a particularly happy professional experience.'

After Dexys' old A&R Roger Ames took over as overall president of Polygram North America, Nick diverted into looking after the Polydor label and Polygram Music Publishing. When, at the tail end of the '90s, the company was bought out, he found himself on gardening leave, kicking his heels in Los Angeles, unable to work for a period of time. 'But the UK kept calling me back.'

In 2001, Nick became president of Island Records, a position he held for seven years, during which time the company had many hit records. 'We had an amazing run there, starting off with pop things like Sugababes and Busted and McFly, before Amy Winehouse and Keane. I worked really closely with Amy, particularly on her debut album, *Frank*. She was a total force of nature, but probably the purest artist I've ever worked with. She had zero consideration for sales, for commerciality. She couldn't care less. She just wanted to be a jazz singer. She just wanted to be a Jewish mum in north London, raising kids and singing jazz. That was her dream.'

Nick went on to be headhunted by Terra Firma, the new owners of EMI, to run the creative side of the company. Success would come in the form of Katy Perry, Tinie Tempah and Swedish House Mafia. Then came a tenure as chairman of Sony Music UK. Since leaving the corporate world, he's since been focused on being an angel investor in tech start-ups and offering consultancy to the music industry. The landscape is now barely recognisable from how it appeared back when he first blagged his way into the corridors of power.

'When I started in the business and became head of A&R at EMI as a young boy, the directors went away for a think-tank and we built in a five-year plan. That's laughable now. There are barely five-*week* plans. Breaking artists at the global level now is near on impossible – at least, not within the time frame that's acceptable when you've got shareholders and quarterly reporting.'

Before Nick and I part – him to stay under the club's cooling ceiling fans, me to step back in the fierce heat of the streets of London – I'm keen to serve him with a counterfactual conundrum. Had he become a record executive a year or two earlier, and had he been charged with the task of being Dexys' A&R man, how would he have responded to the band's approach to *Don't Stand Me Down*'s release? Would he have tried to persuade them to release a single?

'It's a difficult thing, isn't it? There is an unwritten contractual obligation between two parties. The record company is there to do right by the artist's music, to make sure it's disseminated worldwide and to make sure it's promoted. An artist is there to be creative, but also to promote. That's what I'd say. It was kind of a brave decision not to release a single, but also a foolhardy one. I'm sure Kevin could quote back examples that had worked brilliantly. Nobody wanted to release "Bohemian Rhapsody" because of its length, but someone took it to radio and Kenny Everett played it four times in a row or whatever. Also, Kevin hadn't endeared himself to the music press, who were still an important part of the equation. I totally understand about protecting creativity, but give the record company an opportunity to actually sell it. Don't put up too many roadblocks.'

Finally, forty-odd years on, does the musician who put down his instrument to become the company man still play? Nick downs the remainder of his water and scoops up his phone from the table, ready to relocate to the quietest, most discreet corner of the members' club to make some calls.

'Yeah, I play bad cocktail jazz piano in the privacy of my own home, but you'll never hear it.'

His mouth spreads into an easy smile.

'Unless things get really bad and I'm forced to take work in some dodgy hotel near Heathrow . . .'

Reminisce #9

9 Rue du Théâtre, Montreux

For such a well-heeled place as Montreux — reassuringly expensive and blessed by crisp, clean, faultless sunshine — it's the most unsalubrious of entrances. A locked and bolted door, which clearly hasn't been opened in many years, in front of which sits a wastebin. Graffiti is plastered across the adjacent walls. All of it is on a theme. Here, in a variety of languages, and via a variety of permanent marker pens, love and devotion has been expressed to Freddie Mercury and Queen. Mercury's face has been drawn on the walls a few times too.

For this side entrance is the former portal into Mountain Studios, the recording studios, set inside a lakeside casino, which were once owned by the band and where they recorded seven albums, including Jazz and A Kind of Magic. Many others used its facilities too, Bowie, the Stones and Iggy Pop among them.

In 1984, throughout the month of May, Dexys Midnight Runners darkened this door every day, the latest incarnation of the band and its most esoteric line-up yet. Among them was a flares-wearing, piano-playing survivor of the early '70s rock scene, along with Wilson Pickett's drummer from New York.

The sessions were far from super-smooth, partly because of the studio's huge dimensions but mostly because of the band's insistence on recording live as a large ensemble. Having emerged blinking into the Swiss sunshine after several weeks with just that sole finished track, 'Listen to This', to show for their efforts, the band retreated to Blighty, where more studios were booked and more band members came and went. Those largely unproductive weeks in Montreux remain unacknowledged, unsaluted, by the graffiti artist's pen. The walls carry not a single mention of that visit.

There's no reference to Dexys in the permanent exhibition inside either, reached via the main entrance of the casino round the corner. Aside from the studio's old mixing desk and its tape machines, this is another shrine to Queen — and Mercury in particular, with several of his stage suits on display. Not that the other band members are ignored. A quote from the drummer Roger Taylor is reproduced in large letters on the wall: 'I think we are probably the best live band in the world at the moment and we are going to prove it.' Shot through with supreme confidence and determination, again – as with that Henry Higgins line in *Pygmalion* – these could be the words of Kevin Rowland.

There are other words on the exhibition's wall, one bilingual message being particularly noticeable. 'N'oubliez pas de signer le mur extérieur de l'exposition,' it instructs. '*Remember to sign the wall.*' The graffiti on and around the side entrance is being actively encouraged. The tributes to Freddie Mercury keep coming. One day, one day, Kevin and the gang will also be remembered in indelible ink, a message for all eternity. Bring a permanent marker if you're ever in town.

21

Julian Littman

Mandolin, 1985

'I was sitting on my own in the middle of Wessex Studios, just me and my mandolin in one of the biggest recordings studios in London. Hilarious.'

In a basement flat on a street just off the King's Road, two men are sitting at a kitchen table, huddled over a laptop, watching a video on YouTube. It's a twelve-and-a-half-minute music video, one shot both on the streets of New York and in a film studio in downtown Wembley.

It opens with two other men having a conversation in a Manhattan apartment before the action shifts, a couple of minutes later, to that studio set where, as the song explodes into life and the lights flash on, an eleven-piece band is revealed.

One of the men at the kitchen table leans forwards, scrutinising the players. He pauses the action, his eyes flickering left and right. He's looking for something. He's looking for someone. At the back of the shot, next to a pair of saxophonists, he finds what he's looking for. He finds himself.

His name is Julian Littman and he played mandolin on 'This Is What She's Like'.

He and I are in his rabbit warren of a Chelsea flat, where he's lived since before the video was shot nearly forty years ago. We're turning the clock back to the time when he was, in theory at least, a member of Dexys Midnight Runners for a few fleeting moments.

Julian's services weren't engaged long enough to have played any live shows with Dexys. This video is the only public record of his short association with them. In fact, the day this video was shot was the day he first met the band. At this point, he'd only made Kevin Rowland's acquaintance. That had been a couple of months earlier, when he'd recorded his mandolin parts for a handful of songs for *Don't Stand Me Down* in north London.

'I didn't record with the rest of the band. I was sitting on my own in the middle of Wessex Studios, just me and my mandolin, in one of the biggest recording studios in London. Hilarious.'

Julian had been charged with adding colour and texture to what had already been recorded, with Kevin giving him free rein to improvise over the top. And he was to do so blind, hearing the songs for the first time as he played. 'I asked Kevin what the chords were. He said, "Ah, don't worry about them. Just go and do it." It was pretty spontaneous. I didn't know what was coming next.

'I don't think he had any notes for me. And I don't think he ever said, "You should be playing this here and that there." He just let me play. And he was very gracious about it as well.'

On the slower numbers, Julian's playing is empathetic, non-invasive. On the more upbeat songs, he fires into action, never more so than on the spirited denouement of 'This Is What She's Like'. It's extraordinary that he didn't record it live with the others, his mandolin so perfectly interweaving and duelling with Helen's violin, both musicians playing with controlled fury.

Julian sets the video playing again, watching Kevin, Billy and Helen at the front of the band and asking what each is up to these days. He hasn't necessarily kept up with the band; he's unaware that Helen has written her memoirs, or that Kevin has recently released a new Dexys album. He points towards the long-haired piano player on the left of the screen. 'That's Vincent Crane, isn't it? What's he doing these days?' I have to break the news to Julian that the former Atomic Rooster pianist took his own life back in 1989.

The song carries on through its quiet movement, the passage featuring the Beach Boys-inspired close harmonies. Then it cranks up the pace again, rushing towards its climax. And there, eleven minutes in, is the younger Julian, no longer a distant figure at the back next to the sax players. He now dominates the screen all on his own as he wigs out, hair flying as his fingers flutter like hummingbird wings over the mandolin's strings.

The video is paused again. Now at the dawn-break of his seventies, Julian isn't exactly looking into a mirror – the hairline has receded a little and his locks no longer spill over and beyond his collar – but he is fascinated by what he sees. 'Oh God! You know, I don't think I've ever seen this bit. I can't have watched it this far before.' There's a twinkle in his eyes.

The video ends and he immediately embarks on a hunt on YouTube for the other tracks he played on. 'There was one called "The Waltz". And another, a spoken-word thing called "Reminisce (Part 2)".'

He starts typing. 'Re-mi-ni . . .

'Is it S-C? I-S-C-E . . .'

The song starts with some melancholic mandolin chords and semi-bluesy piano, over which Kevin recalls a story of young love in late-'60s north-west London, a love affair soundtracked by the hit records of the day, those by Jimmy Ruffin, the Kinks, the Fifth Dimension . . . Towards its close, Julian's mandolin drifts off in a more free-range direction, shading the song with the colours of pain and regret, of sweetness and warm nostalgia. It's just beautiful.

YouTube suggests playing 'One of Those Things' next, the song that Kevin very strongly modelled on 'Werewolves of London'; Warren Zevon's lawyers would later insist on a writing credit. 'Am I on this one?' Julian asks. 'Might be.' We fall quiet to see if we can make out any mandolin. 'I think there's a little bit there. They used me sparingly on this one . . .'

The fact that Julian recorded his parts alone, with only Kevin and, presumably, an engineer for company, suggests the addition of mandolin was an eleventh-hour decision. It was a well-judged one, Julian's tasteful playing adding further depth and seasoning. They scouted him well.

'I got booked because I used to do lots of ad jingles for Jeff Wayne. Dexys were putting out feelers for a mandolin player and Jeff's booker, a woman called Isobel Griffiths, knew I played mandolin. Dexys wanted the top rock mandolin player and I was the *only* rock mandolin player. Or, at least, the only one who was available.

'I'm actually in a book that George Martin wrote about instruments.' Julian scurries off across the flat in search of it, soon re-emerging with a weather-worn copy of *Making Music: The Guide to Writing, Performing & Playing*, published back in 1983. He starts flicking through it. George has profiled some of the greatest musicians of the age and their favoured instruments: the likes of Eric Clapton, Quincy Jones and, on page 195, on the single page dedicated to the mandolin, a certain Julian Littman. 'All the greats, all the greats. And me.'

Julian's association with Dexys lasted longer than that session at Wessex Studios and that day's filming in Wembley. But not much longer. He has hazy memories of accompanying Kevin, Helen and Billy a few months later to a small studio in the south-east London/ Kent borderlands — either Sidcup or Sydenham. (His haziness is somewhat cleared when I later ask Kev Adams for clarification. 'Yes, that would have happened. I can't remember the details, but the last throw of the dice was to make a new single version of "This is What She's Like".') Despite Julian's lack of clarity on the details of that episode, he recalls how it made him feel: 'On that little trip was when I actually felt part of it, when I had a slight sense of belonging. I thought, *This is what they're about.*'

No matter how short his tenure in Dexys was – if 'tenure' is remotely correct to describe such a brief, unofficial association – Julian interpreted the phone call asking him to contribute to *Don't Stand Me Down* as the latest positive step in his career. 'At that time, I was doing a show at night called *Pump Boys and Dinettes* at the Piccadilly Theatre with Paul Jones, Gary Holton, Brian Pro-thero, Kiki Dee and Carlene Carter, Johnny Cash's stepdaugh-ter. We were both the actors and the band. I was on quite a high at the time as me and Charlie Dore had written a song for Sheena Easton that was in the top ten of the Billboard Hot 100, a song called "Strut". It didn't do anything over here.'

While Julian's role in Dexys was largely as a bit-part player, his career either side has been one of the more colourful of the band's alumni, one in which he's been both actor and musician, often operat-ing at the convergence of both callings. 'Guitar was my primary instru-ment. I joined Gerry Rafferty's band after "Baker Street" had been recorded. And I did loads of sessions and bits and bobs with all kinds of people, including singing with Richard and Linda Thompson.'

His working relationship with singer-songwriter Charlie Dore, she of the late '70s hit single 'Pilot of the Airwaves', continues to this day, having started when they were sixteen-year-old drama-school students. Julian is eager to show me one of their early engagements as actor-singers and flips open the laptop again. What he shows me is a revelation.

He's called up an episode of the kids TV show *Rainbow* from 1973, specifically a clip of the programme's regular musical turn. But these are the days before Rod, Jane and Freddy. Their predecessors are familiar. Alongside Charlie Dore is a hirsute twenty-year-old Julian in a checked cheesecloth shirt and flared jeans, showing his dexter-ity as a finger-picking guitarist on a song about a horse: 'Riding fast, riding slow / Over the hills and fields we go.' The lyrics aside, it's a fine slab of country-folk, reaching deeper into musical tradition than their successors ever did. Completing the trio on second guitar and harmonica is the actor Karl Johnson, possibly best known as a thick-accented policeman in *Hot Fuzz*, the one whose words require translating in order for Simon Pegg's sergeant to understand him.

'Charlie and I had been working in children's theatre in Newcastle when we got the audition for *Rainbow*. We did about two years on the show. The regular pay packet was nice, but Karl wanted to do more serious stuff. They offered us to stay for the rest of time, but we were anxious not to get stuck on there, so we hung up our dungarees. Rod, Jane and Freddy did it for years and years.'

Julian went off to do more acting, both stage and television, while Charlie made music her primary career. But they kept working together. 'We had a bluegrass outfit and then she formed a kind of electric country-rock band. Then one day, her guitarist couldn't make a gig, so I filled in. And then I stayed. We worked together through that whole pub-rock circuit thing in the '70s. Everyone else was turning into the Clash or the Pistols or the Blockheads, but we were country-rock.

'Then Charlie got a record deal with Island, so we went to Nashville to record it at J.J. Cale's studio. This was 1978. Elvis had died the previous year and a lot of his band were out of work. So we recruited a few of them for the album. We did the record, remixed it in Los Angeles and got it back to Island. Chris Blackwell hated it. He said it was too country. "Hold on, you just sent us to Nashville . . ."'

Julian is halted mid-flow by his phone ringing. He glances down to see who's calling. Just as 'Come on Eileen' had made a timely appearance on Kev Adams' radio when I was in Bridgnorth, here's another coincidental interruption.

'Hey Charlie! You all right? Your name's been taken in vain . . .'

They share the quickest of conversations, spoken in the kind of shorthand that's fluent for two people who've been working together for more than half a century.

'Alan Parker put me in loads of scenes with Madonna because
I chilled her out.' Julian Littman's time with Dexys was a fleeting
chapter in a vivid and varied career as both actor and musician.

With Charlie forced to re-record the album – this time without
her old friend, as the new producer, presumably as a cost-cutting
measure, would be playing all the instruments – Julian went on tour
with Gerry Rafferty instead: 'That was amazing, flying on Concorde to go and do *The Frost Show* in New York.'

Punctuated by that brief engagement with Dexys, Julian's dual
careers as musician and actor continued into the 1990s. That

decade, he received what is arguably his biggest acting role to date: he was cast as Eva Péron's brother in Alan Parker's film *Evita*, regularly sharing scenes with Madonna. 'That was quite an experience. I got on really well with her. Really well. We became friends for that period of time – and a bit longer. Me and my then wife went out to dinner with her a few times in London. The one time I remember most was just before the film's premiere. Donatella Versace was very keen that Madonna should wear her dress, her clothes, for the premieres in both Los Angeles and London, so she threw a dinner for her in a private room at the Ivy. And Madonna invited us. We were the only people there you'd have never heard of. There was Elton, Pet Shop Boys, Trevor Nunn, Lynda La Plante . . . We were ushered into this room to have dinner with Madonna. And I sat next to her.

'Alan Parker put me in loads of scenes with her because I kind of chilled her out and we had a good laugh. Alan would say, "Are you on the call sheet for tomorrow?" "No, I'm not on it." "Well, Madonna is, so you'd better be in that scene." So he'd bung me on.

'We shot it in Buenos Aires, Budapest and then at Shepperton. In Buenos Aires, I had this bloody great Winnebago. In Budapest, I had a little caravan, like your Uncle Norman might have had. And then in Shepperton, I had a gloomy closet. Literally just a cupboard. After that, I tried my luck at being a movie star. So me and my then wife, Loveday Smith, kept going out to LA. Three times we went in '98. But by then I was forty-five and I didn't want to start again. It would have meant getting a tiny place in the valley and auditioning and all that stuff. So I decided to stay here and did loads of acting, including a couple more movies. I played Al Capone in a thing called *Al's Lads*, as well as all kinds of theatre stuff.

'Then I was in the Queen show, *We Will Rock You*, for a year. I played an old character called Pop, who was originally played by

Nigel Planer. He's supposed to be the guardian of live music. It was great. And it meant steady income.'

Then came a role on the Tim Burton film, *Charlie and the Chocolate Factory* – albeit one not in front of the camera. Julian was charged with making sure the songs featuring the Oompa Loompas were musically in time, teaching guitar and drum techniques while also working alongside a choreographer and lip sync specialist. It wasn't an army of Oompa Loompas he was working with. Tim Burton wanted to film just one actor, but duplicate and multiply his efforts digitally. It was a long process. It took five months. The whole affair was made trickier by a certain rule that Burton instigated. 'Tim said, "Oh, by the way, I don't want Oompa Loompas to blink." So I had to be constantly on blink patrol.' There are definite shades here of Kevin Rowland's no-smiling rule.

The music-performing part of Julian's life was far from abandoned by all these film and theatre jobs. 'In 2010, Steeleye Span were looking for a new guitar player. They tried me out for a tour and I've been with them ever since. Because Steeleye tour twice a year, I can't sign up for a West End show because those contracts require you for a year. Between those Steeleye tours, I'll do what I can if I'm offered it. Of course, I've got to get jobs, but it's hell for actors at the moment, post-COVID.'

Julian closes the lid on his laptop, closing the lid on that blink-and-you'll-miss-it moment in the sun with Dexys. He doesn't mind a trundle along memory lane, a revisiting of his colourful life and times, from *Rainbow* to Madonna and beyond. But, in his seventies – and with looks and a bright voice that suggest someone notably younger – he remains both jobbing musician and jobbing actor. 'I'm always auditioning.'

He leans in conspiratorially. 'I shouldn't say anything about this, but I'm hoping to play Django Reinhardt in a play.' He's certainly got the guitar chops for the role, but will it involve, in order to be faithful to Django's story and to his art, losing the use of a couple of fingers?

'It's like that old joke when you're offered to play Long John Silver in panto.

'"It's twenty grand a week and you start on Tuesday."

'"If it's twenty grand a week, I'll start on Monday."

'"You can't. You're having your leg off on Monday . . ."'

22

Mick Talbot

Keyboards, 1980

'Kevin asked me to be the musical director, which I reluctantly took on. I thought he had enough of an idea of what he wanted himself.'

Two months to the day before *Don't Stand Me Down* was unleashed upon a largely disinterested, apathetic public, one particular former (and future) member of Dexys was experiencing the polar opposite: he was playing live at the largest concert in history.

It's lunchtime on a Saturday in July in 1985 and Wembley Stadium is crammed to bursting under sweltering sunshine. The crowd are gratefully receiving the benefit of having refreshing hosepipes turned on them. It certainly isn't blazer weather, but nobody told Mick Talbot. He's there on stage, in front of an estimated television audience of many hundreds of millions, wearing a decidedly natty red-and-black-striped blazer and white chinos. And he's working up a sweat, charging through the Style Council's fourth and final song, 'Walls Come Tumbling Down'. He's attacking his organ, his passion making it unsteady, making it wobble. Then it's suddenly over, the final whistle. Their moment in the blistering sun, their fifteen minutes of Live Aid fame, are done.

Time for the backstage post-match interview, the instant reaction. Short of breath, pink-cheeked and sweating, Mick tells Janice Long and her microphone that it was 'very nerve-wracking before I went on, but we went out there and once you saw that crowd, you just had to enjoy it really'.

Thirty-eight years later, Mick's take on the day is less breathless, more considered. But the anxiety remains a central theme. 'We were very, very nervous. We were fortunate in so much as, once we knew Live Aid was on, John Weller – our manager, Paul's dad – got us a lot of big gigs leading up to it. His reckoning was that we'd be match-fit for doing a gig of that size. But there was no getting around the fact that it was just a once-in-a-lifetime thing. We were the second act on. Status Quo were a very crowd-pleasing band and a hard act to follow.'

Nonetheless, the Style Council had other things to distract them that day, unmoveable bookings that were already in their diary. After a swift photo session with David Bailey backstage, they boarded a bus to Maidstone to record a TV show with a live orchestra. Then it was back to London, where Mick was due to be a guest on Radio 1's reviews programme, *Roundtable*. 'The traffic was so bad that I had to do half the show on our plugger's phone. Fortunately, although it was 1985, he had a mobile phone, one of those things that looked like a car battery with a handset on top. So I was broadcasting live from his car in the middle of a traffic jam. I think we got to the BBC with five minutes of the show left, but then had to be back at Wembley for the finale.' Calm contemplation of the day and its significance would have to wait.

And Mick is someone who does calmly contemplate. Today he's at home in south-east London, guiding me over the undulating road, the rolling gradients, of a lifetime spent in the forefront of popular music. He's got a headful of stories. 'I'm just a vessel that you've got to steer, you realise that, yeah?'

Appearing at Live Aid with the Style Council might represent the zenith in terms of numbers and exposure, but he's learned both craft and life lessons with a wide array of bands and collaborators. It all started with the Merton Parkas, the mod revival band he'd founded with his singer/guitarist brother Danny. In the summer of '79, their single 'You Need Wheels' grazed the top forty, earning them a *Top of the Pops* slot. But they never went higher. By the following summer, they'd decided to part.

'We'd been dropped by our label. We realised we were sort of box-office poison and I think the four of us thought that, if we wanted to maintain our presence in the music industry, we were probably better off dividing and going elsewhere.' Mick, at least, was able to maintain his presence in the music industry almost immediately. Dexys made his phone ring.

'It happened pretty quickly. We called it a day in early August and about a week later I got a phone call. It was quite fortuitous. I'd first met Dexys about a year before when they supported the Merton Parkas at Eric's in Liverpool. I remember watching their soundcheck, and them watching ours. I couldn't help but notice they had a lot of soul covers in their set at the time.

'"Your arrangements really remind me of Geno Washington."

'I think Kevin said, "JB [aka Geoff Blythe] used to be in his band so that's probably why the arrangements are similar." They didn't have "Geno" in their set at that stage. They seemed a pretty good band then, but their image was quite different. They were sort of dressed as superheroes or circus trapeze artists – a lot of capes and tights and things. Kevin has since said he thinks he was ahead of the curve. He thought it wasn't dissimilar to what was called New Romantic a year later.'

Twelve months on and Pete Saunders had left the band for a second time, on this occasion involuntarily. Mick detected a sense of urgency. There were live dates in the diary that needed honouring.

'I was really pleased to get the call. I was surprised that Kevin and some of the band had paid attention to a muck-about and a run-through in Liverpool a year earlier. He remembers me playing a Ray Charles thing. "I didn't realise there were many people of our generation playing Ray Charles." That stayed with him and was a lot of the reason why he thought of me twelve months later.

'I came up to Birmingham to play with them and to see if it could work out. Pretty soon after, they said, "We like what you did. Do you think you can learn our set in five days because we're going on a European tour?"

'*Searching for the Young Soul Rebels* had only just come out and it was really unusual. It had such a sort of English identity – or Irish, I suppose, with Kevin – but it was obviously built on the building blocks of so much music that I loved from the States. It wasn't like a few bands around at the time, like the Q-Tips, or any sort of Blues Brothers-type bands. It wasn't a pastiche. It felt like its own thing, just with very obvious roots. I guess it's not dissimilar to what Jerry Dammers did with ska with the Specials. Dexys just did that with soul. And both bands were quite clearly from the Midlands. They weren't pretending they came from Alabama or anything.'

It was a slight culture shock for the lad from Merton dropped into the West Midlands, having to learn the slang and the in-jokes, and 'having to appreciate the subtle differences between someone from Birmingham and someone from Bloxwich or Walsall or Wolverhampton. I had to adjust a little as the only Londoner in the band. But you pick up on things.'

After the '60s suits favoured by the Merton Parkas, there was also a new uniform to wear. Mick made sure this was on his terms, though. 'I didn't get fitted out for a woolly hat. I got a suede jacket and some black Sta-Prest and a white T-shirt. But I understood the whole longshoreman thing. I know some people say it's *Mean Streets*, but to me it was harking back to *On the Waterfront*.

'There was that image and that gang mentality. I understood it and I knew what it was about. They created a lot of self-mythology about bunking on the trains and all of that, but I just said, "I won't be doing any of that. I'm not twelve or thirteen." I was fairly young, but not that young. They made too much of a song and dance about it. I just thought, *Oh, how rebellious*.

'When I came up for the audition, I mentioned to Kevin about seeing their manager to get my train fare paid.

'"Didn't you bunk the train?"

'"No."

'"Why not? We do that all the time."

'"I don't want to risk getting nicked. I'm not here to learn how to be a criminal. I'm a delicate little flower who plays music."

Signed up to the cause, if not to all the cash-saving travel arrangements, Mick did indeed learn the set in five days flat and promptly set sail on the European tour. A festival in eastern Belgium was the first date on the itinerary before the Dexys charabanc headed for the Netherlands, Scandinavia, Germany and Switzerland. After the neatness and economy of being a quartet with the Parkas, playing in a full-throttle eight-piece was a new experience, akin to travelling aboard a juggernaut opposed to a more compact splitter van. The power of the Dexys sound was undeniable.

'It was a treat to have a whole horn section. The trombone seemed to be more prevalent in a lot of ska music, but using it in a more soul way just gave the sound its own thing. I know that JB did quite a lot of the arranging and Jimmy did quite a lot of the writing, but Steve Spooner played a really important part too. If you took his alto out of that three-part section when they were doing a soundcheck, you lost a lot of the grit. He had a tonal thing that really gave it a lot of aggression and oomph. They all blew really hard for a long time and had immense stamina. It was very passionate.'

Footage of a three-song performance on Swedish TV in early October 1980 has popped up online in recent years and shows a band at the peak of their hard-blowing, hard-playing powers. And, stage left, Mick very much looks the part, radiating nothing to suggest he was a recent recruit. It's the only footage that remains of him playing with this line-up; he never did any British TV shows during his three-month spell. 'I only ever played one gig in the UK with them – a closed-shop thing for EMI. Mick Jagger and Sheena Easton were on the front table about three yards in front of us. It was a bit weird, but we still gave it the full experience.'

Such was the unswerving commitment the band was showing on stage, no one in the crowd would have had an inkling that there was something rotten in the state of Dexys. Mick had spotted it not long after joining.

'There was a bit of unrest between people. I had to catch up with two or three years of history to try to understand why and to try to make judgements about who was in the right and who was in the wrong. Or whether there even was a right or wrong. The fact that they looked like an eight-piece band to the outside world, but only three of them were signed, was a bit odd. So I could see where the unrest was coming from, but it was hard to untangle exactly. I don't know if I ever quite got to the bottom of it anyway because, before you knew it, the band was all over anyway.

'At the end of that tour, Kevin just disappeared and got on a plane. We were getting a boat back home, travelling in a minibus that didn't have any heating. And I do mean a Transit with some seats in it. We drove down freezing Scandinavia in that. Kevin leaving didn't bode well. The rest of the band were saying, "I think that's going to be it. And we've got a few ideas about maybe getting a new singer. Are you up for it?"'

Mick was indeed up for it and the five of them ('Initially there were six of us. I think Jimmy Paterson wanted to be part of it, but then he changed his mind') sloped off and became the Bureau. Like Pete Williams and Geoff Blythe and Steve Spooner and Stoker before him, Mick was bemused with the record company's priorities, especially considering their not-inconsiderable financial investment in the Bureau, and especially when 'Only for Sheep' was doing so well Down Under.

'We should have gone to Australia,' Mick laments. 'I'm a great believer in showing the love to the people who are showing you the love. We should have gone out there. But we were committed to supporting the Pretenders at the time in the States.' Again, like Pete Williams and Geoff and Stoker, Mick still fondly remembers the headline act's generosity. 'The Pretenders were very supportive of us. When they were doing radio interviews, they'd always say, "Come down early. Don't miss the Bureau." And Archie and Chrissie used to do a duet at the end of the Pretenders' set if they got an encore. They used to do a Jackie Wilson cover together and be joined by our horn section. So it did feel good. But the album didn't even come out in the States, so I don't know what we were actually promoting.'

After being stranded and struggling to afford their ticket home, the dissolution of the Bureau felt inevitable. Recalling the experience actually causes Mick to laugh. 'That made it three acts who'd all been dropped one way or another while I was a member of them. Three on the trot. You sort of think, *Hang on. This might be the universe telling me I've got to go back to the real world.*

'They created a lot of self-mythology about bunking on the trains and all of that, but I just said, "I won't be doing any of that. I'm not twelve or thirteen."' Mick Talbot recalls his short first tenure in the Dexys ranks.

'That's when the game seemed up. I'd run away and joined the circus, but it hadn't worked. I sort of clung on, though. Although on paper it looks like the Bureau shrivelled up and died at the end of '81, we did make it into '82. I was picking up a few random dates here and there with some friends' bands, and a few pubs around Tooting used to have R&B bands that I could sit in with and get a bit of money. I also went to Germany with a friend's covers band, but there wasn't that much going on. But then summer came and I got phone calls from both Paul Weller and Dexys' manager Paul Burton within three days of each other. Two buses turned up at once and I had to make up my mind which one to get on.'

Of course, he'd stepped aboard one of these buses before and it had broken down very soon after. But his replacement in Dexys, Micky Billingham, had served his notice and there was the possibility of Mick getting his old job back. However, the path for the prodigal son wasn't completely clear.

'Kevin didn't want to meet me in person and that sort of screamed out at me a bit. Paul Weller rang me up himself and he met me in person. Kevin got his manager to ring me and then he didn't turn up. Apparently, he thought I might be bitter or upset. I hadn't actually said anything to him since he got on a plane and disappeared, so why would he think I was bitter?

'Anyway, I listened to what they were saying. Both conversations were full of fruitful promises, but instinctively I felt more on a par with Paul. I had worked with the Jam in the late '70s and a bit in 1980, and I felt I had more in common with him. We were born in the same year and he's from vaguely the same neck of the woods. I lived in south-west London where it bleeds into Surrey, and he was from a bit deeper into Surrey. And when we chatted about our roots, we found we both played a similar circuit of British Legions and working men's clubs as teenagers. We compared notes on our pasts and discovered we had plenty in common.

'The meeting was supposed to be for an hour but it turned out lasting about five hours. We spoke about music and books and plays and films and clothes and so many other things that had influenced us. I felt a real connection with Paul on quite a deep level. I may have got that connection with Kevin if he'd actually turned up.

'I think Kevin was genuinely concerned about me being upset. But I thought that if Paul only realises half of the ideas he had, it was going to be amazing. And it was. He was very open to so many sorts of things. And he was very trusting. He had everything – and I had nothing – to lose.'

And what Paul was offering Mick with the Style Council was a partnership, a duo. Had Mick returned to the Dexys fold, he would be back to being one voice among eight. Actually, with the Emerald Express now attached too, he'd be one voice among eleven.

The Style Council set-up offered elasticity, imaginative thinking and open-ended possibility. The blueprint had been only lightly sketched out. 'Paul said he didn't want to bother with putting a complete line-up of a band together. He just wanted to write songs and demo them, and then see if he knew any people who'd be suited to them. I quickly got into that. I like to get a bit pretentious about it, seeing Paul as a sort of Orson Welles calling up the Mercury Players. We were going to be the musical equivalent of that, bringing people on board every now and then. I created a parallel in my mind of a film director casting the right people for the part. That's just part of my pretentious nature, and Paul was a bit like that too. We were sometimes wilfully pretentious, but it didn't mean that we weren't serious about the music.

'We'd look around and cherry-pick people. The fact that we weren't concerned with going on the road in the first year gave us a lot of liberation and freedom.' In comparison to the frenetic fire and fury of both Dexys and the Bureau, the more relaxed nature of the Style Council suited Mick. It gave him the time to nurture his ideas until they were fully formed. And it meant the absence of sitting aboard a ropey minibus skidding its way through a sub-Arctic landscape.

'Paul had been very keen on a studio in Marble Arch that Polydor owned. He took it over and that became Solid Bond Studios. So we had a studio where we'd go Monday to Friday, like it was a nine-to-five job. Very rarely did we begin at nine, and very rarely did we finish at five, but we went there regularly, like it was our place of work. But the meter wasn't running because Paul owned the studio. That was another liberating factor.

'We were very privileged to have an A&R man called Dennis Munday who sensed that we needed to have some space to do our own thing and to try something different. He was a bridge to Polydor. He helped build a moat around us to keep too many interfering people away until we'd got the finished product.'

And the finished product benefitted from the prolonged gestation period that this protection gave. The first eight Style Council singles – from the organ-led bounce of 'Speak Like a Child' to the angry, diamond-hard groove of 'Walls Come Tumbling Down' – made the top twenty, all but two securing berths in the top ten. The first three albums – *Café Bleu*, *Our Favourite Shop* and *The Cost of Loving* – were all certified gold, each enjoying the view from the highest altitude of the album charts.

Mick issues some caution here, rebutting any notion that the Style Council was an unmitigated success. 'We more or less had a six-and-a-half, seven-year span. If you look at it with hindsight, I guess the first three years clicked and the last three didn't. I don't think our approach ever changed. It's just that people were with us for some of it and for some of it they weren't.

'We made an album that Polydor refused to release. We'd been working on it quite hard. With all these things, whether they're classic albums or duffers, at that time you're really invested in them and you believe in them. They're your babies and you want to see them go out into the world. And even if, in retrospect, they're not very good, they mark where you were at the time. They're a diary of where you were at.

'If we'd known they weren't going to put it out, maybe we'd have called it quits earlier. But that studio was a real hive of activity at the time. It was fun. The joke is that I was working on Dee C Lee's thing, a project called Slam Slam that Dr Robert from the Blow Monkeys was producing. I was working on the early demos for the Young Disciples' first album. And I was working on stuff for Dr Robert's own material. I was working on four albums at the same studios at the same time. Three of them saw the light of day. The only one which didn't was ours . . .'

The first half of the '90s saw Mick busier than ever, in demand to an extent he'd not experienced before. His phone was perpetually ringing. The range of his work had widened, too. He was doing loads of dance remixes, creating extended versions of the records of people like Luther Vandross, Janet Jackson and Sounds of Blackness for the UK market. He was also deeply engaged with the acid jazz scene, playing more Rhodes and clavinet, which suited this new genre down to its Italian-made brogues. Mick also spent the best part of five years as an integral member of the Galliano live band.

'I wasn't left idle,' he smiles. 'I even participated in a few of Paul's albums. I co-wrote a song, "The Strange Museum", on the first one, and played on the second album, on a track called "5th Season". And I'm on a couple of tracks on *Stanley Road*.

'In about '98, I became part of Jools Holland's Rhythm & Blues Orchestra, which is a wonderful thing to be asked to do. I did that for two or three years when his brother Christopher took a break from playing Hammond in the band. But the real treat there was being on *Hootenanny*, playing with people like Dr John or Ronnie Wood or Slash or Tom Jones . . .'

Into the new millennium, Mick reconnected with some former bandmates at that Bureau reunion in Newcastle. Prior to the meet-up, that search for the elusive and now middle-aged Steve Spooner – involving the ad in the *Birmingham Evening Mail* that Steve had possibly interpreted as a request to clear a backlog of childcare payments – was intriguing the rest of them. 'He was the missing man,' says Mick. 'It was almost like a thriller. Archie Brown was the voice of doom: "I'm sure he's come to an early demise."'

On the agenda at the reunion was the possible release of that Bureau album. This wasn't a reissue. It had never come out in the first place. 'We met and talked about it. "Well, if they put it out, do you fancy some live work?" By the time it came out, I suppose it was 2005. We did do a couple of dates around it and we enjoyed them. And we even did a new album. That took until around 2008.'

There was another consequence of the Bureau reunion: Mick's reconnection with Pete Williams. 'He said to me that he'd had a few enquiries from Kevin, who was trying to put a band together. He said, "I feel I want to namedrop you. You've got a real breadth of experience now and I think it would work really well."

'So I met Kevin in person, which was fine. I think EMI were preparing to do the greatest hits, and I think he wanted to get out on the road and do a retrospective. Kevin always likes to put a spin on the way these things are presented. I don't think he liked calling it a greatest hits tour, although it looked like that on paper to me. We had a couple of new tracks, like "Manhood", but for the most part, it was a sort of best of, taken from the three principal albums.

'Kevin asked me to be the musical director, which I reluctantly took on. I thought he had enough of an idea what he wanted himself. I said, "Well, that makes you the sheriff and I'm the deputy, am I? Then I've got to second-guess exactly what you want. Or, I'm likely to lead people down a path you don't want to follow." I'm a great believer in the idea that if you get the right line-up and put together a great band – and that was a really good band – everyone will know what their job is and they'll just do it. And whoever wrote the songs will just have a casting vote on the finer details. But I think Kevin liked the idea of giving people badges and roles. So I reluctantly took that badge and tried to do my best with it.

'We did a lot of dates and then, after a gap, we got offered some European shows. But there was a clash – I was busy with a few other things. I told his management that I wasn't the only keyboard player in the world and that they shouldn't pass on such a lucrative European tour. I had no God-given right for that seat. But Kevin didn't want that. He wanted exactly the same line-up and so passed on those dates. Perhaps he had a point. It wasn't a case of "Go and learn these songs". The way the show was structured, there were a lot of cues and breaking off into different monologues. At certain times, it's almost as if you were in a musical or a play. But I thought it would be good to try, even without those European dates, to get the core of the band together to record Kevin's new material with a view to doing an album.

'He said he was going to take a brief break, but his focus was kind of on scriptwriting by then. I think he had a cousin who was an actress and they'd written a comedy or something. A sitcom, I think. It sounds like I'm making this up . . .'

The man who demanded his band never smile on stage turning his hand to a sitcom certainly would be an unlikely turn of events.

'That's as I understand it. I think his cousin was a successful actress in Ireland and they'd co-written something and he wanted to put his energy into that. I wasn't quite sure of the time frame. As it turned out, it was about five years until I heard back from him. When I finally heard back, it was as if it had only been a month since we'd spoken. "You know you were talking about doing an album while the momentum was still there? It's not a bad idea."'

That album, *One Day I'm Going to Soar*, eventually came out in 2012. Kevin's sleevenotes saluted Mick's steady hand on the musical tiller. 'I couldn't have done it without you,' he wrote. 'You worked so hard and got right inside the songs with me. Your commitment, talent and support took it to another level.'

'He was very kind in crediting me with what I did,' says Mick. 'Kevin's got a particular way of working on things and it doesn't always make sense to people, particularly really busy, experienced musicians. It can throw people. Once again, I had the badge of musical director thrust on me. I had to translate what Kevin wanted to other musicians, some of them older and vastly more experienced than me.'

Mick's not worked with Kevin since that record and the subsequent live shows at London's Duke of York's Theatre that were documented in that Paul Kelly film, *Nowhere is Home*. But he's not been putting his feet up. The pipe remains on the shelf, the slippers in the cupboard.

With his old mates from Galliano, he's formed the backing band for many visiting American soul dignitaries over the years. 'It all started with Candi Staton somewhere in the mid-2000s and then we got asked to do loads of others – Motown people like Kim Weston, the Velvelettes and Brenda Holloway, and rarer soul people like Ann Sexton, Debbie Taylor and Richard Caiton.

'It's dreams coming true. I ended up doing Martha Reeves on two or three separate occasions. When I was nineteen, I used to be in a band that would play in a pub called the Two Brewers in Clapham and we used to play "Nowhere to Run". All these years later, I'm here, playing it with the woman who did the original.' There are undeniable echoes here of Stoker sharing that recording studio space with Aretha Franklin.

Alongside this, there's been work with the Blow Monkeys-affiliated collective Monks Road Social and with Stone Foundation, which has found Mick in the company of fellow former Dexys man Paul Speare. Most recently he's been playing on a new record from his old Style Council pal Dee C Lee that's coming out on the Acid Jazz label. Friends old and new drift in and out of his working world. Another phone call from Kevin Rowland can never be ruled out.

Mick Talbot remains that delicate little flower who plays music, a man who can still take as much pleasure from sitting in with a band in a small club as he did that particular Saturday lunchtime in 1985 at Wembley Stadium. Have organ, will travel.

'It's not been all plain sailing,' he concludes. 'Sometimes the world wants three of you. Sometimes it wants none of you. It can be feast. It can be famine.'

Reminisce #10

Duke of York's Theatre, London

At 650 seats, the Duke of York's Theatre is dwarfed by many West End venues. Indeed, five of them can hold more than three times as many. The Palladium is the granddaddy of them all, able to swallow up more than 2,200 high-dollar-paying theatre-goers.

But, with 650 backsides on seats, the Duke of York's is perfect, scaled-down, intimate. And seat A9 in the Royal Circle is arguably the best seat in the house – dead centre and elevated. It's the perfect spot from which to get lost in the intensity of tonight's production, Shirley Valentine, *with Sheridan Smith taking the play's only role.*

Exactly ten years ago tonight, it was also the perfect spot from which to get lost in the intensity of the opening night of Dexys' nine-date residency here on St Martin's Lane, a suitably theatrical affair with Kevin Rowland doing as much acting as soulful singing. Pete Williams was also in thespian mode, appearing both as Kevin's verbal sparring partner and as a full-uniform police sergeant, while Madeleine Hyland played the focus of Kevin's flirtations, fantasies and frustrations. It was as close to musical theatre as a gig gets.

While Sheridan Smith will have the whole stage to herself tonight, the ten-piece Dexys were a little more cheek by jowl – but all the more engaged and engaging for it. Nowhere to hide, as lost in the moment as the misty-eyed audience was.

The reformed, reshaped Dexys came home that night.

23

Jim Paterson

Trombone, 1978–82, 1984

'I've walked out more than once. But if I get the phone call, I'm there.'

To get to Portsoy, you first need to get yourself to Inverness. If you're travelling northwards, then turn right, head through handsome towns like Nairn and Forres and Elgin, before steering towards the coast. Jim Paterson's cottage is on the outskirts of the village, looking out over a gently inclining hill and rolling fields.

Jim lives a long way from the rest of the world – and that's no problem for him at all. But he doesn't live a long way from where he was born. In fact, he came into the world in this very cottage. This was the house in which he grew up and the house in which his parents lived from their wedding day onwards, a gift to the happy couple from Jim's father's father. After years of globetrotting as a professional trombone player, the magnetic pull for Jim is clear: 'As well as being a roof over our heads, it's my spiritual home.'

Today he's been giving the spiritual home a fresh lick of paint, redecorating both the hall and the landing, while also trying to master the tricky task of the stairs in between. You'd think Jim's height would serve him well in such a mission, but he's not a fan of ladders. It's further for him to fall.

He's therefore only too pleased to down tools and put the lid back on the paint pot to instead trace the arc of his musical life and times for the next couple of hours. It's an arc with one particular constant: other than Kevin Rowland, Jim Paterson is the only person to appear on every album made by either Dexys Midnight Runners or the slimmer-of-name Dexys. 'I want to keep that run going,' he smiles. 'If he does another one, I'm getting in there first. I'm on it.'

A relationship that continues to this day was born back in the autumn of 1978, on the morning he stepped off the overnight train at Birmingham New Street station. Having finished his musical training in Leeds, he was looking for an escape route from the Highlands.

'After college, I did a summer season at Butlin's in Filey before coming back here to Portsoy to work in the mill where my dad worked – and where he'd worked all his life after the war. I was quite enjoying that, but still had a hankering to do music. There was nothing up here musically. I was playing in the county orchestra and brass bands at school, but that was all the experience I really had.'

The spoils of his brass band days remain on show, three modest trophies sitting atop a cabinet of cassettes here in his little home studio in the spare bedroom. 'I was quite good until I started spending more time in the pub than practising. I think I won that middle one in the Scottish under-14 solo category. I have a newspaper clipping that says I beat ninety-three other competitors, but I honestly can't remember.'

Jim's mother went in to bat for her son, writing letters to those who could potentially revive her son's stalling musical career – to cruise-liner companies like P&O, to the Scottish jazz trombonist George Chisholm, even to the BBC – but to no avail. Instead, thanks and praise should be extended to the Portsoy newsagent who ensured that the weekly music papers travelled all the way to this fishing village in the Highlands.

'They stocked *Melody Maker*, *Sounds* and the *NME*, and I bought them all. I didn't know what I was actually looking for. There were ads for trombone players for the cruise liners and the dance bands, but then there was the Dexys one in *Melody Maker*. I didn't know where they were based and the wording of the ad didn't give me much of a clue, either. It actually took quite a bit of courage to phone up. I always went to the pub at the weekends and I phoned up on the Friday night. Pete Rowland told me to call back on Monday when I was sober.

'I'd only been to Birmingham once before. It was blind faith, I suppose. But I was willing to try anything. I was twenty-one, twenty-two and full of bravado. And if you're a musician, if you love music, you'll go anywhere.'

A freezing early morning in the second city ahead of his audition wasn't improved by Pete Saunders' beverage-making skills ('He gave me a cup of coffee with sugar, which I hated'), nor by that excursion to gather mushrooms in the park. 'The grass was soaking wet, my feet got wet and I was even colder than ever. Then he took me to the audition, which was in Pete Rowland's garage. They were all huddled around a single two-bar fire. I thought, *This is not going to go well.*

'But then they started playing and I almost started crying. It was just so powerful. I knew at that moment that I wanted to be part of it. The energy, the commitment . . . It was just a wonderful experience. I'd done a few auditions before, but that was something totally different. It was unlike anything else.'

Jim was delighted to have passed the audition with flying colours and be handed his metaphorical conscription papers. 'It was almost like being in the army,' he agrees. 'I was on duty. It was about discipline, it was hard about work. But I enjoyed it because I love playing. I'm at my happiest when I've got a trombone in my hand. Time flies past when you're enjoying yourself like that. It doesn't feel like hard work. I could have played all day.'

Once he'd moved to the West Midlands, Jim found that playing all day every day was to be the modus operandi – as was signing on. 'I'd saved up a bit of money from my job at the mill, and also from my time at Butlin's, so I had a bit of cash, but that didn't last long obviously because nobody else had money so I was buying them the fags and the beer.

'In the first couple of weeks, we were rehearsing in Kevin's cousin's house in Wolverhampton, just up the road from Molineux. I was staying there as I didn't have a bedsit yet. We'd get up about ten o'clock and I'd make a pan of porridge for whoever was staying there. This caused a problem. Half of them took sugar with it. I thought, *How the hell am I going to get on with this lot?*

'But we quickly became a gang. We looked out for each other. We used to go out shopping – or shoplifting, I should say – and to pubs dressed up in the donkey jackets and woolly hats. People thought we'd escaped from somewhere. We looked quite menacing.'

Until this point, Jim's experience of playing with other musicians outside of an orchestra or a brass band was limited to a single-gig, holiday-cover slot in an outfit called the Seventh City Soul Band. And whatever the format, he was used to being in the background, away from the limelight. The horns being front and almost centre in Dexys was something of a revolutionary act. 'Up until that point, I'd always been stood at the back or sitting on a seat when I played. In an orchestra, the trombones are often stuck behind the clarinets or the bassoons. Standing at the front was totally different and kind of alien. And it took some getting used to because I'm quite shy.'

Rehearsals, as we've heard from everyone in that first incarnation of the band, were taken as seriously as gigs. 'Everything was belt and braces, as Kevin would say. He's a genius when it comes to thinking of ideas and how to get the best out of performances – like the theatrical stuff he's doing now. He just never stops. And we were all willing participants because it just added to the spectacle.'

The dedication that all eight members gave to the cause, and the originality that pumped through the band's collective veins, suggested that their forward momentum would inevitably carry them to some kind of glory, some kind of commercial success. But ask Jim whether there was a point at which they were destined to make such an impact both culturally and commercially, and he feels uncomfortable.

'You know what – and this is the God-given truth – I just don't think like that. I've never felt like that. I just always think, *I'm enjoying this and I don't want it to stop.* That's just the way I am. I've never had any expectations. I've never been ambitious. I've always just thought, *I'm in the moment. Let me enjoy this.* It probably wasn't until we got a manager that I thought that it was starting to become a bit more professional. The two Kevins would go down to London and negotiate contracts and stuff, but I never said to myself, "Oh, this is going to become big and we're going to be successful." Start thinking like that and you get disappointed.'

Nonetheless, Jim must have detected a significant reading on the barometer when the band headed to BBC Television Centre for the first time to mime to 'Dance Stance'. 'I was in a kind of dream because *Top of the Pops* has always been my favourite TV programme and part of the reason why I carried on with music. Seeing Alice Cooper on there doing "School's Out" changed my life. It was inspirational. Being on it was surreal. I'm just a shy boy from a little place in north-east Scotland and you don't expect things like this to happen. It's different if you live in London and you're walking down Carnaby Street every weekend and seeing all these famous people and wanting to be part of it and going to the clubs and stuff. That just didn't happen up here. It's a different world.'

A sense of the different world of pop stardom came once 'Geno' planted its flag at the peak of the pop charts. And the effect was felt in little old Portsoy. 'My mum and dad were getting stopped on the street: "Oh, I see your James is at number one." My dad's head was held high. They were both proud. And everything I did was for them. If you need a reason to do anything, just do it for your mum and dad, that's what I think.'

An occasional user of the social media platform formerly known as Twitter, Jim once posted the observation that 'success to me was phoning up my mum and dad, and telling them they didn't have to send food parcels any more'. I was presuming that was when the widespread radio airplay of 'Geno' gave him a slice of the cash coming Dexys' way. But, of course, the shenanigans and internal politics of the band would have put paid to that. 'I got my first royalty cheque from "Come on Eileen",' he confirms – thus, *after* he left the band. 'I wasn't destitute, but I was relying on my girlfriend, then my wife, because she worked and so supported us both for a while when I was living the dream and not getting paid for it. I can't remember at what stage the band came off the dole and started getting a wage. But it wasn't a lot. It was enough to buy fags and booze and a sandwich every day. But that was fine because we had faith. That's another really important thing that you need starting out: faith that it's going to work.'

Jim really is a gentle giant, his words and actions shot through with humanity and modesty. Those infrequent tweets reveal the essentially shy, humble man behind the trombone. When a Dexys record has been featured on Tim Burgess's Twitter Listening Parties, Jim's contributions have been unremittingly sweet, without a single note of bitterness.

'What Kevin, Dexys and EVERY member of the group has given me is more than one man deserves,' he once wrote, 'but I take it with love and acknowledge I am blessed.' Talking about the *One Day I Going to Soar* album, he posted: 'I've just read the credits. Shit. Kevin says I'm his greatest songwriting partner. I'm lost for words.'

Aside from his emotional astuteness, his tweets also show just how funny he is.

'If music be the food of love, I'm a fat bastard.'

'I fear that if I punched Gavin Williamson, it wouldn't be hard enough.'

'There will always be anger in the world as long as there is clingfilm.'

An alternative career writing humorous aphorisms for greeting card manufacturers has been left wanting.

While 'Geno' was lingering in the foothills of the chart, ahead of its assault on the summit, the band decamped to Chipping Norton. 'I enjoyed that. It was a beautiful studio and we did it so quickly. I think it only took two weeks. There was a Scalextric set upstairs, so if you weren't actually recording, you could go and relax. And there was a barrel of free beer called Hook Norton. It was weak as piss. It was horrible. But I was drinking about fifteen pints a day of the stuff. And the other distraction was the squash club next door, which sold proper alcohol, so every chance I got, I was in there. I suppose it did affect my playing a bit, but I think the LP itself couldn't have been any better.

'One of the proudest moments of my life is when Kevin says "Big Jimmy!". It's the first thing you hear on the record. It still blows my mind.'

The attractions of the squash club possibly had an effect on Jim's participation in the stealing of the master tapes. 'I was so pissed they probably had to carry me into the van. I was a bit upset about something and put my hand through a window and cut it really badly. I was preoccupied by trying to stop the blood while everything else was going on around me. People were running past me, shouting, "Jim, Jim – get in quick! Get in the back of the van!" I remember going pretty fast up the M40. I'm a nervous passenger anyway, even though I was drunk. I suppose it was an adventure, but it wasn't one of my favourite moments. Still, the actual heist itself was a brilliant idea. We're still talking about it more than forty years later.'

There then was the post-album split, where the famed sense of collectivism turned out to be a carapace. 'It felt like it was going to be a democracy,' Jim recalls, 'but Kevin was definitely starting to become more than a leader, shall we say. Maybe a bit dictatorial. He was taking over too much and nobody else was getting a say. I'm sure it happens in a lot of bands, that somebody starts taking over. There was this three-man nucleus as well, which didn't help.

'I was going to go with the others. We were all going to go and leave Kevin on his own – or maybe Kevin Archer was going to stay. But I was definitely going to go to the Bureau. Then Kevin phoned up: "Can I come round and buy you a drink?" I thought, *Well, that's weird because you've never bought me a drink before.*

'He took me to a pub in Kings Norton and told me the rest of the band had left. I thought, *I know. I'm leaving as well.* Then he said, "I need you, Jim." There was something in his voice, something that just made me think that he did need me. And that I needed him, I needed Dexys. It was one of those weird situations where your heart rules your head. So I stayed. I like to think I'm loyal to the cause. To me, Dexys has always been a cause – a calling, even. I had to tell Geoff and Steve and the rest that I wasn't going to join the Bureau. I think I made the right decision for me and for Dexys. It was a hard one, though, as I was letting down my friends.

'They were disappointed, but they managed to get another trombone player, Paul Taylor, who's very good. To be honest, the tour they did in the States supporting the Pretenders would have finished me off. I couldn't have survived that. I would have been very ill. I'd have just drunk too much and that would have been it, a kind of horrible death . . .'

It's a strange point at which to start chuckling.

'I'm laughing now, but it really would have been that bad for me because there was no discipline. They were all getting ill. Pete Williams got a liver disease or something. In hindsight, I made the right decision.'

'As well as being a roof over our heads, it's my spiritual home.'
Jim, his wife Sandra and their dog Storm in Portsoy in the
Scottish Highlands, in the house in which he was born.

Jim's decision to remain on board, to not ride off into the sunset
with the other five, was arguably the point at which he and Kevin
Rowland truly bonded. He'd been the hard-drinking trombone
player until that point and now, particularly after Kev Archer
removed himself too, he'd been promoted to the position of Kevin's
chief collaborator, his new songwriting partner. A bond was tight-
ening. Building on their respective heritages, Kevin dubbed them
the Celtic Soul Brothers.

'That was definitely the point at which we started getting closer,
yeah. We talked more personally about beliefs and stuff. I mean, he's
Catholic and I'm Protestant, but we believe a lot of the same things.
And we come from similar families. Our dads were hardworking

and our mums were beautiful women, inside and out.' Jim pauses for a second or two. 'I'm getting a bit emotional here.'

As the new first lieutenant, Jim was heavily involved in populating Dexys' second chapter, in particular the recruitment of the two new sax players, Paul and Brian. Like several others in the band at the time, he also laments the fact that this line-up never got to record an album of their own before the strings were added and the tracksuits shed in favour of the dungarees.

'It's one of those things, I suppose. Kevin was already planning six months ahead.'

After the unsuccessful experiment of the brass section doubling up on strings, and the subsequent addition of the Emerald Express, the alarm bells began to sound ever so gently for Jim. The horns were going to have to share the front of stage, and space on the records, to accommodate the violins.

'I wouldn't say it was jealousy, but it felt like I was getting demoted or substituted. Imagine a footballer who's playing really well but gets taken off. It was a bit like that to me. I wasn't upset, and it was nothing personal against Helen and Steve and Roger because they were a brilliant, brilliant addition. I just felt like I was being demoted. I'm sure Brian did too.

'We were rehearsing one day and the night before, Brian had been getting fed up. He wasn't liking something or other, so he just upped and left. The next day, I saw him off at Birmingham New Street station back to Newcastle and it just put it in my head. I thought, *I can't stand this any more.* So I went to the off licence, got a bottle of vodka and went to the café opposite the rehearsal room. There I drank the vodka, went across to the rehearsal room, stomped my feet down and said something like "Right, Brian's left and I'm leaving. You can all fuck off."

'It was "Oh, Jim's on one of his benders again", and Kevin just sort of shrugged it off. I didn't have an exit strategy. I hadn't planned it. It was just me going off on one – a spur-of-the-moment thing. Sometimes I think I regret it. Sometimes I think it was the best thing I could have done for me personally – and for Dexys, because it didn't affect them. Nothing was diminished with either me or Brian leaving.

'We had left halfway through rehearsing "Come on Eileen", while we were still working out the key changes. It was a work in progress. So the manager Paul Burton phoned us up and asked us to finish the album as the brass section. Somebody said we went back as session musicians and just did it for the money. That was the biggest insult anybody could say to me. I would never ever play for Dexys as a session player. I'm as much Dexys as the next person. I couldn't have given a damn about the money. I just wanted to play on the LP and be really proud of it.'

Having stayed on board during the band's 1980 split, Jim now watched from a distance as Dexys notched up their second number one, one that comfortably eclipsed 'Geno' for cultural impact. 'I was a bit sad, to be honest, but I'd made my bed and I needed to lie in it. I always knew I'd be back at some point. I always expect a phone call from Kevin: "Oh Jimmy, I've forgiven you. Come back." That's our relationship. I get a call however many years later: "I'm doing an LP. You want to be involved?" "OK, then." It's as simple as that. I've walked out more than once. But if I get the phone call, I'm there.'

In the past, Jim has likened his on/off partnership with Kevin as 'being Tonto to his Lone Ranger, Robin to his Batman, Snowy to his TinTin'. The faithful sidekick, the dependable deputy.

Jim, Brian and Paul reconvened to tout their services as a freelance horn section. But not any old horn section. It turned out that the passion, fire and commitment that membership of Dexys had pumped through their veins was hard to lose as the TKO Horns. Not that they wanted to lose it. 'We always had this Dexys sound, this persona. Session players go and read the dots, get their money and bugger off to the next job. We couldn't do that. We weren't like that at all. We had our own personal sound and it was a real compliment that Elvis Costello wanted us.

'With Elvis, we did the UK and Europe and the States. It was an absolutely brilliant tour. Then we came back and did a few little one-off things, like Howard Jones. But I didn't enjoy that much. I like to get involved and be part of something.'

Jim didn't have to wait too long to be invited to be part of something again. And not just something. *The* thing. Kevin Rowland needed his old mucker to be part of the sessions that became *Don't Stand Me Down*. Jim's phone rang. 'He didn't need to persuade me. "Jim, I need you on here." "OK. When? Where?"'

'I did feel a bit more remote and a bit more alone, though. There did seem to be more and more session players, people who probably wouldn't have been in Dexys otherwise. I loved Vince Crane. He was a lovely man and a brilliant piano player, but I had no idea why he was in Dexys. From Atomic Rooster to Dexys is quite a leap, isn't it?'

Nonetheless, Jim was delighted to be back in the fold, later describing it as 'falling into a giant tub of ice cream with dislocating jaws'. He laughs when I remind him of that quote. 'Oh yeah, gobbling it up. I loved it. Those songs were amazing songs to play. Technically bloody hard as well – and I'm not a very technical player. We were in Switzerland at Queen's studio. It was part of a casino. I don't gamble, so that wasn't a problem, but there was a bar . . .

'There were big names involved and I could have felt out of my depth, but I didn't. For some strange reason, I felt really comfortable doing that LP. And although I felt quite lonely at times, I just really got into the music. I didn't contribute any songs to *Don't Stand Me Down*. With every LP, Kevin has had a different co-writer. It was Kevin Archer for the first one, me for the second, Helen and Billy for the third, and then a mixture for the rest.

'I didn't get involved in the look, in what they were going to wear. I'd have loved to have gone to New York and done the video with them for "This Is What She's Like". I think that's a brilliant video. When Billy and Kevin are walking along the street, it's just perfect. I wish I'd been there to do that. But I'm still proud of it. I'm proud of everything that Dexys and Kevin do, whether I'm involved or not. I'm part of Dexys. That'll never go away.'

Into the second half of the '80s, Jim continued to work extensively alongside his TKO Horns partner Geoff Blythe, whether in that funk band the Neighbourhood or with the reconvened Blue Ox Babes as they finally cut their long-awaited album. Then, in 1993, Jim was called up for the next tour of duty in the Dexys division. It was a short engagement, part of that appearance on *Saturday Zoo*, where Jim ditched the trombone to share co-vocals with Kevin on 'Manhood'.

He laughs at me bringing it up. 'Call that singing?! Well, I did sing when I was a kid. And I was good around eight, nine, ten years old. I used to sing at the Banffshire Music Festival and I've still got the certificates and a few prizes. But I didn't feel comfortable doing *Saturday Zoo*. I did my best, but I was very shy and I wasn't drinking.'

Giving up alcohol in the '90s was a major lifestyle choice for Jim. And it wasn't the only major element that disappeared from his day-to-day existence. 'I stopped playing completely. I didn't see my trombone for the next sixteen years. Then one day a friend from Ireland said, "Oh, my daughter's having her confirmation. I'd love you to play 'Danny Boy'." So I got the trombone out, started practising and played "Danny Boy" at her celebration at the pub up the road from me in Acton.

'About a week later, I got a phone call from Kevin. "I'm doing a new LP. Do you want to meet up?" So we met up at a Thai restaurant in Chiswick. He'd brought a bag of '40s clothes with him. I loved them and thought, *I could get into this.*

'"So, do you fancy it?"

'"What do you think?"

'And that was it. I knew immediately that it was meant to be. I'd just started practising again after sixteen years. It was one of those coincidences.'

The sessions were for *One Day I'm Going to Soar*, which found him not only reuniting with some of the songs he'd previously co-written but which had yet to find a home, but also reuniting with a couple of old pals in Pete Williams and Mick Talbot. 'That was good. I didn't feel quite as estranged as on the *Don't Stand Me Down* sessions. It felt like coming home. But I was a bit critical at the time to Kevin. I said that this was far too personal an album to be a Dexys LP. It was more like a Kevin album with some Dexys colour to it.'

Jim was also part of the live band that played that mini-residency at the Duke of York's Theatre. One of the most poignant moments in the *Nowhere Is Home* film is when Jim steps forward to take a solo towards the end of 'I'm Thinking of You'.

As the last lonesome note from the trombone fades, Kevin says, 'Thank you for doing that for me, Jim' and shakes the hand of his old Celtic soul brother. He's not just thanking him for the solo. He's thanking him for being there time after time, for answering in the affirmative on each and every occasion that he calls with a plan hatching in his head.

Prior to this particular reunion, Jim wasn't exactly a workaholic; at the time, he shared with Kev Adams an affection for Australian soap operas, dedicatedly catching each daily episode of *Neighbours* and *Home and Away* while his wife was at work. He'd also be tinkering away in his little home studio, writing tunes. That cabinet of cassettes is testament that he didn't exclusively spend these times glued to daytime television. 'Nothing's finished,' he confides, 'but I keep beavering away.'

He composed, and still composes, using Cubase software, which he first encountered when Kevin asked him to produce his second solo album, *My Beauty*, at the tail end of the '90s. Jim would head down to Brighton, where Kevin was living, for two or three days at a time to work on the record, but the dynamic of that particular working relationship didn't last the course. Jim beat a hasty retreat. 'It wasn't an argument. We don't actually argue. We've got nothing to actually argue about. And we don't have any musical differences. I don't know, it's just . . .' His voice trails off, a precise definition of the pair's relationship eluding him.

Jim also beat a hasty retreat from west London in 2017. 'The year before, my wife Sandra had a massive stroke and so I dedicated the rest of my life to looking after her. We moved back to Portsoy and she's a lot better now than she was – and than she would have been if we'd stayed in our second-floor flat in London. That's the main reason for moving back here: her recovery.' That recovery has been further helped by the couple being joined in their cottage by Storm, their chocolate-brown springer spaniel. The fresh air of Banffshire is pure and bracing, and its dark skies provide a widescreen vista for amateur astronomer Jim and his telescope.

Despite playing on – and contributing four songs as co-writer to – the latest Dexys album *The Feminine Divine*, Jim was an absentee from the accompanying live dates. The year before, he'd been very much up for a *Too-Rye-Ay* revival tour on the occasion of its fortieth anniversary, but those plans were shelved when Kevin suffered serious leg injuries in that motorbike crash in Thailand. This time around, though, Jim had to honourably decline.

'I realised I couldn't do the tour because I'd have to leave Sandra on her own, which I can't do. Including rehearsals, it'd have been three months altogether, I think. We could have possibly tried to move down to London for those three months, but that would have just been too much. And I certainly wouldn't have put Storm into kennels.'

In his late sixties, Jim has got his priorities and his life balance right. I'm reminded of one last tweet of his: 'I think I've gotten to the stage, or age, where I feel it's ok to put off 'til tomorrow what I could do today. Music is a hobby, so I don't *have* to practise or write. All I have to do is take care of my wife and dog, and myself. Cutting the grass? Hanging pictures? Tomorrow.'

That paint pot, those brushes, that ladder. I suspect they're done for the day.

'I've always just gone where I've been taken. If I come to the crossroads, I don't have to make a choice. If the wind takes me left, I'll go left. If the wind takes me right, I'll go right. Or straight on. Or backwards. And if an alien spacecraft comes and zooms me up, I'll go upwards. It doesn't matter where I go because I'll always end up where I'm meant to go.

'I've nothing to be bitter about. I've had a brilliant life, a fantastic life. I'm here and I'm happy. My mum and dad taught me to always be content. If you've got something and you're happy, then just appreciate it.

'You can't go wrong with that.'

24

Kevin Rowland

Singer, 1978–86

'These days, I take criticism far less personally.
My general attitude is "Fuck 'em".'

It's half-past four in the afternoon and Kevin Rowland is running late.

He's not actually running, but he is striding with great purpose along Somerset Street in Bath. Tonight is the last date of Dexys' current UK tour and he's late for the soundcheck. He might be late because of First Great Western's timekeeping, or he might be late because of the time he took to get ready this morning. He's looking effortlessly stylish: herringbone cap; long, navy-coloured woollen coat over red sweater and denim jacket; burgundy scarf loosely looped around his neck. The turn-ups in his jeans are tremendously generous. They come halfway back up his shins.

Through the stage door of the Forum, the Art Deco former cinema that's tonight's venue, the band has already struck up. They've just started playing the intro to 'It's Alright Kevin' from the new album *The Feminine Divine*, a song known in a previous life as 'Manhood'. But they await their singer, their leader, their guiding light.

Andy the Kiwi has other ideas. A Brummie by way of New Zealand, tonight will be the sixth date on the tour at which this superfan has been in the audience. At each of the previous five – York,

Manchester, Wolverhampton, London and Brighton – he's failed to get a photo with Kevin. All of his pals have managed to but, until twenty seconds or so ago, Andy had drawn a blank. This last night of the tour was his last roll of the dice. But now he's nabbed Kevin in the street. Handshakes are swapped, selfies taken, with Kevin obliging with an upturned thumb pointing towards Andy. Andy then asks me to take one of the pair, a full-length shot this time, one that does Kevin's attire full justice. Got to get those turn-ups into shot.

Andy tells me he's spent the past two hours padding his way around Bath, staking out every café and tea room in search of Kevin. He discovered that there are a great many cafés and tea rooms in the city. Two hours of scoping and scanning, searching for the not-so-young soul rebel. Not a trace. Nada. Then a wander back towards tonight's venue and who should come striding down the street . . .

Kevin dashes off into the dark belly of the venue and Andy punches the air. I ask whether, underneath his tracksuit top ('I wore the gold one for him. Wolves, innit?'), he has a tattoo of his idol on his chest, in the manner of Alan Partridge's obsessed stalker.

'No, I haven't got a tattoo,' he smiles. 'But I know people who have.'

Andy's phone rings. It's his wife. He ecstatically recounts the story of his past two hours, culminating in telling her about the funny thing that happened on the way to the Forum. Apparently, his wife has just awoken from an afternoon nap, during which she had a premonition that Kevin Rowland had suddenly appeared before Andy, like a spirit, like an apparition. It was just how it happened.

Another dedicated Dexys fan wanders up to the stage door. He's wearing the uniform of the 1981 incarnation: burgundy hoodie, grey tracksuit bottoms, boxer boots. His silver hair is even tied back into a ponytail. He's on the same search as Andy the Kiwi. I don't have the heart to tell him he's missed Kevin by just a couple of minutes.

Through the stage door, the band have now launched into 'Plan B'. Their singer has yet to step up to the mic.

A funny thing happened on the way to Bath Forum. The author grabs a photo with an ever-stylish Kevin Rowland ahead of that night's show.

*

Andy the Kiwi had been searching all afternoon. I'd been searching for months.

I didn't introduce myself at the stage door. I pretended to be nothing more than a fan who'd stumbled across him in the street. Kevin Rowland has already given me his answer.

In addition to the past members of Dexys with whom I'm now on good terms, Kevin and I have a close acquaintance in common. I'd decided that using our mutual friend as a conduit would be the most fruitful way of directly getting to my quarry, sidestepping the barbed wire and armed sentry posts of PRs and management. Plus, there are rumours that Kevin is currently working on the second draft of his own memoirs. I need to bring my A game.

As with that original missive to Kevin Archer a few months back, I tried to be as reassuring as possible in the email that goes off to Kevin via my go-between: reassuring about me, about my intentions, about how any interview with me would simply form a snapshot of where he is now and wouldn't tread on the toes of his own book telling his own back story.

I thickly lay on the charm. Possibly too thickly. I drop certain phrases into my email – 'all that you've achieved over the past forty-five years' . . . 'one of my favourite bands since I was a nipper' . . . 'I truly hope this is agreeable to you'. I press what I think might be Kevin's buttons by suggesting we meet in the Pump Room here in Bath for afternoon tea, his taste having become more refined since the days of the Apollonia and the Little Nibble.

The email is sent. Appendages are crossed. *Don't stand me down.*

But the charm offensive fails. Kevin's reply is polite, but short and very much to the point. He will not be meeting up with me. The conciseness of his words indicates no wriggle-room for negotiation, for further attempts at cajoling. Shut down. End of.

Of course, he was going to turn me down. With his own book supposedly in the middle distance, no amount of persuasion was ever likely to work. Yes, he's been doing a good few interviews of late around the tour and the release of *The Feminine Divine*, but these have been for more ephemeral outlets – on-the-hour TV, daily newspapers, monthly magazines. Confessing all for a book, for something that lingers longer on the shelf, perhaps even for a generation or two if it's loved enough, is a different matter. If and when Kevin Rowland's story comes in book form, it'll be him who tells it, and him alone.

*

Big Jimmy Paterson was once asked who would play Kevin Rowland in a biopic of his life. His answer was instant. 'De Niro.'

On the very day in August 1953 that, in an apartment in Little Italy in Lower Manhattan, young Robert De Niro was blowing out the candles on his tenth birthday cake, more than 3,000 miles away, in the Wolverhampton suburb of Wednesfield, Kevin Rowland was taking his first breaths. An exact decade separates them.

There's no astrological significance here, no deeper forces at play. It's mere coincidence. But nonetheless, into adolescence and young adulthood, Kevin gazed admiringly in De Niro's direction, drawing upon the confrontational, me-against-the-world stance of his various characters, especially Travis Bickle in *Taxi Driver* and 'Johnny Boy' Civello in *Mean Streets* (from whom Kevin would also draw sartorial inspiration, namely Civello's leather coat). Just as De Niro would become renowned for his method acting, Kevin also undertook the complete immersion in his role, the absolute absorption. He wasn't now playing the part; he *was* the part. Even when 'Geno' was number one, he still saw no reason to use the services of a British Rail ticket office. (Not that, of course, the behaviour of this adversarial outsider was all for show, all for the stage. Before music had channelled him, Kevin had notched up more than a dozen arrests for various crimes. 'I was the best-dressed kid at the juvenile circuit,' he later quipped.)

But, as the years unravelled, De Niro couldn't remain the angry young man. Indeed, some of his choices of role have been the diametric opposite of Bickle and Civello, especially in his late-career move into comedy. The title role in *Dirty Grandpa* is possibly the furthest distant.

By the same token, Kevin Rowland has mellowed too. Spikes can't stay spiky forever. The interviews around *The Feminine Divine* have seen him keen – possibly even happy – to explain the concept and the vision behind this sixth Dexys album. It's a scarcely recognisable approach from the young man at the typewriter, drafting these words for a full-page ad taken out in the *NME* the same week that *Searching for the Young Soul Rebels* was released:

> From now on, Dexys Midnight Runners will not take part in any interviews with the *New Musical Express*, *Melody Maker*, *Sounds*, *Record Mirror* or any other music papers.
>
> Instead of filling these pages with the usual boring LP adverts, we have decided to use the space to accommodate our own essays which will state our point of view.
>
> We are doing this because we are totally disillusioned with the music press. We have attempted at least one interview with each of the papers but have never been represented properly. Instead, these 'journalists' conduct their own two-hour schoolboy analyses which always reflect their own, oh so predictable, personalities.
>
> Though some descriptions of us have intended favour, we have found them so persistently inaccurate, patronising and standardised, that it is obvious to us that these 'writers' are so out of touch, they should be frightened. They are probably not. Instead, they try to cover their lack of understanding behind a haze of academic insincerity.
>
> We won't compromise ourselves by talking to the dishonest, hippy press. We are worth much more than that.
>
> Dexys Midnight Runners

Perhaps he regards me as a member, or at least a latter-day descendant, of the 'dishonest, hippy press'. Certainly, the abrasive relationship he had with some journalists during the '90s did little to dispel his opinion of them.

That particular decade contained trying, turbulent times for Kevin. There was cocaine addiction. There was debt. There was a brief flirtation with Brahma Kumaris, the self-described 'worldwide spiritual movement' accused of being an apocalypse-believing cult ('I was already a guilt-ridden Catholic,' he told *The Times*, 'and this just doubled the load.') There was even time spent on the dole, the story going that the queue at the unemployment office once broke into a rendition of 'Come on Eileen' when they realised who was among their number. Fold into the mix the press reaction to his solo career – and their preoccupation with his choice of clothes at this time – and matters were only further compounded. 'I'd be turning up to interviews and they were asking me about some track I did fifteen years earlier,' he told the Quietus. 'They were shocked at what I was wearing because they were comparing it to what I used to wear, but there were fifteen years in between. I just felt like a new artist. To me, there was no continuation. If anything, I react against what I did in the past.'

Therapy and rehabilitation helped him make peace with former members and apologise for his previous behaviour. By the end of the century, he could see his past self and identify the faults. 'I turned tyrannical,' he confessed to the *Observer* in 1999.

At the turn of the millennium, there was another indication of Kevin's mellowing in an interview for *Young Guns*, that BBC documentary dedicated to the turbulent times of Dexys. 'When I look back now,' he told the camera, 'I could have had a good time. It would have been nice.' He acknowledged that positioning themselves as outsiders who didn't interact with other bands wasn't necessarily a healthy approach. 'It was all so intense and uptight. I wish that I hadn't been like that. I missed out on an awful lot, you know. Yeah . . .'

That angry young man has excused himself from proceedings over the years. 'I'm more honest now,' he told the *Guardian* in one of those interviews conducted around the release of *The Feminine Divine*. 'I'm more aware of other people. I'm definitely more aware of myself. I don't think I had any awareness whatsoever, really, of what life was about back then. I had no real interest in it either: I was quite a control freak and obsessive – and I still am – about work. These days, I work hard at keeping that obsession at bay, because it's not creative, especially when you burn out. I'd like to think I have left that kind of all-consuming attitude behind.

'These days, I take criticism far less personally. My general attitude is "Fuck 'em". I'll just enjoy them getting wound up because they're the ones with the issues.'

After years spent within a pebble's throw of Brighton beach, Kevin now lives alone in Hackney. Unlike the homes of other members of Dexys, there are no gold discs on the wall. He's facing forwards, rejuvenated after further trying times. In 2016, he found himself burnt out by the struggles of making the *Let the Record Show* album; his mother passed away the same year. Near-certain that he would never make music again, he made an extended stay in Thailand, possibly in search of spiritual – and personal – enlightenment.

According to its press release, *The Feminine Divine* more than hints at some degree of enlightenment. It's 'a personal, if not strictly autobiographical, record portraying a man whose views have evolved over time – and not just on women, but the whole concept of masculinity he had been raised with'. Kevin has returned refreshed, ready to interrogate and diffuse possible notions and ideas he used to hold. This is one aspect of his past he apparently is willing to engage with.

Rowland the auteur, the Scorsese of popular music, has never wanted to occupy the same patch of ground for long, those itchy feet setting him moving in a new direction, often – as we've heard from various past bandmates – with a detrimental effect on the band at that point. Then again, as a few have also indicated, such restlessness has benefitted the long-term survival of the Dexys name, of a band with a reputation for near-constant renewal.

Alexis Petridis's review of *The Feminine Divine* in the *Guardian* noted that while the Dexys sound has moved on – the second half of the record takes on a deeply electronic hue – some recurrent themes are present, including Kevin's excoriation of his younger self. There's one particular killer line in the review: 'complaining about painful earnestness on a Dexys album feels a bit like complaining that a sandwich shop has just sold you a sandwich'. Petridis does, however, acknowledge that Kevin is once again refusing to stand on ground he's occupied before. 'It is a dramatic left-turn that feels like business as usual precisely *because* it's a dramatic left-turn.'

Musically, aside from the rebranding of 'Manhood', there's another definite reprise. The first single from the album, 'I'm Going to Get Free', uses the same tune that was adopted for the version of 'Tell Me When My Light Turns Green' played on The Bridge tour back in '82. Then, it was set against lyrics that complained about powerlessness; now, it's become an anthem of liberation. It chronicles the protagonist's changed regard for women, but could just as much be a celebration of Kevin's calmer, brighter outlook and his survival through decades of torment.

As much as he would love to exclusively face the future, the elastic pulls Kevin back to decades past. He can't completely ignore them, so it's an act of compromise. As he did the press rounds for *The Feminine Divine*, the American music magazine *Spin* wanted to base their interview on the genesis of 'Come on Eileen', the song that defined them as one-hit wonders in the States, as gently lampooned in *The Simpsons* ('You haven't heard the last of them,' Homer tells Lisa). Kevin complied, diving into the song's evolution in more detail than he's ever done previously. 'We never tried to write for a hit,' he concludes, suggesting success was an impure concept that arrived as an accident. 'In the end, it almost wrote itself.'

Journalists and broadcasters ask questions about these songs because they still mean so much to others. Dexys have to play them live in some form, although choosing to not necessarily replicate the old records note for note. On both this latest tour and the *One Day I'm Going to Soar* live dates a decade earlier, these later-period LPs, both of which are loose concept albums, were played in their entirety during the first half of the evening. Then, come round two, the gloves were off and the old numbers revisited. As John Edwards said, Kevin got his hits out.

Even then, though, those hits would often – as with the salsa version of 'Geno' – be reframed to avoid them being mere carbon copies, as Kevin told the *Shropshire Star*: 'If you're playing the old songs, you have to find a new connection to them, otherwise you can't do them. You can't recreate the past. You can't look like you did when you were twenty-five or twenty-six. Or sound like you did. You can't do that unless you're willing to make a bit of a fool of yourself.' Robert De Niro would certainly agree. Who could countenance a reprisal of Travis Bickle, De Niro's silver locks shaved into a mohawk?

Kevin is resolute on this. 'Good luck to those people on the nostalgia circuit. It's better than sitting at home or going back to the factory or warehouse. Why not?

'But I would hate it.'

*

Inside the Forum, the pre-show music is largely as you'd expect – a tasteful, warming selection that includes Marvin and Roxy and Van, Aretha and the Fureys. The Unit 4 + 2's 'Concrete and Clay', as covered by Kevin on *My Beauty*, also gets an airing. Gently warmed by these selections, the gathering punters don't need encouragement to have a good time tonight. 'It might be the last chance to see,' someone whispers behind me.

Plenty of people are sporting oversized flat caps and artfully tailored jackets, inspired by Kevin's look around the time of the

Let the Record Show album. Reflecting an earlier period, there are also more dungarees in the place than at a convention of ex-*Playschool* presenters.

When he takes to the stage, Kevin has swapped his woollen coat and turn-ups for a green suit that's the polar opposite of skin-tight, under which he wears a Breton shirt. A white sailor's hat completes the look. This man is seventy. No other seventy-year-old dresses like this. And no other seventy-year-old leaps onto speaker stacks with such agility either.

The first half is that faithful recital of *The Feminine Divine*, a record that feels like he's slipped into the psychiatrist's chair, the call-and-answer of the band acting as the prompt of the shrink. When it's played before a couple of thousand people, it's like a mass therapy session. Forty-five revolutions around the sun after those very first Dexys auditions, the confrontation's gone, the friction's been defused. Kevin Rowland appears at ease with the world.

Whether he likes it or not, there's a palpable sense of relief at the half-time break. 'So now we're getting to the good stuff,' declares a south Bristol-accented voice behind me. 'Yeah, the old gear,' agrees his mate. 'That's really what we want to hear.'

For all his new visions, his new songs, music is still a balancing act between the past and the present, the then and the now. Kevin and the band play along. When they skip into 'Jackie Wilson Said', the big screen reprises that old *Top of the Pops* gag, showing a picture of the darts champion Jocky Wilson. This time he's shown in the bath, his darts held up for the camera. When Kevin reaches the line 'You in that dress' in 'Come on Eileen', a photo of him in *that* dress from the Reading Festival in 1999 appears on the screen. It's another measure of how relaxed Kevin is these days, bearing in mind the pain and ridicule he suffered from that particular sartorial choice, the one that prompted the *Observer*'s sub-editors to use the headline 'Frocky horror'.

The band plays the game by unleashing the big hits, but they finish the evening not with a bang but with the melancholic, deeply reflective 'Carrickfergus'. Nostalgia's embrace is still in Kevin's control. Its limits remain defined by him.

And he knows how to pluck the heartstrings. As 'Carrickfergus' closes, there are tears in the eyes of grown men, grown men who look like they can handle themselves, grown men who aren't used to sobbing so easily.

Eyes dried, some of them are among the crowd gathering at the stage door afterwards, keen to pay their respects. Andy the Kiwi doesn't need to camp out here anymore. He's got his treasure. He's got his photos. He's also missed his last train back to Birmingham. One option is to get a hotel ('I'm not paying £250 for a Travelodge. That's what it is round here'). Another is to walk the streets of the Georgian city for a few hours until the first rail service in the morning, the 5.43 back to New Street. That's a measure of his commitment, his devotion. And if he chooses the latter option, he can spend the night mulling over the proposition that some of the other superfans have just dangled before him: heading to Amsterdam for the Dutch date of the band's European tour in three weeks' time. He's sorely tempted.

Kevin Rowland's magnetic pull not only finds musicians coming back into the fold after long absences (Jimmy, Pete Williams, Mick Talbot, Helen for the Commonwealth Games . . .) but also, out here on the street, sees punters braving some seriously chilly temperatures on the off-chance of the shortest, possibly the most awkward, of interactions with their hero.

These fans are in their fifties and sixties, equally split between the sexes. Freshers-week students, walking past as they chomp on late-night fried chicken, look bemused, puzzled as to why a gaggle of folk their parents' age (and possibly older) are congregating here, down this cold side street in the midnight hour. The roadies start loading out, an unpleasant duet of shouts and clanking metal. The fans shift onto the kerbside to avoid injury but are otherwise unmoved.

A member of management tells them it's going to be another couple of hours before the band will emerge as they're having an end-of-tour party upstairs. The crowd thins a little, a few slipping away into the night. But a hardcore decide to call his bluff and hold their position. This hardy half-dozen shall not be moved. The strong devoted.

They're still searching. And so am I. To us all, Kevin Rowland remains this enigma, the phantom disappearing for a soundcheck, the behind-closed-doors figure avoiding the after-show pavement gathering. So it's kind of correct, kind of poetic, that my search isn't a complete one, tied up with a bow, those loose ends neatly trimmed. It's entirely in keeping with that observation from Andy Hamilton that for him summed up the dichotomy of Dexys: 'It was almost as if shooting yourself in the foot was seen as a victory,' that notion of snatching defeat from the jaws of victory. The Dexys story could never be complete, finished, perfect. It was always open-ended. There were always abrupt left turns to make, there was always somewhere else to move on to. The future was unwritten. *We're striving, we're striving, we're striving . . .*

Even at the age of seventy, Kevin Rowland still has somewhere else to move on to. Commendably, he sits on no laurels. Like us all, he's still striving, whether for meaning and identity, for creative fulfilment, for personal contentment. The phantom is one of us.

Searching, searching, searching . . .

In memoriam

Two of Dexys' earliest drummers are no longer still with us: **John Jay** and **Bobby 'Jnr' Ward**. Prior to joining the band, Bobby occupied the same role with Subway Sect. Having played on 'Dance Stance' and undertaken a couple of tours, he reportedly sold his kit to fund his heroin addiction. 'Bobby was a great drummer,' Kevin Rowland told the *Guardian*. 'A terrific drummer and a great guy. RIP.' Pete Williams agrees: 'Both of them were lovely fellas.'

Steve Spooner's replacement on alto sax, **Brian Brummitt** (often credited as Brian Maurice), passed away on 2018 on his sixty-sixth birthday. Remembered by his fellow sax player Paul Speare as 'a tough little Geordie' (and a close mate of fellow Tynesider Brian Johnson of AC/DC), Brian was a committed and extremely hard-working member of the band who wasn't slow to express his opinions, often through humorous means. Kev Adams recalls the time the band were introduced to their latest 'uniform'. 'I remember Brian putting on his dungarees for the first time and doing a Coco the Clown impression, running around, taking the piss, saying "You can't be serious" in his Geordie accent.'

'Brian could set the room alight with his sense of humour and have us all in hysterics,' agrees Paul Speare, who spoke at his funeral. 'His speciality was launching into "club" versions of Dexys songs in the style of Tony Bennett. "Plan B" was particularly spectacular.'

With his cascading hair, droopy moustache and penchant for cheesecloth shirts and flares, **Vincent Crane** was a renegade from the '70s who looked an ill fit for the multiple *Don't Stand Me Down* sessions. But his bluesy piano playing brilliantly served its purpose. 'Vince completely got the vision from the off,' Kevin Rowland would later say. 'He just knew how to play it. A genius.' A former member of the Crazy World of Arthur Brown and co-founder of Atomic Rooster, Vincent had suffered from manic depression since the late '60s and took his own life on Valentine's Day in 1989, after reportedly swallowing 400 Anadin tablets.

Lancastrian **Mick Bolton** first came to attention in the mid-'70s when he joined Mott the Hoople on Hammond organ. A decade later, he temporarily replaced the absent Vincent Crane as pianist on the *Don't Stand Me Down* sessions, before returning to the fold as organ player on the subsequent Coming to Town tour in late '85. Mick remained in the line-up to record 'Because of You' the following spring and, a couple of years later, appeared alongside a solo Kevin Rowland on Channel 4's *The Last Resort*, playing 'The More I See You'. Post-Dexys, he became Linda McCartney's personal piano teacher, as well as recording with artists as diverse as La Toya Jackson and Loudon Wainwright III. Mick died in his sleep at the age of seventy-two, on the night that 2020 became 2021.

Acknowledgements

Thanks to . . .

all those former Midnight Runners who were happy to be found, generous with their time and didn't mind a nosy parker prising open long-shut doors on the past. Thank you one and all. Without you, there would be no book.

Thanks to . . .

all of those kind souls who went the extra mile or three in offering assistance, leads or good old-fashioned encouragement once the detective's deerstalker slipped back on: Kev Adams, Luther Boghal-Jones, Mark Elliott, Mark Hart, Rob Hughes, Deborah Smith Lawrence, Barry Mac, Helen O'Hara, Pete Paphides, Siân Pattenden, Steve Shaw, Bob Stanley and Pete Williams.

Thanks to . . .

my sharp and dapper agent Kevin Pocklington of The North Literary Agency for making this book's light turn green. Double figures now, Pockers.

Thanks to . . .

my publisher Pete Selby for his boundless enthusiasm and masterful captaincy of the good ship Nine Eight; and to my editor, James Lilford, for his careful steering through the tight turns of the production process.

Thanks to . . .
the wider Nine Eight team, among them cover designer Alex Kirby, Frankie Eades, Grace Harrison, Paris Ferguson, Rob Sharman and Jane Donovan.

Thanks to . . .
the treasure trove of a website that is dexys.org, an extraordinary repository of all aspects of the Dexys story. Also, Helen O'Hara's sure-footed memoir *What's She Like* was essential in unpicking a large part of the band's complex chronology.

And finally . . .
thanks to the gang at home, to Jess and Finn and Ned and Ralphie. I'm in heaven when you smile.